Big Like

Cascade into an Odyssey

D1282294

WOLF RICHTER

ISBN: 1467967491
ISBN 13: 9781467967495

To Marichan

Author's Note

To protect the privacy of innocent bystanders and guilty parties alike, I changed most of the names. I didn't want to get anyone into trouble with the laws or moral codes of the countries and jurisdictions where the events took place. If you recognize yourself in this book but don't like the name I gave you, please forgive me! You can gripe to me about it through my website: www.testosteronepit.com. I'd love to hear from you.

Table of Contents

1

Airmail From Afterlife

1976

One rainy summer day, I packed my backpack and went to America. I was seventeen. I knew what I was doing: I was escaping from the debacle at home. And I was looking for something. For what exactly, I didn't know, but I'd go look for it in America. There, the heat burned in my nostrils. Lawns were brown. Cars were big and air-conditioned. Girls went gaga over my accent. Guys thought I was cool. And I fell in love with it all.

Three years later, I was paying my way through college in Texas when the notion of home, distant and convoluted as it had become, blew up with gratuitous violence. A Boeing had crashed into a mountain in Turkey, killing all 155 people aboard. I heard about it on the radio. But I didn't connect the dots.

A few days later, I found a message from the operator in my campus PO Box. *Telegram, call Western Union*, it said. I called from one of the pay phones. My heart was pounding in my temples, and I had trouble hearing the lady on the other end.

"I'd read it to you," she said. "But it's in German. I think you better come by and get it."

"I'm fixing to go to work. Can't you try to read it to me?"

"Oh dear."

"Is it long?"

"Two lines."

"Can you spell it?"

"Well, I guess I could. Are you ready?"

I pulled out a notepad and pen. "Ready," I said, though I knew that I wasn't ready, that I'd never be ready for whatever she was about to spell.

"E-L-T-E-R-N new word," she said, "A-M new word M-O-N-T-A-G new word M-I-T new word F-L-U-G-Z-E-U-G new word I-N new word D-E-R new word T-U-R-K-E-I—"

"Stop! Please." I couldn't write anymore. *Parents on Monday with plane in Turkey....* German sentences, even in abbreviated telegram style, had the main verb at the end, but I didn't want to hear the main verb, didn't want to hear it spelled out letter by torturous letter. "Thank you. That's enough."

I'd escaped the debacle at home and had gone as far away as possible. But this wasn't what I'd had in mind. I stood there in a daze, brain dead-locked, numb, clutching the receiver, drowning in abysmal emotions.

Then I went to work. It was just a part-time job, but now I needed the money more than ever. Afterward, I drove to the Western Union office and picked up the yellow slip of paper with twelve lines of all-caps alphanumeric gibberish and two lines of readable text. It was from my sister, sent from the town where she was staying with friends. But it didn't include their phone number. And my brother was on vacation somewhere. So there was no way to reach him either.

The next morning, I woke up sopping wet, having just sat next to my parents on the plane as it went down. My mother was sleeping with her mouth open. My father was snoring. I knew we'd crash, and while I was wondering if I should wake them up, we crashed. Seats, people, and luggage were flying forward past me, and I watched the expressions on the faces of my parents.

I was rattled for hours. But in class I paid attention, took notes, participated. It was sanity, and I clung to it by my fingernails. The next morning, a similar scenario played out in my dreams. And the morning after that. But one morning, I woke up after six hours of sleep before the nightmares had set in, and for the first time in days, I didn't feel tormented. From then on, my inner alarm clock would go off after six hours of sleep, and I'd wake up refreshed and ready to go.

Then I found a letter in my PO Box, one of those flimsy baby-blue airmail envelopes with red and navy diagonal stripes around the edges. I stared at the address, at the handwriting. It was from my dead mother.

I hated it when the obvious was irrational. I was scared. What if my universe wasn't what I thought it was? What if the deceased could send airmail from afterlife?

I opened it, gingerly pulled out two sheets of bluish translucent paper, and unfolded them. They were covered with my mother's impulsive handwriting, where entire words degenerated into horizontal lines. My eyes fogged over.

Be rational!

There had to be a rational explanation. There always was. You just had to look for it long enough. That's what my father, an engineer, used to say. I tried to focus, cut through the fog. And I willed myself to look. At the date. Okay. A rational explanation. A huge relief. She'd written it before her departure. It had taken nine days for this letter to make its way from Nuremberg, Germany, to my campus PO Box in Wichita Falls, Texas.

I read the first two lines. They were too brutally irrelevant, and I couldn't read on.

Weeks later, another flimsy baby-blue letter arrived, this one from the family friend with whom my sister was staying. The remains of my parents had been transferred from Turkey to Austria, he wrote. The funeral would be in Achenkirch on—

"Tomorrow?" I muttered.

I rushed to the nearest travel agency. The woman, seeing the state I was in, went through the motions with her flight schedule book. "Out of DFW, let's see, you got TWA, Pan Am, and Lufthansa—but you won't be able to make today's flights. And tomorrow's flights arrive day after tomorrow."

It was impossible. Even if it had been possible, it would have been impossible. Tickets cost a fortune, and I was living hand to mouth and had to save for tuition. So I missed the funeral.

As for my brother, the day the plane crashed, he and some friends were driving around Turkey in a rust-perforated VW Bus. When he learned of a plane crash nearby, he didn't connect the dots either. He was twenty-two.

He found out two weeks later when he went home and his roommates told him. But he didn't miss the funeral. As for my sister, the authorities located her the day after the crash and informed her. She was eighteen. She didn't miss the funeral either.

By law, I was in the US on a student visa, and after finishing my coursework, I'd have to leave the country and go home. But *home* had become a theoretical construct associated with *debacle*, and the idea of going home had become an absurdity. During the turmoil of these days, even when I wanted to weep to find relief from my conflicted emotions, my eyes remained disdainfully dry. But something else was working itself to the surface, a magnetic and at once an ominous thought: I was finally free.

2

MAGIC WORDS

1995

The bus I'm on is idling in front of the double-arched Beaux-Arts facade of the train station in Tours. Our guide checks her watch, says something to the driver, then grabs the microphone. "We'll wait a few more minutes," she chirps in French and English over the PA system. "A passenger is still missing."

That I have so much time on my hands is hard to believe. The big day was last Friday, August 31. I shook hands with the man who owned the place, wished my successor good luck, turned in the keys to my demo, and said good-bye to some people on the way out. Ginger, in sunglasses, tank top, and miniskirt, was leaning provocatively against her red Mitsubishi 3000 GT, her fine blond tresses tousled by the hairdryer breeze. Two dozen salesmen milled around on the porch, smoking, watching the spectacle. I waved at them and climbed in on the passenger side. After ten years of working lousy jobs while getting my BA, MA, and MBA, and after ten more years of working seventy hours a week as general manager at the Ford

5

Superstore, I was finally free. At least to the extent possible in a modern, responsible sense.

I'd met Ginger a few months earlier. When I told her I was going to quit my job and go to France for seven weeks, she was puzzled. The very concept was alien to her. "You don't quit a dream job like that," she said. "And why do you have to be gone for that long?" She'd never been out of the country. And she wanted to start a family. Yet she tried to be supportive. "Get it out of your system," she said with dubious enthusiasm. As there was still some slack in the relationship, we arrived, to use Don Colson's term, at an unspoken verbal agreement: during my absence, she'd do her own thing, and I wouldn't ask any questions afterward.

My friends didn't mince words. "You're nuts," they said. They thought that quitting would ruin my career, that I'd be damaged goods. They thought it was because I'd turn forty this year. I should deal with it and tough it out and get over it, they said.

But there's nothing to deal with or tough out or get over. I didn't plunge into a spiritual black hole. I'm not racked by depression or a nasty divorce. Heck, I'm not even married. I'm not interested in long-term anything, to the point where I've made extra principal payments on my fifteen-year mortgage to get out from under it sooner.

My friends told me to overcome my aversion to debt and marriage. "They're part of life, like death and taxes," they said, "and the way to win is to submit to them gracefully." Of course, these dear friends of mine have been reshuffling spouses, fighting custody battles, and unscrambling upside-down mortgages under the supervision of the courts. Others have child support and alimony obligations out the wazoo. The irony is that they recommend the same program to me and call me cynical for not embracing it wholeheartedly.

Quitting occurred to me during Larry Hester's funeral—a man of fifty taken out by cancer. He wasn't the first of my friends or family to die, but he was the first to cause me to think about my life and its potential brevity. *What if I die at fifty?* I stared at the neck in front of me—graying hair not quite covering the skin folds bunching up against a starched white collar. There wasn't even a guarantee I'd make it to fifty. *What if I die at forty?* For years, I'd been in survival mode. Then, for another decade, I'd been in success mode—but what was the point now?

Something gave way inside me, a wall of sorts, and on one side was my analytical mind, and on the other I discovered my heart. I couldn't stand this kind of horseshit and almost jumped up. I was losing control. I'd never thought my mind and my heart had been disconnected, or could be disconnected, or that I even had a heart or whatever other than the big pump that kept me going. But now I saw they'd been disconnected for decades.

Maybe that's how I'd gotten through the debacle at home. My mother was fifty-one, my father sixty-five, when they went up in flames. I could go for years without giving them more than a fleeting thought. The few photos and letters I had were in an envelope I rarely opened. When I did think about them, I was invariably glad they were gone from my life—a thought that suddenly confused me, and for the first time, I didn't know what to do with it.

The eulogy at my parents' funeral must have made them seem like good and loving people who'd done their best. But I wasn't there and didn't hear it. If the eulogy had been recorded, would I listen to it now and give it a chance? Would I *give them a* chance?

A stunning question. Not that I was stupid enough to run out and search for reconciliation or the meaning of life or whatever. Instead, I went back to work, where I ping-ponged around, useless and distracted. At 5 p.m., I got in my demo, drove home early for the first time in ten years, and went for a long run down by the river to sort out what was troubling me.

I ran fifteen miles, but even that wasn't long enough to sort it all out, though it was long enough to make a decision: I'd quit and go to France for a while. I needed some time to gain perspective. And I wanted to open myself up to new possibilities. I had no clue where this would lead or what would come of it, and for once I had no projections and spreadsheets, no list of assumptions, no five-year graphs. All I had were sore legs from my run.

"Voilà," Stephanie says over the PA system, "our missing passenger."

An Asian girl in jeans and salmon blouse jogs across the parking lot, her black hair whipping behind her. She climbs on the bus, hands Stephanie her ticket, and makes her way down the aisle. She scans empty seats, stops, can't decide where to sit. Her silky blouse seems out of place among everyone else's sweaters and jackets. She exchanges a slight nod with an older Asian man and alights on the seat in front of him.

He speaks to her. She twists back to face him. Minuscule pearls of sweat glimmer on her nose and upper lip. He talks. She nods at polite intervals.

And when she turns around to listen to Stephanie, who's peppering us with the turbulent history of the châteaux of the Loire Valley, her eyes pass over me as if I didn't exist.

At the Château de Chenonceau, the Asian man asks her to take pictures of him with his big Minolta. He poses in front of Catherine de Medici's bed, offers to take pictures of her with her camera, tries to make conversation, but she gravitates to a delicately carved dresser and consults her guidebook, melancholic smile at the corners of her mouth.

In the Grand Gallery, she drifts away from the group, swiveling in the ballroom's elegance and immensity. I sidle up to her and search for something to say, something intelligent preferably.

"Isn't this checkerboard floor exquisite?" I say.

She seems to nod.

"It looks modern, but it's four hundred years old."

She lowers her eyes to examine it.

"Tufa and slate tiles, classic building stones of the region."

She raises her eyes to evaluate the woodwork of the ceiling and floats away from me.

Isn't this checkerboard floor exquisite? I mean, come on. Cobbling together pickup lines is the oldest form of mental gymnastics and is responsible for the very survival of the species, but even after all these years I'm still, as the French say, *nul* at it.

Yet there can't possibly be a more romantic venue for picking up a girl than this illustrious château. In 1547, King Henry II of France, twenty-eight, gifted it to his mistress, Diane de Poitiers, a seductive redhead twenty years his senior. His wife, Catherine de Medici, had to endure their hanky-panky for twelve years—until he was killed in a tournament. Now Regent of France, she finagled to expel her rival from the château and then remodeled it in the hot new style imported from Italy that we call Renaissance. She bequeathed the château to Louise de Lorraine, wife of her third son, King Henry III. Upon his assassination, Louise de Lorraine retired to the château and immersed herself in prayer and reading. Thus commenced a period of four centuries during which women owned or ran the château.

We walk out the front portal into a cold drizzle. I'm a few feet behind the Asian girl. She pulls in her shoulders and crosses her arms. On the other side of the bridge over the moat, she whirls around to view the ornate façade—and her eyes land on me. She brushes a strand of hair from her face, surprised someone is at the very spot I occupy.

"Do you like the château?" I ask.

"I love it. It's obvious that women built and remodeled it. Everything is designed to please the eye. It's a beautiful loyal residence."

"Loyal residence?"

"L or R?"

"Oh, royal, with an R."

A shiver runs through her body.

"Let's get some coffee to warm us up before we go back to our bus," I say.

"Our bus?"

"We've got twenty minutes."

"*Your* bus?"

"*Our* bus. We're on the same bus."

That's how it goes with girls. They don't even know I'm there. But now we're talking. We crunch through wet gravel to the museum café. I open the door for her. She halts.

"I'd rather stroll in the gardens," she says.

Alas, I absolutely have to use the restroom, but before I can fashion this into an eloquent response, she strides into the mist and disappears between plane trees, bushes, and hedges glistening with moisture.

When I get on the bus, she's in her seat, listening to the Asian man. At the Château d'Amboise, I climb off the bus right behind her.

"Have you seen any of the other châteaux?" I ask.

"Yes, several. I was here a few days ago with a different tour but didn't have time to look for Leonardo da Vinci's grave."

"His grave is here?"

"He was hired by King Charles VIII to remodel the château, and she died here."

"Who's she?"

"She?"

Now we're both confused.

We follow Stephanie into a surviving wing of the formerly vast castle. From a roof platform, she points out a wrought-iron balcony on the other wing. Twelve Protestants were hanged from it in 1560 during the repression of the Huguenot Conspiracy. A thousand Protestants were beheaded on the marketplace. Others were drowned in the Loire. A select few were quartered.

"To inspire loyalty to the Catholic Regime of France," Stephanie says with an ironic curve to her lips. European history, incomprehensibly bloody since time immemorial, is part of the fun of traveling, and tour guides depict it with gusto to jack up their tips.

The group disperses for lunch. The Asian girl and I buy ham-and-butter baguette sandwiches. With our napkins, I mop rainwater off a bench in front of the château, and we settle down. Izumi is her name. She's in France for a week and has to go back Saturday.

"I came to study the history of the châteaux of the Loire," she says. "I did a lot of reading in preparation. Actually, the trip is sort of a birthday gift to myself."

She's twenty-six. The sun comes out. Sparrows peck at the crumbs between our feet. She works for a venture capital firm in Tokyo, one of the largest ones, and I've never heard of it. I tell her I'm doing a two-week homestay where the lady of the house gives me French lessons.

What I don't say is that living with a functional family has a salubrious effect on me, that I observe with astonishment how parents support their kids, how they resolve conflicts, how they respect each other, and how fear, denigration, and violence aren't the foundation of their relationship.

"I'll do another homestay near Marseille," I say. "Then I have three weeks on my own."

"I wish we had vacation this long."

"We don't have vacation this long either. I quit my job."

"Quit your.... Why?"

"Midlife crisis.

I'm joking. I'm too young to be in any kind of crisis. She doesn't think it's funny. She doesn't know the term. I define it. She grapples with it, digs a 1,340-page Bible-paper English-Japanese dictionary out of her purse. But *midlife crisis* isn't in it. It doesn't exist in Japanese. Japanese men don't go through it. They have other problems and commit suicide.

Then she doesn't believe how old I am, and I have to show her my passport.

"Aren't you worried about your future?" she asks.

"I'm excited about it. I feel like a little boy with all possibilities still in front of him."

"Cool. I envy you."

We stroll around. By the ramparts and in front of da Vinci's house, she asks me to take pictures of her with her camera. But she doesn't take pictures of me; she hasn't elevated me to that level yet. And I travel without camera. During my last summer in college, I took rolls and rolls of film of the Rockies and afterward couldn't remember what I'd seen because I'd seen everything through my camera—but didn't have the money to get the photos developed.

We sit together on the bus and walk through the châteaux together. Back at the station in Tours, we coast away from the bus in an uncertain direction. She's schlepping a bag with three bottles of Chenin Blanc she bought at our last stop, a wine tasting in Vouvray. It's 5 p.m. In theory, we'll part ways here, and I'll never see her again. So I ask her to join me for an espresso. She checks her watch and says, "I could do that." We head to a café across the street and order espressos from a wordless waiter dressed entirely in black except for his maroon mini-apron.

"I used to dream about a job in venture capital," I say. At her age, I'd just finished my MA in English and was rolling burritos at a Taco Bueno. "You have an awesome career ahead of you."

"Not awesome. I manipulate numbers. My development project in Sri Lanka is so over budget it'll require a third round of funding. It'll never be profitable for the limited partners. Yet I have to make it appear profitable to—" she pulls out her dictionary "—to lure investors."

"Luring is the crux of business. We call it selling."

"It doesn't inspire me."

"You want a job that *inspires* you?" I'm incredulous.

"And I want to work with culture and languages and live in other parts of the world."

"Like where?"

"Southeast Asia or Latin America."

"And the US?"

"I haven't thought about it." She thinks about it. "Probably not."

"How about Europe?"

"I've been going to Europe for years. It's not new enough."

"Interested in dinner tonight?" *Aventure de vacances* the French call it, a fling on neutral territory with no loose ends dangling off afterward.

"I have an appointment."

"A date?"

"Not date. A retired American military guy and two Japanese girls from the hotel."

"Oh." I need to pronounce the magic words that will lead to more words, which will lead to the next step so that it won't end here.

"Actually, I need to hurry," she says. "I need to get ready."

"Tomorrow night?" My magic words. They're all I have.

"I'm not available."

"Not available?"

"I'm meeting a friend in Paris," she says.

The dipstick of a waiter takes my money, drops the change on the table, and wads up the check while staring at five chicks that greet each other with *bises*—air kisses on each cheek.

"I have to call him to confirm. I called her twice already, but he wasn't there, so I left her a message. If I can't reach him, I can stay in Tours one more night."

Her personal pronouns can give you whiplash, but I know better than to ask, *He or she?*

"If I don't go to Paris," she says, "I'll call you tomorrow, and we can have dinner."

A face-saver. She won't call. She'll have her own *aventure de vacances* in Paris. "That would be awesome," I say and write the phone number of my homestay into her guidebook.

Outside, there's an awkward moment. Shake hands? Say good-bye, without anything? Do *bises?* She extends her hand, and I shake it. It's tiny and soft. The hand of a child.

Instead of taking the bus, I hoof it back to my homestay in Fondettes on the slope across the Loire. Jeanne is cooking when I arrive. Nicolas has commuted home from Paris. "The hour on the TGV is my daily ration of peace," he explains while their four boys noisily set the table.

"Lettuce, carrots, and onions are from my garden," Jeanne says as we sit around the table, all seven of us, a veritable dinner party at my place.

"Twelve years ago, when we moved in, this was just a brick shell with a roof," Nicolas says. "We installed hardwood floors, tiles, doors, and lamps. We stuccoed and painted."

"We enjoy physical work," she says.

"I'm glad it's done. Next year we might even go on vacation." He eyes her wistfully.

"My garden requires daily care. I can't—"

The maroon phone on the buffet jangles. She frowns, gets up, and answers with a dry *"Oui?"* Her sons aren't permitted to use the phone during dinner. "Yes, an instant," she says in her English and motions with the receiver to me. I don't expect any calls. Izumi, if she calls at all, will call tomorrow. I excuse myself, squeeze through between Nicolas and the wall, and curve around the table to the phone.

"Wolf?" A feathery voice.

I see stars. I got up too fast. I brace myself against the buffet.

"I couldn't reach my friend in Paris. I can stay in Tours one more night," she says.

The entire family listens to my side of the conversation, and no one eats. When I hang up, I excuse myself again. Jeanne is icily silent. Philippe and André, the pubescent twins, giggle. Romain, who's in lycée, asks if she's my girlfriend. Paul, who's in college, tells him it's none of his business. I shrug like a Frenchman, the only possible answer.

After dinner, the boys do the dishes. Jeanne retreats upstairs. Nicolas reads a magazine on the couch. I sit on the back porch amid odors of moist earth from the vegetable garden. The moon hovers behind racing clouds, an oscillating silver stain on the black sky.

I've come to France to improve my French. I want to graduate from mere Francophile to that elusive level the French call Francophone. And meeting a French girl would help those efforts along nicely. I haven't come to France to meet a Japanese girl. Yet all I can think about is Izumi.

3

HARVEST MOON

The drizzle in front of the Hôtel de Ville is so fine it wafts up underneath my umbrella, while I'm wondering if Izumi has changed her mind. But then I spot her. She walks fast and every few seconds falls into a brief trot.

"Sorry," she says as she comes to a stop in front of me. Her radiant smile excuses everything, even the interminable wait in the drizzle. "I had to find a sweater." She tugs on her thin black sweater. "I borrowed it from a Japanese girl at the hotel. I didn't bring any warm clothes. It was hot in Tokyo, and I didn't think it would be cold in France."

We meander through the historic center and talk about what we see. At the New Basilica St. Martin, I tell her the neoclassic structure is a third-generation replacement of a much larger basilica from the fifth century when Christianity coexisted with Roman and Gallic deities. I'm on shaky ground with my deities, periods, bishops, and emperors, but she listens with interest.

At the Tour Charlemagne, one of the remaining towers of the old St. Martin, I point out layers of architecture superimposed on each other. She follows my finger across the weathered stones, and her eyes sparkle. "Transitions fascinate me," I say. What fascinates me is her body. And the way to her body is via her brain, and her brain is endlessly curious and thirsty for cultural tidbits.

It's getting dark. We're wet and hungry. Conversation has switched to food. I translate menus posted outside. Some restaurants are packed with young people, and it would be fun to have dinner there, but I'm looking for something romantic. And voilà: a menu by an old wooden door, stone stairs down to a medieval vault with massive columns and, between them, tables decorated with candles and exotic blossoms.

We order Kir Royale. She has me translate every item on the menu and every nuance of every herb and sauce, handicapped as I am by fuzzy knowledge.

"The *daurade rôtie au fenouil* sounds interesting," she says. "What is it?"

"It's fish." I know because it's listed in the fish section.

"What's *fenouil*?"

"It's what comes with the fish."

And so on. But she can't decide and has to go over her top choices again, narrows them down, and after a painstaking process, chooses the *daurade rôtie au fenouil* anyway. I order duck breast, beef having been expunged from menus due to the mad cow fiasco.

Agilely picking fish bones from her lips, she chatters about her hard-working high-school years and hard-drinking college years, and about her dizzying social life. It's her turn to immerse me in cultural tidbits. Wine emboldens her in her feisty struggle with English, and her words become more fluid and her syntax more tangled. For dessert, she wonders about the *île flottante.*

"Floating island," I translate.

"Sounds romantic."

When it comes, she gasps at its size, pokes her fork into the mountain of meringue floating in *crème anglaise*, loses interest, and raves about the infinite entertainment options in post-bubble Tokyo. She's on a roll. She's passionate about Japan, and her passion is infectious.

I've been all over the US and Europe. I have a reasonable command of French and German. I studied European history going back three thousand years and American history going back five hundred. But I know little about the rest of the world, and I'm ignorant about Japan. Is this, I wonder as I eat my *tarte Tatin*, a flipped-over apple pie, the result of our educational system? My college in Texas only offered Spanish, French, and German.

Why not Japanese or Chinese. Why not Arabic? Why was my education so Eurocentric?

"I want to go to Japan someday and study Japanese," I say when she pauses.

She doesn't react. She has heard it before. Travel acquaintances say this kind of blather. She knows it isn't a promise, that I won't follow through, that distance and exigencies of life at home will prevail.

"In Japan, nothing was built to last," she finally says. "We accept the transitory nature of things. For us, fires, earthquakes, tsunamis, volcanoes, and landslides are certainties. Tokyo used to be built of wood and paper, and it was destroyed on average every sixty years."

When we step outside, the drizzle has stopped. Streets are bathed in moonlight. People mill around. We circle back to Place Plumereau. At one of the sidewalk cafés that line it, we get a waitress to towel rainwater off a table and a couple of chairs for us. I order two shots of Calvados.

"I've never had Calvados in a glass," Izumi says.

"How do you normally drink it? From the bottle?"

"I've had it in pastries."

We drink to the moon, which is huge and astounding.

"Harvest moon, the brightest full moon of the year," she says. "Can you see the rabbit pounding rice cakes?"

"The what?"

"The rabbit pounding rice cakes."

"Where?"

"In the moon! Can't you see it?"

I strain to see it but don't know what to look for. Turns out, you have to be Japanese to see it.

She explains the Japanese writing system, jots the hiragana into a small notebook, and intones them in a rhythmic rhyming chant. "Your first Japanese lesson," she says, tears out the page, and slides it across the table. "We also use kanji, which are Chinese characters. And katakana for foreign words."

"Your keyboards have got to be one big mess."

"Not at all. Japanese can be written perfectly well in hiragana—"

"So why don't you write it in hiragana?"

"Some people do, but it looks uneducated."

"But you use hiragana keyboards?"

"No. We use the same alphabet keyboards you use, but with software that converts letters to hiragana, and hiragana to kanji or katakana."

"You type Japanese in the Latin alphabet?"

"Of course."

"But then, why don't you *write* it in the Latin alphabet?"

She looks at me perplexed.

"I mean, without all this crazy converting and artificial complexifying."

She still looks at me but now is speechless in the face of so much ignorance.

"Maybe that would be too easy," I backpedal and order another round of Calvados.

At about 2 a.m., the waitress begins stacking chairs upside down on the tables around us. We're steeped in conversation. Her fingers toy with the shadow of her shot glass that the moon is casting on the tabletop. I put my hand on her hand. She sucks in a puff of air, holds her breath. Her fingers twine around mine. Her eyes burn into mine.

"Let's go," I say.

She nods.

We amble vaguely toward rue Nationale. I have no clue what to do or where to go but seem to be leading her. Suddenly, I know what to do. I pull her into a dark corner and kiss her. The mellow ethereal flavor and pulpy texture of her mouth engulf my thoughts. The warmth of her body seeps through my clothes. She sinks into my arms, abandons herself, and if I weren't holding her up, she'd sink to the cobblestones. When our lips separate, I speak my magic words:

"Where's your hotel?"

"Over there."

It means *yes*.

She doesn't seem eager, but she doesn't hesitate. Her knees buckle. She clings to me. My arm is draped around her back. Her waist is so narrow that my hand comes to rest on her belly. Her shoulder slips into my armpit. Pieces of our bodies fit together like a puzzle.

At a one-star hotel on rue Pimbert, she roots around in her purse, pulls out a keychain with two iron keys, and unlocks the door. We mount a creaky staircase. She gestures to a toilet down the hall and whispers, "In case you need."

Hours later, I'm still glued to her on the narrow bed. Her skin has the texture of compressed air, her breasts the hue of moonlight. Her hair ebbs and flows over the pillow. She sleeps without a sound. Every now and then, a moped screams by. She'll be on a TGV to Paris in a few hours, on a plane by 1 p.m., in Tokyo tomorrow, and at work the day after. But for us, there'll be no tomorrow.

"Unless I make it happen," I mutter at dawn, worn out by thoughts that won't cease churning. I wake her up, and we make love one more time. I shower in her in-room plastic shower stall and dry off with a sheet, there not being any towels in this joint. She sits on the bed, wrapped in the other sheet, watching me. I don't even know her last name.

"Can I write you?" I ask.

"I'd like that."

"Write me, too."

She offers me her notebook. I write my name, email, and other contact info into it. She writes her info on a blank page, tears it out, and hands it to me.

"I don't have email," she says and dabs at her cheeks with the heel of her hand.

We hug, and she cries in a reluctant manner.

"I'm going to Japan in the spring," I mumble into her hair. This time, it isn't travel-acquaintance blather but a decision. Neither distance nor exigencies of life at home will prevail. "Would you be interested in seeing me?"

"Very much."

It's time to go. As I cross the corridor at the bottom of the stairway, a rough voice barks at me from behind, wanting to know what room I stayed in. I imagine the owner in wrinkled pants and undershirt, cigarette dangling from his lips. I speed up, try not to run. He wants to be paid for the night I spent at his establishment. But I don't want to embarrass Izumi. I blow out the door, rush toward rue Nationale, sense her teary eyes on my shoulders, but don't look back because I don't want to face the angry owner. And I hook around the corner.

Tours is barely stirring this early on a Saturday. I slump into a chair at a sidewalk café on the sunny side of rue Nationale. I'm exhilarated. I'm drained. My knees are shaking. I can't think. I'm triumphant. I'm exhausted. I didn't sleep at all. I see her in front of me, her luminescent breasts, her shoulders that are broad for her size, her hair undulating over the pillow. And there's a vacuum where her body pressed against mine.

4

PILGRIMAGE

The two-axle cog-drive steam engine spews clouds of soot into the immaculate sky as it pushes with hissing rhythmic thumps two carriages at walking speed up the 16 percent grade. I'm a railroad buff, and as a kid, I already loved this little train. It's an apt finale to my seven weeks in Europe—five weeks in France, ten days in Italy, and now Austria.

We curve past modern homes and multistory buildings that look vaguely like the half-timbered Tyrolean farmhouses of yore. *Lederhosen Architektur* locals call that style. But tourists think it's quaint.

The town of Jenbach recedes below us. Jagged peaks and glaciers scintillate in the October sun on the other side of the Inn Valley. Meadows alternate with birches, bushes, and ferns that give way to pines as we climb. The odor of manure mixes with the acrid stench of burning coal. We crest at the village of Eben and coast toward the southern tip of an emerald-green lake wedged lengthwise between rugged mountains, the Achensee.

A two-lane road runs along its eastern shore, carved into the mountain during the thirties and forties, just above the precarious single-lane old road. On the western shore, only a footpath hugs the cliffs, steep forests, and gravel washes. But I take the ferry, the most spectacular way north. It crisscrosses the lake and docks at villages and isolated inns.

I disembark at the Hotel Seehof, a turn-of-the-century chalet of ochre stucco, mossy concrete, and weathered wood set on a promontory among chestnut trees, pastures, and stands of pine.

"We don't get Americans often," says the surprised lady at the reception when I show up with my blue passport and no reservation. She has no reason to know that I'm the grandson of the couple who operated the hotel until 1959 and that the man who operated it for another decade is my uncle.

I pause on the balcony of my room. It faces the lake, and late at night, when all human sounds have faded, you can hear the echo of waterfalls, the frayed silver ribbons dangling down the mountain on the other side. Then I head out and walk north across the hotel grounds.

The chapel where my parents were married is still there, its sagging door locked. The little house where I spent the happier parts of my childhood is gone. The barn is still there. The kiosk by the lake is gone. The boathouse is still there, as is the *Dépendance* where the staff used to live. It's shuttered. The machine house is still there. It used to contain a high-pressure waterwheel and generator that supplied the hotel with DC electricity until it was connected to the grid in the thirties. The equipment disappeared long before my time, but the high-pressure feed pipe to a spring up the mountain supplies the hotel to this day with delicious ice-cold water. The pines, replanted after the war, have become tall.

I continue on the old road to the northern tip of the lake and on to Achenkirch, a straggling village of picturesque farmhouses, pastures, *Pensionen*, and big chalet-type hotels, hemmed in by piney mountainsides into which ski slopes have been cut. In its center is an eighteenth-century church with an onion-domed steeple surrounded by a walled cemetery.

It takes me a little while to locate the grave. Five names are on the bronze plate. Top left are the names of my mother's parents who died in 1959 and 1960 in the little house that no longer is.

Squeezed beneath their names, in smaller font—as if by afterthought, though he'd died over two decades before them—is the name of their son Martin Pfeffer, the most admired man in my mother's life. In 1937, he participated in the third German expedition to climb the Nanga Parbat, one of the eight-thousanders in the Himalayas, all of them unconquered at the time. During the night of June 14, an ice avalanche buried their camp, killing everyone in it, seven Germans and nine Sherpas.

A search party reached the site a month later, and on July 20 they found a tent beneath eleven feet of ice and compressed snow. In it were Martin and a comrade in their sleeping bags. Near them were their journals.

Martin had scrawled his last entry on June 14 at 6 p.m., a description of his solitary climb to the ridge and on to a minor peak, his first six-thousander. Rock pinnacles and glaciers appeared here and there through racing clouds. Later, after he'd returned to the camp, the sun came out, and the view opened up to the Indus deep below them. Hope, optimism, and excitement were laced into his words. Clement weather might finally set in and allow them to advance to Camp V. And he envisioned tackling the summit soon.

The wristwatch his comrade wore had frozen into position at 12:20. The search party recuperated their journals, the watch (which started running again when it warmed up in someone's pocket), and other items, but their bodies are still under the ice, and his grave is empty.

On the right are the names of my parents. They died at night on a package tour. My father had retired six months earlier from Siemens, his lifelong employer, but my mother still sold electric massagers on a part-time basis. This trip was a big event for them. They were going to study Turkey's antiquity. They'd read up on it months in advance and had taken evening courses, and a docent would guide them through the archeological sites and lecture on the intricacies of ancient Asia Minor.

They didn't get very far. They flew to Istanbul, changed planes, and on their way to Antalya, crashed into a mountain. The authorities were able to identify the remains by their wedding bands, which were then delivered— still charcoal encrusted—to my sister in a little plastic bag.

My mother had never been on a plane before. And my father, who believed in numbers like others believe in God, had always said, "Flying is the safest mode of travel." Which it doubtlessly had been, until then.

The grave faces the church. On both sides, mountains against the evening sky. The beauty of the spot in the middle of this valley is stunning. I step into the church. Tyrolean Baroque with frescos, gilded decorations, and paintings. Smells of must, incense, and burning candles. In the pews, an ancient woman in black overcoat and headscarf, murmuring with trembling lips, rosary between her knotty fingers.

I light five candles. Tyrol's dialect is nearly incomprehensible to me, its independent mountain culture impenetrable. I don't come here often. It's far, and for vacation, there are better places to go.

Yet something tugs on me. Here, you can't check your emotions at the door. It's where grief descends on your soul. It's where you try to think of your parents as essentially good and loving people who hadn't been able to overcome their flaws. It's where you try to understand and forgive, even if you know you can't. It's where you come to cry.

My pilgrimage concludes at a nearby Gasthaus with a beer, a bowl of speck dumpling soup, and a plate of goulash with boiled potatoes and salad. The only other patrons are five guys at a table in the corner, talking in their native tongue, drinking, smoking, and slamming cards on the table.

As I nurture a second beer, I realize that I need to do one more thing. Martin, my uncle, was married to Karli. She used to live on the other side of the border, in Holzkirchen, now a suburb of Munich. So I call around to get her number; then I call her.

5

HEROIC TIMES

Awisp of a lady in slacks and sweater, Hermès scarf draped around her neck, opens the door, stares at me wide-eyed, clasps her hands over her cheeks, and breaks into tears.

"Karli?"

"You look just like my Martin," she wheezes.

After a few moments, she collects herself and invites me in. While she hustles about serving coffee and slices of apple tart, I sit on the couch, wondering about the faded indigo cardboard box incongruously situated on the coffee table. It's the size of a shoebox for hiking boots. Clearly, she put it there for me.

I ask about her husband. He isn't doing well. He's in the hospital. She wants to know what I've been up to for the last twenty-five years. I tell her in three sentences. Then I ask about Martin.

"I knew that's why you've come," she says. She tells me their story. She met him while she was my mother's private teacher. He was a dashing elite alpinist. He was strong and fit. He was smart. He was an architect. He was everything. They got married, and by the time he left for India, she was pregnant.

"He knew?" I ask.

"He promised he'd be back before the baby would come."

"You believed that?"

"*Believe?*" she snorts. "Two German Nanga-Parbat expeditions had already failed, and people had died. Every expedition to any of these cursed eight-thousanders had failed. People climbed them to die. But he said, 'Don't worry, this time it's different. We know a lot more about the mountain, and we have the best team.'"

"He said that?"

"These days, I forget a lot, and sometimes—" her eyes dart around the room "—I can't remember where I put my purse. But I'll never forget his words." With the silver cake server, she distractedly repositions the slices of apple tart. "But I believed him. What else should I have done? *Not* believe him and go crazy?"

"Makes you wonder why people risk everything to try to accomplish the impossible."

"Those were heroic times. It was an important expedition. Every alpinist dreamed about it. The Nazis wanted to make a statement. People were still talking about the humiliation of Versailles. God only knows. Just getting to India took a month. The whole world was watching. The Luftwaffe was involved—"

"The Luftwaffe? Interested in mountains?"

"High-altitude experiments. More coffee?" she says as she tops off my cup.

"Thanks. The apple tart is heavenly."

"I thought you might like it. It was Martin's favorite pastry."

"Couldn't he have backed out?"

"Sure. But it was an immense honor. And perhaps he loved his mountains more than—" She doesn't take her eyes off me. But she isn't seeing me. She's looking through me, and beyond me, she's seeing Martin.

"Did you ask him not to go?"

"No. I loved my Martin the way he was. And he was an adventurer at heart. Perhaps the Lord hadn't made him to raise a family."

When she learned he'd been killed, she couldn't envision life without him. But part of him would continue, and so the baby became her source of strength. I don't want to hear the rest. I know vaguely what's coming, heard stories about it. Her words emerge one by one.

"The baby died during birth. Suffocated. I almost died, too. I still don't know why I didn't."

"But you put yourself back on your feet."

"The Lord gives us no choice. I remarried and we had two darling kids. I've always respected my husband. But my Martin is the only man I've ever loved."

"Does your husband know that?"

"Come," she says and gets up. I follow her into the bedroom. She picks up a framed photo from a bedside table, a black-and-white of a young man with a long, narrow face and a big forehead.

"My Martin," she says.

"Your husband has been willing to face Martin every day?"

"Every family has its arrangements."

We sit back down on the couch. She slides the faded indigo cardboard box across the coffee table and places it on her lap.

"I saved these," she says and lifts off the lid. On top are brittle newspaper clippings—articles about the expedition, its catastrophic end, and the search efforts. Then there are letters he sent her. On the bottom are his two expedition journals, rescued by the search party. They're jammed from edge to edge with a looped chaotic cursive that I can't decipher.

Morose and clouded with questions, but also energized and restless, I take a train to Munich and catch the night train to Paris. At the Gare du Nord, at 6:30 a.m., police with automatic weapons pull two dark-haired young men in front of me aside and harass them with questions. Trash skitters in the wind. People glance about. Soldiers with assault rifles patrol in teams of four or five. Luggage lockers are sealed.

ATTENTAT scream the headlines at newsstands. A bomb exploded on an RER train in the tunnel between St. Michel and Quai d'Orsay—the fifth bomb in four months. Everyone is fingering the Algerian Islamists.

I install myself, as the French say, in a café, dunk a croissant into my *grand café,* and think about Martin who died on an eight-thousander in the British colony of India, now in Kashmir on the Pakistani side of the Line of Control. And I think about Karli who survived World War I, the loss of Martin, the loss of their child, Allied carpet bombing during World War II, and who knows what all. And I think about my parents who died in Turkey on a frigging package tour. And I think about my own life, that there have to be answers and parallels, that this has to make some kind of cosmic sense, that there's a nuanced revelation at the end, and I think and think. But there aren't any parallels, and it doesn't make cosmic sense, and no revelations appear. Instead, reverberating in the background is the drumbeat of my unscripted future, and it fills me with excitement.

6

PARADISE

1996

The rickety taxi drives us past rows of stalls. People are sleeping on the ground. Others are cooking breakfast. Our windows are down. The warm humid air is a godsend after a decade on the plane.

We departed Tulsa at noon on Saturday, February 10, changed planes in Dallas—even when we go to hell, we have to change planes in Dallas—and Los Angeles, refueled in Hawaii in the middle of the night, crossed the international date line and lost twenty-four hours that instant, a mind-boggling event that we slept through, and arrived today, Monday, at 5 a.m. at Nandi International Airport on Viti Levu, the main island of the archipelago of Fiji.

I'm euphoric because I got off the plane alive—an irrational euphoria that washes over me whenever I get off a plane, irrational because flying is the safest mode of travel, statistically speaking.

"Is this what they call culture shock?" Ginger asks out of the side of her mouth.

I don't know either. It's the first time for both of us in the Third World.

The driver points out a hotel, an Indian restaurant, a temple, a mosque. "People in Fiji are either Fijians or Indians," he says. "I'm Indian, for example." They putter around in front of tin hovels and moldy concrete buildings clustered at the edge of sugarcane fields. To fill the hours before the departure of our ferry, we've hired a taxi for a tour of the area.

"We're half the population, but we can't own land. Only Fijians can own land."

"How do you make a living?" I wonder.

"We can own businesses. I drive a taxi, for example."

We bounce over the wobbly tracks of a sugarcane train.

"Fijians are lazy. They resent our business success."

Sugarcane fields everywhere.

"I'm Hindu. Other Indians are Muslim. On Fiji, all Indians get along."

The goal apparently is a sugarcane mill, a rusting corrugated-tin hulk. "Managed by Indians," he says proudly. "Fijians can't manage anything." He holds forth on Fiji's coups, which are bloodless, and on the constitution, which reserves top government posts for Fijians and guarantees them an absolute majority in parliament.

His aggravating complexities convert post-flight euphoria into a headache. I'm dreaming of coffee.

"Doesn't sound like paradise," I tell Ginger, who is staring sullenly out the window.

"Doesn't look like paradise either," she says.

The reason we're in Fiji is my travel agent. I asked him for tickets to New Zealand. He proposed an Air New Zealand special with a free stopover in Fiji. "A tropical paradise in the South Pacific," he called it.

By the time the taxi drops us off at the marina, we're exhausted. But before us is the dazzling ocean with distant specks that might be islands, and one of them might be ours. Deckhands heave cargo on a rusty catamaran ferry. We board with two dozen locals and some tourists, and shortly after 9 a.m., the catamaran speeds into the deep blue sea.

We lean against the railing and squint at islands as they draw nearer, at their blinding beaches and swaying coconut palms. Ginger's hair caresses my cheeks. It's even blonder here among so much black hair—kinky for Fijians, straight or wavy for Indians. We've already learned to interpret everything in terms of this duality.

Four hours later, we approach Castaway Island. The sea turns turquoise, and by the pier, it's so crystalline it doesn't seem to be there. Beyond the brilliant sand are coconut palms, and under them are thatched buildings that dissipate into a curtain of greenery.

A Fijian woman in a flowing red robe ushers us to some chairs in the shade while deckhands unload supplies. Two papaya drinks appear.

"Now you're on Fiji time," she says.

We sip our drinks. She inquires about our trip. We groan about the flight. The catamaran departs. A porter carries off our luggage. A diesel generator rumbles behind the staff buildings.

Then she asks for my credit card. Ah yes, money. Even here.

Our *bure*, a Fijian-style cabin at the far end of the campus, has no TV, AC, phone, or hairdryer. Its backside abuts tropical forest. Door and patio face the beach. Trade winds breathe through the glass shutters.

We throw on swimsuits and sprint across the sand and splash into the water, yelling, laughing. The antidote to jetlag.

"That's what a tropical paradise is supposed to look like," Ginger says in the shade of a tiki hut, exuding Coppertone, eyes hidden behind sunglasses, lips sculpted into a smile. Water trickles from her breasts over her belly whose whiteness matches that of the sand. And I gaze at her while I still can.

We shower in our airy bathroom. She sits on the bed, naked. I brush out her wet hair with long slow strokes. It pleases her. A squall drums on the roof and cascades down the glass shutters. She closes her eyes. Amazing what arouses a girl. Not my money, not my lean body, not my eyes, not my equipment. But a plastic hairbrush.

Afterward we lie on the bed with a view of the ocean and distant islands. The ceiling fan is slapping at the thick air. A gecko scurries up the wall, pauses, peers down on us, and disappears into a gap in the vaulted ceiling that is painted with native motifs. Everything is in balance, and there's nothing else I want. I'm happy.

"Fiji time," I say.

She sighs.

My body is in a state of perfect relaxation.

"I'm glad you didn't cancel my ticket when I asked you to," she mumbles into my chest.

I'm wavering lazily between sleep and wake.

"But why can't you fly home with me?"

Now I'm wide awake. The problem is she isn't on Fiji time yet. She's still on her biological clock that is ticking to her version of the future where we're a married couple with kids. I can't blame her. A girl has a right to think that way. But I can blame her for yanking me out of Fiji time.

For the next three weeks, we'll do Fiji and New Zealand. Then she'll fly home. I'll fly on to Australia and Japan. That's our deal. Her plan B will fill my spot. She'll get pregnant because she's ready to get pregnant. She knows a lot of guys and always has a plan B.

For instance, after we met last year, she'd show up at my place at odd hours to fuck, maybe twice one week, then not again for two weeks. A few times, she agreed to go on a date with me but bailed out at the last minute. I was plan B to the guy she was doing. She didn't even hide it. He was a lawyer and snorted coke, she told me. One night last July, she came by at an odd hour and said as a greeting, "I'm tired of his bullshit. You can have me lock, stock, and barrel, if you still want me."

I'd been promoted to plan A.

We went on our first date. Normally, you have two goals on a first date with a hot chick: weasel into bed with her and get another date. The rest, such as the consequences, you worry about later. So you focus. You're sensible and companionable. You make her laugh and feel good about herself. You listen with fascination to her crap and comment only on cue. And for crying out loud, don't offer solutions. You don't have opinions, and if she has opinions, you agree with them. In short, you keep your inner asshole to yourself. And you show in subtle ways that you can provide—for instance, you pay with practiced nonchalance, as if the ruinous amount you just blew had no impact on your vast financial holdings.

All this was, of course, moot on our first date. It was then that I told her I'd tendered my resignation but wasn't searching for another job. She was supportive but didn't like the uncertainty. I told her I'd spend September and October in Europe. It baffled her, but we came up with our unspoken verbal agreement that she'd do her own thing during my absence and I wouldn't ask any questions afterward. I told her I wasn't interested in marriage—an absolute no-no on a first date.

"We'll just have to see," she said.

"And I don't want to have kids," I declared with utmost finality.

She rumpled her brow, held her breath for a few seconds, but then broke into a confident smile. Perhaps she thought it was merely another challenge I'd thrown in front of her, something she could overcome if she read up on it in *Cosmo* and used the correct techniques. But I believe in laying out the issues up front. I wanted her to know what she was getting into before she'd get into it too deeply. Now we have both gotten into it too deeply.

Dinner is underground barbecue, a Fijian specialty. Two wiry guys in shorts and flip-flops wrap a three-foot fish and some veggies in banana leaves, put the bundle into a pit, cover it with burlap sacks and dirt, and shovel a pile of embers on top. Soon, steam and smoke rise from the pit. Guests stand around and watch. A waitress serves drinks.

The fish shows up on the buffet, and by the time we get to it, it's an overcooked mess with bones sticking out at random. But the dining patio borders the beach, and the magnificence of the sunset renders the blandness of the food irrelevant. The dessert buffet tempts Ginger. But she hesitates.

"Go ahead," I say. "You can afford it."

"No way. I'm three months pregnant."

I draw a blank.

"Something not right with your food?" she says.

"Urk—" My brain explodes with useless thoughts.

"Got a fish bone in your throat?"

"*Pregnant?*"

"Oh, that." Her laugh peals across the patio.

"What's so funny?"

"Your face."

"Did you say *pregnant?*"

"Sure. You know, not with a big P. It's the awful plane food. I'm so bloated."

The jackhammer in my temples abates. I'm such a sucker.

"I should have taken a picture of your face to show mom."

"It's still not that hilarious to me."

She puts her index finger under my chin, pulls me closer, and kisses me across the table, which I accept as apology for chopping ten years off my life expectancy. Distant islands turn into black mounds against the night sky.

At dawn, melodies of birds mingle with rustling leaves, flapping wings, sloshing waves, and rhythmic squishing sounds. Rhythmic squishing sounds? I peek through the shutters. A guy with a steel bottle and wand is spraying shrubs with insecticide.

Ginger wakes up also. She puts on her bikini bottom and my polo shirt from yesterday, and we mosey to the beach with our books—where sandflies bite us before we have a chance to slather on DEET. Perfection interspersed with imperfections.

And so it goes for a couple of days. We join a snorkeling tour to the outer reef. We tack up and down in a Hobie Cat. We hike through tropical forest up the hill to the highest point of the island, which takes five minutes. There really isn't much to do on this speck of land, and that's part of its recuperative charm.

At sunset, a French couple in their forties gets married in a Fiji ceremony. They and two witnesses—identical Fiji robes unflatteringly tied around their torsos—parade to the end of the pier that has been decorated with palm leaves. Bride and groom, embarrassed and possibly liquored up, try to repress their irrepressible giggles. A Fijian chorus sings a few songs. Someone films with a camcorder. At the end, we clap.

"Wouldn't it be a blast to get married this way?" Ginger says.

"Yup."

Is she pulling my leg again? She always does that to me. The day before our departure, I stopped by her apartment, envisioning her despondent in the middle of a heap of clothing that wouldn't fit into her daypack and duffle bag—we were going to travel light. However, her daypack and duffle bag sat neatly packed by the door.

"There's also a suitcase in the bedroom with my party clothes," she said.

"A suitcase?"

"Don't be pissed off."

I stormed into her bedroom and saw the red Samsonite. "It's not going to be me who'll be lugging this fucking thing around," I informed her between my teeth.

"A girl needs some party clothes."

"Shit."

She leaned against the doorframe, snickering. I grew suspicious, lifted the suitcase. Empty. And her snickering became a seductive laughter.

In the evening, entertainment is a dance group of topless Fijian guys, including the two underground-barbecue cooks, in hula skirts.

"They're kind of sexy," she says.

"I'm looking forward to the girlie group," I say.

"Me too."

When it becomes evident that there will be no girlie group, we reapply DEET and retreat with our G and Ts to our end of the beach, where there's no one. We drag two chairs from a tiki hut closer to the water. Behind us, palm fronds sweep from side to side, a fricative tinkle in the whooshing of the trade winds and the sloshing of the waves. Above us, a dense canopy of stars. A few lights twinkle in the distance, perhaps boats, perhaps islands.

"Paradise must have been like this," she says.

"Minus the smell of DEET."

"I'm so proud of you. What a Valentine's Day gift!"

JESUS! Valentine's Day! I forgot all about it. The fact that we're here today is pure coincidence. I don't say that, of course. I smile.

"Thank you so much for bringing me here."

I bask in unanticipated glory.

"Every girl dreams of spending Valentine's Day in paradise." She pushes her glass into the sand, stands up, sloughs off blouse and skirt, under which she wears nothing. Silvery curves of a ghost against the inky Pacific. "Who were the two people in Paradise?" the ghost says.

"Adam and Eve."

"Did Adam wear a polo shirt and walking shorts?"

"Don't be silly. He wore a fig leaf when he sat for the painters. Otherwise, he was naked."

"Well?"

Well, the day we have to check out of paradise, we don't want to leave. I ask the lady in the flowing red robe if we can stay two more nights. She names the price, double the rate I paid my travel agent. I ask for a discount. She blows me off. Like, if I can't afford the inflated rack rate, I shouldn't be here in the first place. She has all the salesmanship of a hail-damaged trunk lid.

So we decide to go to Suva, Fiji's capital, on the other side of Viti Levu, several hours by running cab from Nandi. But rather than taking the catamaran back to Nandi, we'll fly; we've seen the contraption every morning. As there are still two seats available, we buy tickets from the lady in the flowing red robe.

A couple of hours later, we watch nervously as the single-engine float-plane splashes down near the pier and taxies toward the beach. It cuts its engine. Two guys wade out and pull it backward into shallow water. Four grinning tourists climb out, shoes in hand. One by one, they shuffle on the floats to the back and step off into ankle-deep water.

A fat Australian couple and the two of us board the same way in reverse. It's an antique. You can see through the gap between the flimsy door and the frame.

The pilot starts the radial engine, guns it. Deafening racket. We move. We move faster. The floats bump over waves. *Frapp-frapp-frapp-frapp.* It doesn't have enough power. *Frapp-frapp-frapp-frapp.* The Australians are too heavy. *Frapp-frapp-frapp-frapp.* But unexpectedly, the floats clear the water. We barely gain altitude and bank around islands instead of flying over them, and islands—deep green cores set in rings of white amid effulgent blues—are scattered as far as you can see. We're grinning, and our hearts are pounding, and we don't talk because it's too loud to talk, and everywhere around us is the most amazing sight.

7

CANNIBAL

On our last day in Fiji, we decide to do something cultural: a guided tour to the Nausori Highlands. Climax, the brochure says, is kava ceremony with a village chief. Our minibus, packed with Australians and Americans, jounces up a dirt road. George, our Fijian guide, teaches us village rules. And Fijian. Or more precisely one word, *bula*, which is what we have to say when we meet the chief.

When the road peters out, we continue on foot past hillside plots of cassava, banana plants, bamboo thickets, and clouds of mosquitoes. At midday, a village comes into sight. George passes out wrap skirts to the women in our group to wear over their shorts (village rule), and we pack away hats and sunglasses (village rule) before we enter the cluster of shacks, some made of corrugated tin, others of grass mats with thatched roofs. They have nothing in common with our beach *bure*.

We line up at the porch of the chief's shack. His current wife, a youngish woman, files out with some of his children, ranging from teenagers to old men. Then the chief crawls out on all fours. George talks with him.

"He's 108," George says to us. "His knees are bad, and he's blind."

One by one, we shake his gnarly hand and say *bula*. George talks some more with him.

"He feels a bit under the weather today and can't do kava ceremony with us," he says to us.

Oh well, there goes our ballyhooed climax. We tour the village. George explains everything. Slapdash wires run from a Honda generator under a tin roof to some shacks. "Now kids can do homework after dark," he says. Barefoot kids scamper around us. "Don't touch their heads. It's a bad omen." The antenna post? Emergency radio link with the government. "Everything is carried up by donkey," he says when a guy leads a donkey into the village.

Puppies are tearing at the severed head of a cow. It grosses Ginger out. "We started eating beef only recently," he explains. "Before, we were cannibals."

She glowers at him. She can glower in a deadly manner. She did it to me the day I stopped by her shop to show her the tickets to our tropical paradise in the South Pacific.

"Cancel my tickets," she said.

"Cancel?"

"Go without me. It doesn't make sense. It'll hurt too much."

"But—"

"Just cancel my fucking tickets!"

I folded up the brochure. If I could find some magic words, she'd loosen up and change her mind. I said, "Think of our three weeks in Fiji and New Zealand as an experience by itself, not attached to anything else, a time to enjoy each other and have fun together regardless of what the future might bring." I can be quite eloquent.

Man. Lips clamped together, she glowered at me the same way she's glowering at George the cannibal.

We take off our shoes at the door of a windowless corrugated-tin shack. Inside, it's semi-dark. The only light comes from the door and from gaps in the tin. Two men greet us. Two women are squatting around a small fire in the back, cooking. We sit down on the dirt floor in a semicircle around the men, and they proffer morsels from their culture.

"We build new houses with tin," the younger man says.

"Tin costs more," the older man says.

"Tin lasts longer and leaks less than grass."

"On sunny days, tin houses get hot inside."

After half an hour of this sort of info, the women serve plastic plates with sautéed cubed meat, cooked spinach, and breadfruit. It's simple but a lot tastier than the food at Castaway.

Kava ceremony commences after lunch. The younger man situates a wooden bowl with stubby legs in front of him ("I want that for a salad bowl," Ginger whispers). No meeting can be held without kava, he says as he adds water from another bowl. He kneads a cloth-wrapped lump into the water, adds more water, kneads. When the water is sufficiently muddy, he dips a coconut bowl into it and hands it to George.

"Watch," George says. He claps once, drinks it, and claps three times.

I'm next. I'm worried about the water of uncertain origin, and I'm worried about the mud, but I drink. It has the texture and flavor of muddy water.

The men expound its medicinal benefits, which range from curing toothaches to healing broken limbs. My lips get numb. Everyone drinks a bowl. The second round is easier. By the third round, nothing matters anymore. If they handed us a bowl of hemlock, we'd drink it, too. Numbness spreads over my body.

Kava makes most people taciturn but others talkative, like the septuagenarian Australian who calls himself Italian. He pontificates on the Italian way of thinking, which is superior to any other. The rest of us conspire to kill him, but we can't move, subdued as we are by kava.

An unknown period later, George tells us that we need to go. No one reacts. He works himself to his feet, entreats us. It isn't easy to motivate our limbs, but one after the other we manage to stand up. Under the blistering sun, we trudge up to a ridge where we feel the first breeze we've felt all day, and beneath us is verdant land bordered by intoxicating shades of blue.

8

MANIAC

Blackwater rafting, whitewater rafting, rappelling into sinkholes, and bungee jumping into canyons are the reasons Ginger has agreed to come to New Zealand with me, not strolling around rainy Auckland, though certain aspects of it she enjoys—Parnell Road, for instance, a historic street with chic boutiques. Her mind works in mysterious ways. She doesn't care about traveling or being in a foreign country, but she likes doing crazy stuff, and not just the sex-in-a-bistro-toilet variety.

As for me, doing crazy stuff is the price I have to pay to prolong our relationship by three weeks. Yet our deal almost fell apart a few days before our departure when she blew through the door with the words "Cancel my tickets." It was the third time she'd told me to cancel her tickets. I took her in my arms and led her inside.

"I don't want to go," she said. "I want to take care of my orchids and ferns."

I sat her down on the couch and poured two mugs of Sam Adams. This would be our final rip-roaring blast together, after which she'd be free to start a family with some other dude. I didn't say that, of course—the consequences of my previous verbiage to that effect still vividly on my mind.

And she didn't want to hear a logical response. She didn't want to hear anything. She wanted me to shut up and just be there. A daunting task for a guy.

"Flying home without you would hurt too much," she said.

I handed her a mug. She took a long gulp.

"I don't want to travel."

I nodded. Nodding is always good.

"I've been all over Oklahoma and Texas, and going farther away is a waste."

I nodded some more. Actually, she'd also been to Arkansas, but this wasn't the moment to needle her with details.

"As they say, if it ain't in Texas, you don't need it."

Her dry humor was bleeding through. A good sign. She drank half her beer. I went to my globe, picked it up—it floated freely on a pedestal of lions—and showed her Texas.

"That's it?" she said, pouting, another good sign.

I leafed through Lonely Planet's *New Zealand* and some brochures and showed her photos of young people rappelling into a cave, rafting down a violent rapid, and bungee jumping off a bridge. She'd seen them before, but she looked nevertheless.

"Would be cool," she said.

"Wouldn't it?" My first syllables in this whole exchange.

So, on our third day in New Zealand, we head into the countryside to do crazy stuff. Pastures, tree farms, deer farms, and patches of bush mark the hills around the village of Waitomo Caves, but underneath this idyllic scene is porous limestone with cavities and subterranean rivers—a veritable mecca for adventure tourism. We go from the bus stop straight to the booking office and sign up for blackwater rafting.

Not much later, a dozen of us adventure tourists decked out in wetsuits and helmets float on inner tubes behind our guide down a creek into a cave. Eerie limestone formations spangle in the beams of our helmet lamps. We negotiate tight passages and paddle across inky pools. When we switch off our lamps, we see above us hundreds of tiny lights, glowworms hanging off the ceiling by silk threads. And everywhere is the echo of dripping, splashing, and disconcerting rushing sounds.

High on awe and dread, we're back in the booking office and stare at photos of what they call Lost World. Day one, you practice rappelling. Day two, you rappel 330 feet into a sinkhole and follow a subterranean creek out. The photos are unreal, the concept insane. It's expensive and risky. I doubt and worry. But the idea of rappelling into the bowels of the earth excites her. We kick it around. Then I plunk down my credit card. It's the price I have to pay to be with her.

At the tavern at night, she eggs me on to chat up the three German girls at another table who were part of our blackwater group. One is an Amazon. The other two are average.

"In German," she says.

"Why? Their English is good enough."

"I've never heard you speak German."

I'm reluctant. The girls are sizing us up. They're discussing us, like we're discussing them.

"They're lesbians," she says.

"How do you know?"

"I just know."

"Do you want to flirt with the Amazon?"

"I want to hear you speak German."

I don't like speaking German out of the blue. I stopped speaking German at seventeen, and when I do speak it, I feel like a seventeen-year-old who has forgotten half of what little he ever knew. It's impossible for me to have a conversation about business, for example, because I lack the most basic business vocabulary.

"Why don't you extend your trip by a week?" I say instead. My time with her is running out, and I don't want to squander it on German lesbians.

"I can't."

"You could at least think about it."

"And what should I do with my shop?" She always says *my shop,* though it's her dad's. They fabricate awnings. She manages the shop. He makes calls, quotes awnings, and installs them with his sidekick.

"Cut your dad some slack."

"No way. Not him. Nuh-uh. Not in a million years. I know how you boys are." She frets over the '56 Chevy on blocks in her shop. "Without adult supervision, he'll work on the Chevy all day instead of making calls and quoting awnings."

We saunter over to the lesbians. Two sentences in German, and I have them laughing.

"What's so funny?" Ginger asks.

"My hilarious sense of humor," I say.

"He has the strangest accent," the Amazon says.

"He doesn't know the German word for *rafting*," an average one says.

"He used *Floß fahren*," the other one says. The mere sound of it causes another round of riotous laughter.

"And he should have used?" Ginger asks when they calm down.

"*Rafting*," they blurt out in unison.

All Germans laugh when I talk.

Wednesday, February 21.

The Lost World group gets together early in the afternoon during a lull in the drizzle. People give their spiel. The guides, Jerry and Mark, both in their late twenties, like their jobs. "Pay is lousy but beer is plentiful," Jerry explains.

A French guy is next. His name is René. He's twenty-six. His plan is to get a chef's job in Wellington.

"Is it that easy to get a job as a chef?" someone asks.

"A French cook can always find a job in an Anglo-Saxon country," he says. "It's the accent that matters, not the cooking, because Anglo-Saxons can't taste the difference." Some people chuckle. Ginger, who is into nouvelle cuisine, and I dislike him already.

Phillip, a thirty-year-old lawyer from Auckland, is solo. His wife hasn't been able to get off work. By his side is Kathleen, well-rounded, eighteen, also from Auckland. "We're just friends," she says without anyone having asked. Beyond doubt, he's committing adultery with her.

There are honeymooners from the UK, a German telecom engineer, a guy from Glasgow who is halfway into his one-year stay—he quit working at a hostel to travel around some—and two Canadian guys on a similar program.

Jerry enumerates safety rules and the dos and don'ts of good abseil form, as he calls it; each violation shall be sanctioned later at the tavern. "And if you hang upside down, it'll cost you *two* rounds," he reassures us. Then we practice abseiling from a scaffold built up against a rock.

I hate heights. But I climb over the edge, and we practice abseiling until we have it down pat. Only Ginger doesn't get sanctioned—she's so cute in her harness and helmet that neither Jerry nor Mark notices her violations. She could be upside down, and they'd give her extra credit. Several rounds of beer at the tavern complete our training.

Back at our B&B, where everything is painted white, even the furniture, Ginger clips her roughed-up fingernails.

"Want my emery board?" I say.

"I've never used one."

"Are you pulling my leg again?"

She doesn't answer, but she doesn't snicker either, so I file the nails of her sensuous fingers and end up making love to her on the bed that squeaks, rattles, and bangs against the wall. I'm unspeakably grateful for every minute with her.

"Maniac," is her last word.

Thursday, February 22.

The entrance to Lost World is a deceptively modest hole in the ground surrounded by dripping bush. Outfitted in wetsuits and helmets, we stand on the metal platform at the rim of the hole and gawk down into an immense cavern. Dim reflections of daylight 330 feet beneath us.

I hate heights. I hate being on platforms and gawking down into voids. Mark hooks his harness to the rope that dangles into the cavern, climbs over the edge, and rappels into the void, swinging ever so slightly in all directions until he's just a dot at the bottom.

"Next," Jerry says.

We struggle with what we've gotten ourselves into.

"Next!" he insists.

No one is next.

"NEXT!"

"Ooooh-kay girls, let's go," Ginger says, hooks up her harness, and rappels into the void. She's just awesome. And then it dawns on the rest of us: the effect of her maneuver is that now no one can chicken out.

When *Next!* means me, I smack my phobia down with logic, hook myself up, and go. I bounce gently up and down due to the elasticity of the rope, swinging and pivoting in the middle of the dome. The bright hole above gets smaller and smaller. Vegetation clinging to the rock thins out. Visual and auditory parameters I took for granted on the surface no longer apply. At the bottom are boulders and the echo of a creek.

Each moment is an intense experience, separated from any other moment, disconnected from my world. Time decelerates. I marvel and absorb. I'm going down slowly to maximize my experience because I'll do this only once in my life. The farther I go, the more I bounce, and when I touch down on a boulder, the rope yanks me up again.

One by one, we accumulate on the boulders at the bottom of the dome. Water is babbling underneath. Jerry passes out sandwiches. We eat under the bright dot that marks the unreachable hole to the surface, this being a one-way trip without possibility of going back.

"I want to go back," says the German telecom engineer.

Edgy silence.

"I don't like caves," he says.

A joke perhaps. We chuckle nervously.

"I've got to go pee," says the Canadian guy.

It only sounds like a joke. We squirm in our wetsuits. We all have to go.

"This is the place," Jerry says, and one after the other, we duck behind a boulder and wrestle with our wetsuits.

We follow the creek from the dome into the dark. Soon, we've left the last glimmer of daylight behind. We crawl through muddy claustrophobic tunnels, leap into unseen pools, and clamber up rocks. The beams of our helmet lamps illuminate fossilized shells and whalebones and at times fade into black nothingness. Glowworms populate some areas.

Anxiety from being in the bowels of the earth is building up with each hour. I'm worried about the persistent rain that might bring up the water level of the creek to where we can't get out. We switch off our lamps, grope along a wall. The darkness is absolute. We touch our noses and can't see our hands. We've been condensed to inconsequential nanoparticles in a vast scheme over which we have no control, a humbling thought.

Ginger is in her element. But as the hours wear on, the dark, the dirt, the cold water, exertion, and sheer dread are beginning to grind on her. Then a distant trace of daylight! We work toward it, wade out into the drizzle, and squint into the murky light that seems bright and welcoming. We're exhilarated because it was terrifying and glorious, and we're ecstatic because we're back on the surface of the earth. And we're not a pretty sight.

In the morning, we roll around in bed. Rain patters on the tin roof.

"At the least we should have received a survival certificate or something," she says.

Even griping about her aches, she's seductive. She has cuts and open calluses on her hands. Her nails are shredded, and there's nothing left to file. Her arms and legs are bruised. Her left cheek is scratched. Her head is resting on my shoulder. I massage her sore hands with gobs of lotion.

"We're having so much fun," I say.

She nods.

"I wish this could go on."

"Hmm."

"Extend your trip by a week."

"I don't know."

"If we have one more week, we can do more crazy stuff."

"Maybe."

"We can do the pipeline bungee jump."

"Hmm."

"It's the highest and craziest bungee jump in the Southern Hemisphere."

"You got a point."

"Call your dad. Ask him how your shop is doing. He'll tell you. Then you decide."

There not being a useable phone in our B&B, she calls from a pay phone on the street while I hold the umbrella over her—and envy her. She can talk with her parents. Okay, they're divorced, so it's a little complicated, but that's a relatively minor detail. If I had a chance to talk with my parents, I'd like to find out what they were thinking back then.

For instance, one evening when I was about five, I heard my father unlock the front door. I dashed out from the back, and as I hugged him, he pushed me off and hit me in the face so hard it knocked me down. Dazed, I dashed back the way I'd come and collapsed on my bed, incapable of wrapping my brains around what had just occurred.

An eternity later, my mother came in and explained that his back had been hurting and that my actions had made it worse. It was a rational explanation that was supposed to make sense to me because it had been my fault.

Other times, my father's or mother's hands would hail down on us until their anger had exhausted itself. They had their idiosyncrasies, though.

He hit harder. She lasted longer. With him, crying made it worse. With her, it helped. Periodically, she'd add a few days of icy silence. Yet, if someone was around, both behaved.

I don't remember when my mother stopped beating me. But with my father, there was a seminal moment. I must have been fourteen. He was about to unleash his hands on me. Instead of adopting a defensive posture, I stared him in the eye, determined to hit back with all my force, even if he killed me afterward. His hand froze in midair, and we stood face to face for the tensest moments of my life. Then he dealt with his anger in some other way. An armistice ensued.

But the damage was done. I hated them and needed to get out. Now, almost three decades later, I'm wondering perhaps for the first time what they were thinking back then. At a minimum, I'd like to understand—

Ginger hangs up the phone.

"Dad's fine with it," she says with an evil grin. "I think I woke him up or something."

She has extended our relationship by a week. On cloud nine, I call Air New Zealand and change our tickets.

We head to Rotorua, two hours east by bus. Sulfurous odors pervade the town. We visit bubbling mud pools and an orchid garden. We soothe our aches in the hot mineral pool at our lodge. Over a cup of Nescafé, the second scourge of New Zealand after greasy and bland food, she confesses that her digestive discomfort of the last few days has blossomed into diarrhea. And we wonder if it might have been the muddy kava water of uncertain origin in Fiji.

On the bus to Wellington the next day, she barely makes it from rest stop to rest stop. No longer suspecting the kava water, we reevaluate everything she has ingested since.

"Yogurt!" she exclaims.

"Yogurt what?" We've been eating it every day as an antidote to the grease in the food. My idea.

"I'm allergic to yogurt."

"No!"

"Mom told me. I haven't eaten yogurt since I can remember. I forgot all about it."

At 8 p.m., Downtown Backpackers in Wellington is full. I call other hostels from its rowdy lobby. Full. I'm looking for something cheap, after the financial sinkhole of Waitomo Caves. She's antsy, has to go to the john, but doesn't like hostels, their smell, their grotty communal bathrooms. I call my fallback hotel, the Terrace Regency, which has a room.

During the trot up the hill, she becomes desperate. She's twitchy at the reception. I unlock the door to our room. She bolts into the bathroom.

"Oh my God, our own real bathroom!" she yells from within. And when she comes out, she says googly-eyed, "You won't believe this. There are towels, soap, and shampoo!"

Monday, February 26.

The ferry steams out of Wellington's harbor, a flooded volcano crater several miles in diameter. We stand on deck and take in the skyline and the neighborhoods that sprawl up the surrounding mountains.

Yesterday, our first sunny day in New Zealand, we strolled along the waterfront. Street performers animated the crowd who'd come to watch a dragon-boat race. Ginger felt great, not having eaten yogurt in twenty-four hours. "I could live here," she said, a momentous statement for her.

And she's still smiling. We cross the Cook Straight that separates the North Island from the South Island and dock at Picton, a quaint Victorian port in the Marlborough Sounds. The onward train to Christchurch—Ginger's first train—is not a great specimen, and only tourists are allowed on it. But soon we're transfixed by the land. Windblown grasses, shrubs, dunes, and the South Pacific on the left. The Kaikoura range on the right. And sheep everywhere.

In Christchurch, we check into the formerly ostentatious Victorian railroad hotel, now budget hotel—the even more ostentatious railroad station is being converted into a commercial complex, and the train terminus has been moved to a suburb. We zigzag through the center and watch street performers on Cathedral Square. We eat at a Lone Star Steakhouse, based on our discovery that foreign-themed restaurants are an effective dodge of the first scourge of New Zealand—though not of the universal surliness of the wait staff. And on the way back we run into the red-light district, a fascinating affair for Ginger, who has never seen one before.

In the morning, a rafting company minivan takes us to a gravel beach in the Rangitata Gorge. Guides prepare four rafts while two dozen tourists struggle with rubberized jackets, life vests, and helmets.

"How bad are Class V rapids?" Ginger asks me.

"I don't know."

"I hope they're bad."

"No worries," says Mike, a skinny kid in his twenties who's the guide of our raft.

On the slow-moving water, Mike teaches us rafting commands—all forward, all backward, stop, right forward, high side, and so on—and we practice until all six of us do more or less the same thing at the same time. The rapids are easy initially, after each rapid we hurrah and clap our paddles together above our heads, and our exuberance grows with the violence of the rapids.

When Mike announces the first Class V, we're already spellbound by the distant thunder and mist. He explains our strategy, at what angle to enter the drop, how to avoid a certain rock. The thunder gets louder. The leading raft drops out of sight and seconds later reappears downstream. People in it hurrah and clap their paddles together above their heads. The second raft drops out of sight. The third raft, manned by Brits who are bouncing up and down for the heck of it, drops out of sight at a funny angle.

The current grabs our raft. Mike yells commands. We stare down into a violent cauldron. Rocks everywhere. Some of us paddle furiously. Others scream and hunker down. The raft is sucked into the chute, tilts forward, plunges. Water collapses over us. Mike is still yelling, but we can't hear him anymore. We broadside a rock, spin around, and shoot backward into slowing water.

Holy fucking cow! We can't believe it. We hurrah and clap our paddles together.

Then we see them. The raft of the Brits is floating upside down. A girl is clawing up a rock near the shore. Others are swept downstream. Their guide flips the raft over. We yell and point at the girl, but they don't hear us; they're busy helping each other back into the raft. Then they notice the empty spot. Oops.

We paddle our rafts to the shore. The guides wave at the girl to motivate her to get back into the water so the current can wash her down to us. But she crouches forlornly on her rock and doesn't budge. Two guides have to rescue her via land, not easy in this terrain. Then she refuses to get back into the raft. She's shaking. Her raft mates entreat her and hug her and promise her things. Which eventually bears fruit.

The river snakes through the canyon, rapid after rapid. A quarter-mile stretch is all Class V. How we survive that, God only knows. Late afternoon, still high on excitement, we drag the rafts out. A minivan hauls some people away on a dirt track. Ginger and I and some Brits stay at the hostel by the river, a clapboard shack from the gold-rush days. We barbecue sausages, drink beer, and play spoons.

At bedtime, my intrepid adventurer stops in the middle of our particleboard room, the only private room at the hostel, and turns into a pillar of salt. She glowers at me in her deadly manner. Something is my fault.

"What?" I inquire.

"Spiders!"

"Where?"

"Everywhere."

"Oh, those."

"Eeeeee. There! On the bed!"

"That's not a bed. It's a piece of foam on the floor with a sheet on top."

"And THERE!"

"Calm down. They're just spiders."

But these sorts of scientific pronouncements don't hold water with her.

"It's not like they're black widows, brown recluses, and tarantulas," I mollify her.

"Shut up."

"They're on our side. They munch on mosquitoes and sandflies."

"GET THEM GONE, EACH AND EVERY FUCKING ONE OF THEM."

And I remove each and every spider. Well, the ones she can see, and she isn't looking very hard because her eyes are closed, and her hand is in front of her eyes because she hates spiders so much she can't look at them. I shake out the sheet, step on things, and make other generic spider-removal noises. When I assure her that they're all gone, she loosens up and creeps under the covers with me, and I have to promise that I'll keep them away from her during the night.

9

POSTPARTUM

Rowdy British and Canadian backpackers plus a quiet Japanese couple populate the bus to Queenstown. We know the driver is Maori because it's the first thing he tells us. He corners brutally, silencing even the Brits, and each time he overtakes another bus, a death-defying maneuver on the curvy two-lane road, he screams over the PA system "THEY HATE ME, THEY HATE ME!"

In between, he provides must-know data, like "In New Zealand, there are more sheep than people, except during the summer, when there are more tourists than sheep." In the background are the ridges and glaciers of the Southern Alps, among them Mt. Cook, the highest mountain in Australasia. Ginger reads a paperback and occasionally expresses impatience.

At 6:30 p.m. we're in Queenstown, a picturesque place wedged between Lake Wakatipu and the Remarkables range. At a Lone Star Steakhouse, we laugh about the universal surliness of Kiwi wait staff. It's so predictable. We try to make the waitress smile but fail. We try to get her to say more than three words but fail. We order another bottle of wine and try again.

At 3 a.m. the bed shakes, and the headboard bangs against the wall.

"What's going on?" Ginger says. Something shatters.

"It ain't me."

,d. I hate to think you're still not satisfied."

each other. The building pops, a horrible sound. I'm waiting

apse.

worry," I say. "It's just an earthquake."

"Oh well, in that case, I'm going back to sleep."

At breakfast, guests are atwitter while they dig into the grease. Everything is fried: eggs, bacon, sausages, tomatoes, mushrooms, potatoes. Even toast is presoaked in butter. It's deadly, and I can't eat it. I eat a banana, the only thing that doesn't have grease on it. Tea drinkers get brewed tea. Coffee drinkers have to make do with Nescafé, which is even worse than dealership coffee. The earthquake is all over the news. A magnitude 5.0 on the Richter scale. The young Japanese at our table shrug it off.

We've come to Queenstown for the pipeline bungee jump. The videos at the booking office are insane, and I'm getting second thoughts. Nevertheless, we sign up for tomorrow's jump. More up my alley is the lake cruise on the steam-powered TSS *Earnslaw* whose posted capacity is 1,035 people or 1,500 sheep—sooner or later, everything in New Zealand boils down to sheep. The spotless engine room is glassed in for viewing. Rods and linkages move up and down, wheels spin, and levers tap to the gentle *pfft-pfft* of the steam.

Ginger stands next to me and watches it for a few moments to humor me. Later, she stands next to me on deck amid the splendid scenery of mountains and glittering waves. But mostly she's inside reading her paperback. I get dreamy with longing. I want to travel for months up some river into a vast continent to the *pfft-pfft* of the steam, my life adjusting to its rhythm and to the sights that glide by and to the people I meet along the way.

Friday, March 1.

"The scariest part isn't the jump," says Te, the Maori driver of the 4x4, as he turns into Skippers Canyon Road. He laughs maniacally, contorts his bulbous body back to us, and bares his teeth. "It's the drive!"

Skippers Canyon Road is a dirt track with steep gradients and tight turns that Chinese laborers chiseled into the canyon walls during the gold rush. Below is the Shotover River. Te takes each curve with a rear-wheel drift. Tires kick rocks against wheel wells and into the canyon. We brace ourselves the best we can. Te guffaws as the 4x4 skids through a blind downhill turn. The outside rear wheel fishtails off the edge. Our hearts stop. We don't want to die down there at the bottom of the canyon like so many Chinese laborers before us.

"You'll thank me for driving like this," he bellows. "It'll make the jump easier."

Some cackle, others bite their lips.

And just as we're coming to grips with the fragility of life, the 4x4 grinds to a halt in a cloud of dust by an old pipeline suspension structure across the canyon. With a catwalk on top of the pipe. The second 4x4 plows into the gravel. Our eyes are fixed on the finger-thin cables. And on the flimsy catwalk. It moves.

Holding on to a cable that serves as the handrail of the heaving catwalk, we advance in single file. 340 feet below is the silver-green Shotover River. Above are bluffs, mountains, and glaciers. I hate heights and jumping off catwalks. The first guy stops. Everyone behind him stops. He clings to the cable with both hands.

"Go ahead," he says, desperate smile on his pale face. He lets us get around him. Then he backtracks to firm land. Down to three guys and five girls.

One of the guys who work there ties a harness around the ankles of the first girl. Another guy instructs her. I'm not listening. I don't want to hear it. Merely being on the catwalk is nerve-wracking. But I'm thinking. The numbers don't jibe. Why are there *three* guys and *five* girls who want to do this? Why are there *any* girls who want to do this?

The girl plunges and screams. Holy baby Jesus, she's fast. I can't even follow her with my eyes. A tiny speck down there, hanging off the rubber band which—now that I'm looking at the end that's tied to the suspension cable—is composed of hundreds of little beige rubber bands of the type you have in your junk drawer, only longer. Whoa! She's coming back up! Why is there *anybody* who wants to do this?

"How many stone do you weigh?" the guy asks me while he straps my ankles together.

"Stone? You've got to be kidding."

He isn't. I tell him in pounds and kilograms. It doesn't mean anything to him. Another girl plunges and screams. He gives me a once-over and says, "Eleven and a half stone." Makes you wonder where these people have been for the last two thousand years. Then he selects a bungee cord based on my weight in stone.

"Scream on the way down," the other guy says. "The sound effects are cool, and you'll feel it better."

"It?"

"Falling into the canyon."

My ankles tied together, I inch to the edge of the jump-off platform jutting out from the catwalk into thin air. It doesn't even have a handrail. The bungee cord linking my ankles to the catwalk loops into the canyon.

"Don't get tangled up in it on the way down," he says behind me. Kiwis can be extremely helpful at exactly the right moment.

I hate, hate, hate heights. And platforms jutting into thin air. I never thought 340 feet would be this far. I'm doing this to be with Ginger. She's somewhere behind me, occupied with her own thoughts. Sounds are blotted out. My vision fails to provide useful information. I worry about getting tangled up in the bungee cord on the way down. I hate that guy. My brain freezes up. My heart races. If I were able to go back, I would, but my fine motor skills are shot, and backing off the narrow heaving platform without handrails, ankles tied together, isn't feasible. I see only one solution—and if I die, so be it.

I power-dive forward to accomplish a neat horizontal position to impress Ginger, but the weight of the bungee cord pulls my legs down. A weird voice echoes at me. Canyon walls fly by. The rushing air draws tears from my eyes. I pray that the bungee cord will hold. It tightens around my ankles, a relief. Blood rushes into my head. I pray that my eyes won't pop out and that my legs won't come loose and that I won't hit the water too hard. I stop above the water, and for a moment I think it's over, but then I'm yanked up. I pray that I won't hit the pipeline from underneath and that I won't get tangled up in its cables. I stop and fall again, yo-yoing until I dangle to and fro, the Shotover River above me, the pipeline underneath, and the sky at the very bottom.

They lower me headfirst into a jet boat that has powered upstream. One of the guys in the boat unties my ankles, and they unload me at the shore by the two girls who jumped before me. I'm high. Others jump. I don't know what's happening to me. We yell and clap. I'm floating above reality. I can't stop smiling. I don't know if what I'm saying makes sense to anyone. They're smiling, too. Ginger is last. Perfect form, body horizontal, back arched, arms spread apart—though she forgets to scream.

The high is addictive and mind altering, and we decide to jump again. But by the time we get back to the booking office, it has worn off, and I have a headache and sore eyes. Instead of signing up for another jump, we complain to a skinny white guy about Te's driving. He just grins. We watch the videos of our jumps. Ginger looks superb, I incompetent: arms flailing, body at forty-five degrees, feet down—until the bungee cord jerks them up.

"Let's just order yours," I say.

"We need both."

"I won't even be home to watch mine."

A completely asinine thing to say based on her glower, so we order both.

Out on the street, I don't know where to go. I'm aching, listless.

"God, I'm worn out by all this insanity," I say.

"Now I know what postpartum feels like," she says.

We do a wine-tasting tour to lift our spirits. Tipsy, we ride the Skyline Gondola to the summit. A stupendous sunset is unfolding. And just as awe is gnawing its way to the surface, she twists herself out of my embrace.

"I miss everything," she says. "I have no idea how my shop is doing. I'm worried about my orchids and ferns. I'm tired of hotels. I'm tired of buses. I have a headache. I want to go home, but I don't want to go home alone. Why can't you go with me?"

"Why?" I think about Asia. I've become a free man, at least temporarily. Life might not offer me another chance like this. "I'll be back in a couple of months."

The precise answer is four months—one in Australia and three in Japan. We've never said a word about what will happen afterward. We've wrapped that topic in silence.

We both know what will happen. She won't wait. Not four months. Not even two months. It's an eternity for her. She'll take her fate into her own hands and mold it to her liking. Her dream is to become a mom, and she'll make it happen. I adore her. I know I'll miss her. And I don't want to let go of her. But I don't fit into her dream, and she doesn't fit into mine.

Tuesday, March 5.

We're having breakfast on the glassed-in back porch of our B&B, a Victorian house way up on High Street in Dunedin. The roses in the garden before us dance in the cold wind. We're talking about Milford Sound, where we kayaked along dark-green rainforest slopes, waterfalls, and dripping mossy cliffs. We're talking about how we've never seen so many sand-flies as at the Milford Lodge where we spent the night. We're talking about the bus rides.

Actually, I'm talking. Ginger is smiling tensely. Her bus-and-sandfly quota has been exceeded. I count the remaining days of our relationship on my fingers. Five.

"Something wrong with your hand?" she asks.

"With my hand? No."

I want to extract the maximum out of each moment with her, but sometimes it gets to me, the finality of it all. She never comments on how few days we have left. She doesn't think in those terms. Maybe I'm not as much of a gift to her as she is to me. Her problem is flying back alone.

"What am I supposed to tell dad at the airport, when it's just me, and he's expecting both of us?" she says, stirring Nescafé into her cup.

"He's old enough. He'll figure it out."

"Figure *what* out?"

"Or you could call and tell him."

"Tell him *what*?"

From our windswept B&B, we wander downhill into the center, whose grandiose Victorian buildings date from the gold-rush days when Dunedin was New Zealand's largest and richest city. We do a boat tour out the twelve-mile-long inlet to Taiaroa Head, the tip of Otago Peninsula.

Dozens of Royal Albatrosses soar in updrafts to the top of the cliffs where their nests are. Others approach a few feet above the waves. They flick their wingtips and play gravity against air with divine grace. Wingspan is ten feet, says Nellie, our marine biologist guide. Chicks hatched last month. Parents take turns guarding their chick and hunting to feed it. In September, chicks will be fledged. They'll practice their wings until a gust lifts them off the rock and over the South Pacific.

Lifespan is that of a human, Nellie says, and couples, despite long separations at sea, are monogamous for life.

Snarling something about being cold, Ginger ducks into the cabin.

But she hasn't lost her deadpan humor. At a yellow-eyed penguin reserve on the other side of the peninsula, we peep from a trench-and-tunnel system at penguins a few feet away. Some stand in the sand, shivering and grooming themselves with their beaks. They're molting. Others wash up on the beach, get on their feet, and waddle up to their buddies.

"Like a bunch of guys waiting to get into a black-tie party," Ginger says sotto voce.

We chuckle because it's so accurate.

"Shhh!" Nellie despises people who lack reverence for her penguins.

And Ginger despises being shushed. You can practically stick your finger into the toxic concoction between the two.

The next day, Ginger reluctantly acquiesces to do the Taieri Gorge excursion train. As the train screeches around cliffs and clatters across iron trestles, she's reading a paperback. I beg her to join me on the open-air platform at the end of our car, and eventually she humors me. But the gorge and the carcasses of railcars jammed into boulders down by the river don't mean much to her, and soon she's reading again while I dream of traveling for weeks on a slow train like this across stunning scenery.

At a photo stop, we climb off the train. She shoots a picture of the gorge then stashes her camera away.

"I don't want to travel anymore," she says.

I take her in my arms to cheer her up, but my hug has lost its curative powers.

"I don't care for trains," she says.

"I understand. Just enjoy the beauty of the land."

"I miss my orchids and ferns. I want to go home, but I don't want to go home alone."

The refrain of our swan song.

Back in our room, she feels perkier due to the bottle of Riesling we've had with dinner. She disrobes by the window facing the rose garden and fingers her nipples. Moonlight turns her pubic hair silvery. I'm an idiot for letting her go, and she's rubbing it in.

Why can't I go back with her? It would be so easy. Get on the phone and buy a ticket. Five minutes. But I'm fooling myself. My dream is to roam. Her dream is to become a mom. She has even given up trying to foist her dream on me. She knows what she has to do: find some other dude. Whether or not I fly home with her is ultimately irrelevant in her scheme of things.

"What are you thinking?" she says as she drags her fingers over her abdomen.

"I'm thinking how much I love you." Which is true.

Saturday, March 9.

Yesterday we flew to Auckland and splurged on a decent hotel because we didn't want to spend our last night together in a budget dump. We went to a crowded Indian restaurant on Ponsonby Road, where they spooked us with friendly service and delicious food. Then we went to a loud bar down the street, where it was possible to forget reality. We joked and laughed, and I considered buying a ticket home but kept my trap shut. I'd been drinking too much to say anything of consequence.

This morning, we take a city bus to Mission Bay Beach. I want to go swimming. She doesn't want to get sand in her hair. So we promenade. People picnic and watch a regatta. We have pasta at an alfresco café by the waterfront. Life could have been so good.

Back at the hotel, she calls her dad and tells him when to pick her up at the airport. She uses *I* instead of *we* and *me* instead of *us* without telling him explicitly. Maybe he notices. At any rate, he doesn't ask any questions. We make love one final time. You'd expect the final time to be an eruption of passion, a culmination of desperate wildness. But her spirit is elsewhere. "You go ahead," she says. "Don't worry about me." It's over for her, and she's just soldiering along.

We ride the shuttle to the airport, have our final glass of Riesling at a bar in the terminal. Words are like lead. We examine the fingerprints on our wineglasses. Thoughts are like lead, too.

"Thank you," she says with a quavering voice.

"Thank *you.*"

At passport control, we hug. She passes through the gate, turns around, smiles, waves. And that's it, my life with Ginger.

I hate moments like these. Years later, hindsight might shed light on just how much you've screwed up. Disoriented, I take the shuttle back to the hotel and wallow in Ginger's faint chemistry still lingering in the room.

10

HOLY MOLY

Without Ginger, I have new freedoms. For instance, I can stay at one of the cheap hostels in Kings Cross, a sleazy area of Sydney that my guidebook promises is full of hookers, brothels, and strip joints. Even the driver of the airport shuttle is reluctant to take me there. He drops everyone else off in lush neighborhoods and at high-rise hotels. It's Sunday morning, and the rainy streets are deserted. When I'm the last one left on the shuttle, he twists back to me.

"Do you really want to go to the Cross?" he says.

"You bet. Orwell and Victoria will be fine."

"Not a problem, mate." And he actually winks at me.

When he lets me off on Orwell Street, the only sign of life is a crew of Asian men sweeping up the testosterone-laced wreckage from last night. My plan is to find a suitable hostel by walking around and checking some out, but it's raining, so I dive into the nearest one, a shabby three-story Victorian house.

The entrance opens to the common room—and to the bitter reek of unwashed humans, sweaty socks, and full ashtrays. A girl, elbows propped on a big rustic table, tea mug in front of her, exhales smoke.

"Are you awake?" I ask.

"I'm trying."

"Do you work here?"

She joggles her sun-bleached dreads.

I sit down.

She's from Denmark and has a degree in architecture. She's doing a yearlong round-the-world trip. "Before I get stuck in a job," she says. She has been to India and Indonesia. She hates Java, had problems with men there, and won't ever again travel to a Muslim region. But she adores Bali, its art and spirituality, and her eyes drift to terraced rice paddies, steep hazy valleys, Balinese architecture, and Hindu temples, and sparks fly, and some of the sparks land on me.

I'm going to Bali, I decide. I'm proud of myself. I'm finally spontaneous. By nature, I'm systematic. I plan everything. But I want to break free from my nature. I want to allow myself to be carried by the moment and do something without a plan. I want to give spontaneity some breathing room.

Two guys in heavy hiking boots galumph down the stairs. Maybe they'll strap on crampons to ascend some glacier down the street. But no! They heat up milk, spoon Nescafé into it, and remove a paper bag marked with skull and crossbones from the fridge. They're Germans. Three Japanese guys tiptoe down. Other people begin puttering around. Two Brits scoop a vile tarry substance out of a jar and spread it on their toast.

"What's that?" I ask.

"Vegemite," one of them says.

"An Australian delicacy," the other one says.

"Everyone eats it," the first one says.

The Germans with their open-faced ham-and-cheese sandwiches and Nescafé lattes scrunch up their noses. Not everyone eats it.

A thin guy with a goatee swaggers in with a loud "G'day." Obviously, he works here. I ask him if he has a bunk for a few nights. He extracts a ledger from a desk in the corner, flips through the dog-eared pages.

"Reckon, mate," he says. "Room four."

It's upstairs and sleeps twelve. The fug is thick. Some people are still sleeping. I step over backpacks, shoes, and clothes, toss my duffle bag on an empty bunk, and flee.

The rain has stopped. I zigzag on foot from Kings Cross through Woolloomooloo to central Sydney. I haven't done that in a while, walking alone, not holding Ginger's hand, and my hand feels empty. As I replay our four weeks in Fiji and New Zealand, I try to think of locals we met. But aside from drivers, guides, and others in the tourist trade, we didn't meet anyone.

I have lunch in the Rocks at the foot of the Harbour Bridge. The sun comes out. I climb the two hundred or so stairs to the Lookout in one of the bridge pylons and gaze at waterfronts and coves, at the extravagant roofline of the opera house, at the skyline, at the urban area broken up by greenery and amoebic shapes of blue across which catamaran ferries draw white double arcs. I wish Ginger were here with me. I miss wrapping my arm around her, miss her hair caressing my face, miss every aspect of her, and it converts this moment of beauty into melancholy.

Friday, March 15.
I need to scoot. I bought tickets to Bali, and my five days there have to be subtracted from my time in Australia because I have to be in Tokyo by April 10 when my language course starts. Time, which I thought I had in unlimited supply, is suddenly the only thing I lack.

Sticking to the proven traveler strategy of staying away from locals other than those in the tourist trade, I took a backpacker bus from Sydney south along the coast to Melbourne, a two-day ride. Now I'm in a similar conveyance for the three-day ride to Adelaide. No Australian ever sets foot on these garishly painted worn-out things. Only backpackers stoop this low.

The atmosphere is subdued. Some people are sleeping. Others are hung over. Eventually, some Brits come to, and when they reach critical mass, they encourage the pudgy girl next to me to moon the bus behind us. She goes to the back, stands up on the bench, lifts her skirt, and exposes her big lily-white derrière out the rear window. Pandemonium. They prod her to flash her knockers out the rear window. Utter pandemonium. She considers it. Is tempted. Almost does it. Sits back down. She's eighteen.

"Kodak moment," someone yells above the din.

The driver hits the brakes. A kangaroo-crossing sign. Someone hasn't seen one yet, though they're everywhere. We get out, and while people take pictures of it, I throw the boomerang I bought earlier. It came with instructions. The correct side has to face up, and you have to hold the correct end just so. After a few flops, it flies out, arches up, pauses, and comes back whoosh-whooshing above my head. Totally addictive.

Even more common than kangaroo-crossing signs is kangaroo road kill, but none of these bulges with two fearsome legs and a monstrous tail triggers a Kodak moment. At the first mob of live ones, however, mayhem breaks out, and everyone screams "Kodak moment."

In Torquay, we stop at a surfing-gear outlet mall. Before letting us off the bus, the driver tells us where the deals are.

"And one more thing," he says, "Aborigines get paid their allocations on Fridays. Some might use the cash to buy alcohol. Some might start early. They might be drunk already. They might get a little loud. Just be cool."

They loiter in groups, some barefoot and in rags, drunk and sad, out of place in their own country. They taunt us and yell at us, but we're cool. And shocked. This isn't the Australia we've come to see, and it throws a pall over shopping for surfing gear.

Torquay is also the beginning of the Great Ocean Road that twists along Shipwreck Coast, a limestone escarpment carved up by wind and waves. At a Kodak moment, I can't resist the temptation and throw my boomerang from the edge of the cliff toward one of the rock pillars that the surf is pounding with exaggerated drama. Twelve Apostles they're called, these surrealist leftovers from where the coast used to be. The boomerang flies out, arches up, pauses, and returns above my head, but its trajectory doesn't amount to a micron within this scene, its *whoosh-whoosh* is drowned out by waves slamming into rocks, and the incomprehensible might of the Southern Ocean that is grinding this magnificent coast into sand renders my efforts risible. Humbled, I stash the boomerang away.

We stop for the night at a hostel. Before letting us off, the driver makes another one of his announcements.

"Barbie night, on the house," he says. "There's piss in the Esky. Count your stubbies and pay me in the morning."

If you have trouble with the native tongue, you do what others do: they jostle around a cooler on the back porch and fish out bottles of beer while the driver is frying a pile of hamburger patties and sausages on a griddle.

But sleeping in a hostel is an acquired art. Bunks are close together. The air is putrid. People stomp in at all hours. Some switch on the light. Others make do with a flashlight. A girl trips, crashes, cusses, giggles. A guy snores. Another digs frantically through his effects at 3 a.m. then gives up without explanation and goes back to sleep.

Saturday, we veer inland to Grampians National Park and stop for a scenic hike.

"I love Australia," says a tall girl as she shoots a photo of a koala slouching in the fork of a tree, eminently satisfied with life. She has short brown hair and wears a baggy purple shirt and tie-dyed pants. "If it were up to me, I'd never go back to Germany."

"I know how you feel," I say.

"Unfortunately, I've got to go back next week and do some paperwork."

"And if you don't?"

"They'll cut off my unemployment compensation."

"What a reprehensible thing to do!"

"*Ja.*" Two tattered emus stalk by, eyeing us with derision.

"Any plans other than paperwork?"

"Thailand. Have you been there?"

"I haven't been anywhere yet."

"What I *should* do is look for a job, but it's hard when they pay you to travel."

"I wish they paid me to travel."

"I'm thirty-three. If I goof off much longer, I'll become permanently unemployable."

As for Ginger, she'll be jetlagged, but she won't sit around and wait. She isn't that kind of girl. She'll make it happen. In that respect, we're kindred souls. While I miss her, there are people around me, and we shoot the breeze. One of them is Susi, the unemployed German girl. So I try to make something happen beyond backpacker camaraderie, but it's impossible because there are always people around.

And I've stayed in touch with Izumi. During my homestay in la Fare les Oliviers, three weeks after our *aventure de vacances*, I received a letter from her. Six pages of soft pink paper with gold flakes. Touching them was like touching her silky skin.

Whenever I come into contact with culture, art, nature, and history, and whenever I have a chance to talk with someone who is open-minded and romantic, I feel very happy, she wrote. *I want to live a life with such emotions. I think about your vision and what we shared in such a short, wonderful time. But working for a venture capital firm is too different from what I want.*

She wrote that talking with me had motivated her. She might quit her job and take coursework to become a teacher of Japanese to foreign learners.

I'd like to become a window through which they can see Japan. And through them,
I want to see their cultures.

A couple of weeks after I got home from Europe, I finally decided to reply.

Dear Izumi, I wrote and stared at the blinking cursor. How do you start a letter to a chick you had an *aventure de vacances* with two months earlier? *I spent some unforgettable hours in Tours with a ravishing woman I seem to have met in a dream.* And the words started flowing. I wrote about the rest of my trip and how the Guimet Museum of Asian Arts in Paris had galvanized me. I added that I wanted to go to Japan to take a language course and if possible see her again.

Since she didn't have email, I tried to fax it, but it didn't go through. I printed it and stuck two Marilyn Monroe stamps on the envelope. Bills got Richard Nixons. Neutral or friendly mail got classic cars, locomotives, or flowers. Izumi got Marilyn Monroes.

Ten days later, I received a four-page word-processed fax from her. *The hours we shared seem like a dream, too short and too beautiful. I was a bit scared the vision of you would fade. But your letter reminded me that it was not a dream. I could feel you from every line and every sentence.*

She'd resigned but would stay through December. She was worried her family and friends would consider her irresponsible. There was a hilarious section on how she'd rearranged her room by dragging and pushing her furniture around. She wrote about Italy, which she adored, and compared Western fairy tales to Japanese fairy tales.

I was ambivalent about her decision to resign. I admired her for grabbing the bull by the horns. But she'd graduated from prestigious schools and had gotten her foot in the door to the antechamber of Japan Inc. It wasn't rational at her age to quit this kind of job over a few quibbles. Yes, she was doing the same thing I'd done, but it wasn't the same thing. I was forty and had run a frigging car dealership for a decade.

Sunday morning, I sit next to Susi. Across the aisle is Wouter, a skinny Dutch guy in faded red T-shirt and khaki shorts. He has a degree in journalism and has been traveling around the world for a year. "Oz is my last country," he says. "I'm flying home in three weeks."

"Sad it's over?" I ask.

"No. I'm eager to launch my career."

When I introduce him to Susi, he switches to German. So do I, to her giddy astonishment, and every time I say anything at all, she laughs.

"Why do you speak German?" she asks me an hour into it, though she doesn't ask Wouter. It's okay for him to speak it, but I have to justify myself.

"We Americans are a polyglot bunch," I say.

"Bullshit," Wouter says. "You Americans never speak anything but English."

"Well! Thirty-one percent of us speak another language at home. And eleven percent don't even speak English." When my hackles are up, I can pull numbers out of my ass as well as any Wall Street economist.

"They don't count," she says. "They're immigrants."

Europeans can kick you in the balls without compunction. But if you shut up, they soon kick at Turks in Germany and at Moroccans in the Netherlands, and you're off the hook.

At 8 p.m. the bus pulls into Glenelg, a seaside suburb of Adelaide. Before disbanding to the hostels where we have reservations, we agree to meet tomorrow afternoon on the beach down the street. I have dinner at some eatery when Wouter trundles in. We drink a few beers together, and he talks about Russia. To avoid the leftover Stalinist restrictions that tourist visas still impose on travelers, he bought a business visa through some outfit that specialized in selling them. With it, he could stay three months and go anywhere. And he went all the way to Sakhalin"Where's Sakhalin?"

"It's an island off the Pacific coast." He raves about Russian hospitality and inescapable vodka binges. "You've got to go to Russia," he concludes.

"I'm committed to Japan. I signed up for a language course in Tokyo."

"When you're done, take a ferry to Russia. It's just like next door."

Tuesday, March 19.
Wouter beams when I drop on the sand next to him. I ask him about Russia. I can't hear enough. As he's telling me a Siberian tale, a tall chick in a bikini walks along, face shaded by a floppy hat. She carries a bag in one hand, sandals in the other. Her boobs sway and her hips swing and her inner thighs rub together as she puts foot before foot in the loose sand.

"Look at that babe," he says.

"Holy moly," I observe in my perspicacious manner.

She changes direction, zeroes in on us. Subject to genetic programming, we become speechless. He sits up straight to appear bigger. In the span of two seconds, we've flipped from friends to competitors. She stops a few feet away, smiles. Pubic hairs wriggle out from under her bikini bottom. We stop breathing.

"*Hallo*," she says.

Susi. Practically naked. We only knew her in baggy traveler clothes. We breathe, pretend nothing has happened. Then the cursed backpacker camaraderie sets in and douses any possibilities with traveler talk.

Hours later, we take the antique tram into Adelaide's colonial center. We've dressed up for the occasion: Wouter in polo shirt and the khaki shorts he always wears but with the zip-off legs zipped on; Susi in a cocktail dress; I in a wrinkled dress shirt and winkle-free khakis. She wants to go shopping. Wouter and I tag along, first to the Central Market, then from shop to shop. We eat at a trattoria, and when it closes, we migrate to a bar.

Susi flirts with both of us. We've switched back to English, flirting in German being simply too torturous. It's our last evening together. We laugh and carry on. We dance, miss the last tram, walk back. His hostel is the first one up, and we come to a halt in front of it.

"Why don't you guys join me on the Wayward Bus tomorrow to Alice Springs?" I say.

"I can't," she says. "I'm out of time."

"Oh man, it's too expensive," he says.

"It takes eight days. If you average it out, it isn't bad."

"I'm not doing the Alice," he says. "It's too far and too hot."

Her eyes shift from him to me and back to him.

I like him, and part of me is sad I won't see him again. The other part of me is leering at Susi in her cocktail dress.

"So—" His face twitches into a smile. He has come to grips with his fate. We're in front of his hostel, he has to go inside, it's over for him, she'll be mine.

"See you around," he says to her.

"*Ja.*" She wavers, wants both of us. "See you." They shake hands.

"Good luck with your trip," he says to me.

"Good luck with your career," I say to him. We shake hands.

And she's mine. We dawdle through the neighborhood. The air is buzzing with anticipation. She's swiveling and swinging her hips.

"There's my hostel," she says about a building half a block away.

We hesitate, slow down, stop, turn toward each other. She inhales, projects her boobs toward me.

It would be easy to hook my fingers behind her arm and draw her to me. The rest would follow. Instead, I struggle with logistics. We both have roommates. The beach is lined with multistory buildings. We don't even have a beach towel. While I'm juggling these complications, anticipation fades. We stand around, undecided, uncertain, silent, incapable, and then we say good-bye, regretful because this is something that should have led somewhere.

11
WOUTER'S WISDOM

The wiry guy with the parched face and immobile lips is Duncan, the driver of the Wayward Bus whose cargo bays are jam-packed with tents, canisters, equipment, Eskies, boxes, and crates. Backpackers mill around. Then Wouter comes around the corner, expedition backpack on his back, daypack dangling off his hand. Instant brouhaha. Turns out, he changed his mind.

We sit together. In front of us are Tammy and Travis, Aussie retirees in their fifties, an odd addition to the twenty youngish foreigners. Duncan introduces himself. He has taken off from his teaching job to do this. He introduces the girl by the door, Mandy. She does all the hard work. He introduces the bus, an oldie but goodie. He establishes the ground rules for the next eight days and introduces the route. The Stuart Highway is the fastest way to the Alice, a thousand miles north across the desert, but we'll stick mostly to small roads and tracks.

Then he drives. Mandy rides shotgun and does paperwork. A guy behind us, Dennis, blows into a hollow six-foot pole. A didgeridoo. You can buy them at tourist shops, just like boomerangs. When he gets it right, it emits a monotone aspirated drone. But mostly it emits his hissing breath.

We pass vineyards and orchards. Duncan introduces bush flies, what they eat, where they lay their eggs, and how many of them there are, and we buy fly nets at the next general store.

We stop at a campground near Hawker, a railroad town back when the Ghan still ran through it.

"Count your stubbies and pay me in the morning," Duncan announces.

We lift equipment, crates, and Eskies off the bus. He assigns us tents, and I rent a grungy sleeping bag from him. We pitch tents with missing stakes and torn cords, set up kitchen equipment, cut mountains of vegetables, and cook in vats on industrial propane burners. At last, we're eating. Travis slaps at his arm.

"The mozzies are coming out," he says, wiping his hand on his pants.

He and Tammy teach us Strine, their mother tongue. Aussies don't hike; they bushwalk. Kangaroos are roos, and the grill guards on our bus are roo bars. The smelly building to the left is a loo.

Later, after all the dishes and vats are washed and put away, two girls slink out of the dark, stubbies in hand.

"You must be the Dutchman and the American," one of them says.

Wouter and I look at each other.

"We know all about you," the other girl says.

"We got our spies out there," the first one says.

"Have a seat," I say, and they sit down on the dirt with us.

"Actually, Susi told us," the other one says.

"You know Susi?" Wouter says.

"She was in our room at the hostel."

"She was totally wired when she came in last night."

"She wouldn't let anyone sleep."

"She told us we absolutely had to meet the Dutchman and the American."

They're Beverly and Sharon from Canada. They've been in Australia for six months, and their plan is to find work on a ranch near the Alice.

"Have you ever worked on a ranch in the desert?" I ask skeptically.

"Nope, but it'll be a blast," Beverly says.

"I'm flat-out broke," Sharon says. "I must get a job, like, within days."

"And if you don't?"

"I've got to call mom and ask her to wire me some dough. That would be a bummer."

In the morning, everything is complicated: dislodging hung-over people from their tents, fixing Nescafé and tea, cooking breakfast, washing dishes, kicking stakes that have been driven into the ground too deeply, loading the bus. Cockatoos in the trees comment on everything.

We drive north to Wilpena Pound, a basin in the Flinders Ranges. Some decide to bushwalk up a dry creek bed. Dennis and his buddies decide to practice didgeridoo. The rest decide to bushwalk up St. Mary's Peak.

Brigitte, a shapeless German girl in her thirties who has been sitting on the bus by herself, stops to catch her breath, then sprints to catch up, then exhausted, stops again—and eventually falls hopelessly behind. I wait for her. I don't want her to be alone on the trail.

"Interval training?" I inquire.

"I'm breathing."

"You're walking too fast. Stay behind me." I set an excruciatingly slow but steady pace.

"I can't do this," she says after an hour.

"You're doing great. You're just not used to hearing yourself breathe."

"I want to go back."

"No you don't. What you want is to get to the top."

The sun is brutal. She runs out of water. I give her a quart of mine. She wants to stop, she wants to go back by herself, she can't go on. But she goes on.

"Enough," she sighs at the Tanderra Saddle.

"Look how far you've come. We're almost there. You can't give up now."

She makes it to the top, a bleached rounded-off rock, sinks down next to the others with a profound *aahh*, and takes in the mountains that encircle Wilpena Pound and the desert beyond them that fades into a purplish haze.

Everyone is waiting for us at the bus. It has taken us seven hours. She snatches a bottle of water from an Esky, slumps into her seat with an angelic smile, and doesn't budge again until we arrive at Angorichna station, a former sheep ranch with bunkhouses that have been converted to tourist accommodations.

Friday, March 22.

Clouds of fat black bush flies surge out of nowhere the moment the sun edges over the horizon. Bush flies don't bite. They do something even worse. They try to get into your mouth, nose, eyes, and ears to feed on the protein therein. If you kill a thousand every second, it won't make any difference.

But on the bus, they aren't the problem. The few that got in cling feebly to the glass. The problem is Duncan. Face redder than normal, he's castigating us because we didn't help Mandy enough. When he's through, he puts the bus in gear and drives.

Wouter tells stories about his train trip from Russia to China.

"Why did you skip Japan?"

"It's too expensive. A month in Japan costs the same as a year in cheap countries."

"How are you funding your trip?"

"My parents wire me money when I need more, but it's not unlimited."

"That's generous."

"It was their idea. After I graduated, they encouraged me to see the world."

"You've never worked?"

"Not yet."

"Not even part-time in college, or a summer job?"

"Why would I want to do that?" He looks at me as if I'd come up with my zaniest idea yet.

At the Leigh Creek pit coal mine, a gargantuan festering cancer, Brigitte sidles up to me while Wouter is taking pictures. She also sidles up to me at the Ochre Pits where Aborigines quarried rock for pigment. She has bonded with me though I'm not interested in her. I'm interested in Beverly, who's joined at the hip to Sharon, and they're embedded in the last row of the bus among hung-over party boys from the UK.

In Marree, I evade Brigitte by climbing into the carcass of a diesel engine, knowing she'd never follow me into this man toy. I investigate the inline-six motor, turbo-charger, gauges, and levers. For a railroad buff, an abandoned engine on a track that's sinking into red sand is a lugubrious sight.

Camel rides for tourists and a defunct railroad are all that remain of a once thriving transportation and communications industry. In 1872, the two-thousand-mile transcontinental telegraph line from Port Augusta to Darwin was completed, a risky enterprise in the largely unexplored continent. Marree was one of the repeater stations and maintenance hubs.

As the settlement grew, a camel industry sprang up. Camels, originally imported then bred locally, hauled everything from wool to pianos through the desert. Afghan cameleers led these caravans, and Marree became the camel capital of Australia. In 1884, the railroad arrived and added oomph to the local economy, while camel caravans continued to ply routes not serviced by the railroad.

But in the 1920s, motorized trucks arrived and annihilated the camel industry. After World War II, the telegraph line was superseded by modern technology. And the rail line that connected Adelaide to Alice Springs, well, it crossed a vast inland floodplain, and sporadic rains elsewhere could get trains stranded for weeks. So in 1980, a more reliable line farther west entered service. The Ghan, as it's affectionately called after the Afghan cameleers, was shut down. And Marree was rightsized into a near ghost town that scrapes by as minor tourist spot.

Our next stop on the dirt road is the dingo fence, the longest fence in the world. It divides Australia in two. We get out, and people shoot photos of it.

"On which side are the dingoes?" I ask Duncan.

"On both."

"So, what's the purpose?"

"Keep out the rabbits, originally."

"On which side are the rabbits?"

"On both."

"What's the purpose *now?*"

"Keep out the dingoes."

"But they're already on both sides."

"Yeah."

Duncan is useless. You're better off not listening to him.

At Lake Eyre South, fifty feet below sea level, the lowest point in Australia, we squint across the brilliant salt crust to discern where it ends. But it doesn't end. It fuses with the white flickering sky.

"It teems with aquatic life," Duncan says. "Certain animals bury into the slushy lake bed under the salt crust and survive for years in a state of suspended animation. When the water comes, they surface, and pelicans and other waterfowl show up to feed on them."

Suspended animation. I mean, come on. I no longer believe anything he says.

Back on the bus, he explains that we might be able to see Ayers Rock, weather conditions permitting, though it's five hundred miles away. It'll be a fleeting image. The phenomenon is due to the Heisenberg effect, he lectures, inveterate teacher that he is. Something to do with the ionosphere. He scans the land.

"There!" he says and brings the bus to a halt in a cloud of dust.

A hump near the horizon. Ayers Rock! Bedlam breaks out. We drape fly nets over our hats and scramble off the bus, and people take pictures of the fleeting image. Then we drive on. The image dissolves but recurs a few miles later, larger. Excitement comes to a boil. The next time, it's even larger, and people take more and more pictures.

Then we see it again, and people are still taking pictures though it's increasingly clear the hump isn't a fleeting image and has nothing to do with the ionosphere. It's a real rock a few miles away.

"Bullshit," Wouter says and sticks the lens cover back on his camera.

Even Tammy and Travis have been duped. Duncan's lips are fixed into a thin line. Reini, a twenty-year-old German, has a cow. He used up his last roll of film "on a normal fucking rock," he climaxes through the fly net against a swarm of frustrated bush flies.

"Losing your lolly?" Mandy says.

"Here you go," Sharon says and stuffs a roll of film into his breast pocket, which shuts him up.

We pitch our tents at William Creek, an ex-railroad town now down to eight inhabitants, a diesel generator, and a pub. At sunset, the bush flies disappear, a moment we've been looking forward to all day, though no one can tell us where they disappeared to, and we know better than to ask Duncan.

"I made lots of friends in Russia," Wouter tells me at the pub, "but there's no one like Inga in Irkutsk."

"Where's Irkutsk?"

"In Siberia. You should know. Didn't you pay attention in history class?"

"I thought I did. Why?"

"It's the former capital of Alaska."

She's twenty-five, speaks fluent French, and lives with her parents. He stayed with them all June. "For a few bucks a day," he says. "You can't beat that."

"Was she the reason you got hung up in Irkutsk for a month?"

He raises his eyebrows, writes her address into his notebook, tears off that corner of the page, and offers it to me as if it were his most valued treasure. "You've got to go see Inga in Irkutsk," he says.

Sunday, March 24.

Ayers Rock! The real one! We're parked at the official sunset viewing point. The brown sandstone monolith rises a thousand feet from the flickering plain, isolated and solitary. As the sun sets, it turns crimson, then grayish purple, and it darkens until it's but a black silhouette against the night sky.

Viscerally, you understand why it's sacred to the Anangu people, on whose real estate it is, and who call it Uluru. People use up rolls of film and have hushed reverential conversations.

At the camp in Yulara, a tourist town a dozen miles from Ayers Rock, post-climactic lethargy sets in. The ice in the Esky has melted, and the beer is hot. No one has the initiative for drinking games. Dennis elicits monotone drones from his didgeridoo. Michael and Terry try out theirs.

At midnight, Wouter and I stretch out on our sleeping bags outside the tent, hoping for some kind of breeze, but there's none. Heat radiates from the baked earth. Ayers Rock is out of sight, but its solitary majesty is still moiling inside us. Occasionally, we say a few words. Sometimes it's gibberish, other times sort of profound.

"A traveler who leaves home alone, must go home alone," he says with a rueful resonance.

"Wouter's wisdom?"

"Ancient traveler wisdom."

"Explain."

"If you uproot a girl, she'll wither. Or she'll use you. Either way, you lose."

"Is that what you were afraid of with Inga in Irkutsk?"

Silence.

To let him know I'm waiting for more, I whisk a bug off my chest. Something always lands on you or crawls up on your sides or squiggles into your shorts. But that's it. He has gone as far as he can go in sharing his emotions.

At sunrise, we're back at Ayers Rock. A linear smear leads straight up the rock along a cable you can hold on to. People coalesce into a huge drove at the bottom of the cable and inch up one by one in a solid line. Wouter and I race up a few feet away. By the time he gets to the top, I'm through reading the directional panel.

"You surprise me," he says, out of breath, face as red as the rock under our feet.

"Why?"

"You beat me."

"Did you think I was some old dog?"

"Well, the way you crept up St. Mary's Peak...."

Our eyes wander across the red harsh land to mountain ranges, some of them at the limit of visibility over a hundred miles away. What we can't understand is why people ever settled here, or stayed here, or survived here. Yet archeologists have found signs of human habitation dating back 22,000 years.

"I should have brought my didge," Dennis laments when he makes it up. "Here is where it's meant to be played. Here, I'd be able to connect."

Wednesday, March 27.

We drive north on the Stuart Highway and learn the meaning of *road train*. Passing them—one is a sixty-six-wheeler—is quite an event. And I always thought eighteen-wheelers were big.

"What's it like to travel for a year?" I ask Wouter.

"It's the best fucking thing I've ever done."

"In what way?"

Three camels stare at us. We stare back.

"They're feral," Duncan says over the PA system. "They're a pest. They eat up sparse native vegetation and multiply like bloody rabbits."

"Build a camel fence across Australia," someone shouts, and we all whoop and clap.

"It can't be explained," Wouter says after the noise has settled down. "You have to live it."

"So why don't you keep going?"

"I've reached the end of my road."

"How do you know?"

"I saw a sign. Every traveler runs into it. I ran into mine at a corner in Sydney. A guy in a suit was talking to another guy in a suit. Behind them was a big red sign. 'END OF ROAD' it said. I didn't want to be the guy in dirty shorts anymore. I wanted to be like them, you know, be productive."

The end of the road for the Wayward Bus is Alice Springs, a town of 20,000 souls, the bull's-eye of the Red Centre. We loop up and down the main drag and get off at hostels and lodges with our backpacks, didgeridoos, and Aboriginal paraphernalia. Based on Duncan's recommendation, we'll meet for our last supper at Bojangles. Except Duncan and Mandy. He has to wash the bus—a nightmare, the condition it's in—and she has to coordinate the next tour. Theirs is a job with a capital J.

We trickle into Bojangles, showered and dressed up. Wouter has zipped the relatively clean legs to his unspeakably filthy shorts. Brigitte commandeers the chair to my right. Beverly's spaghetti-strap dress displays her tangible assets in their bountiful glory. Even Sharon wears a dress and makeup. Michael comes in with my boomerang, scuffed and nicked from daily use. I purposefully left it on the bus because I wouldn't be able to throw it anymore.

"Duncan found it," he says. To appear grateful, I have his first beer put on my tab.

Our dishes—in my case, a chewy kangaroo steak—are delectable after a week of camping meals. When a rock band begins playing, Tammy and Travis get restless. "We're ready for a real bed," Travis says.

They've been wonderful though it must have been peculiar to tour their own country with a bunch of foreigners. We exchange addresses, promise to stay in touch.

At midnight, Brigitte asks me to escort her to her hostel. It's by the Todd River. She has been cautioned not to walk back by herself; Aborigines live in the dry riverbed! I want to party and make another run at Beverly but can't leave Brigitte to twist in the wind.

"I guess that's it," I say to Wouter. I'll catch the 6 a.m. van to Darwin. It's the moment to say good-bye and exchange addresses.

"I don't exchange addresses anymore," he says. "I've done it with hundreds of people, and nothing ever comes of it. It's a senseless traveler ritual. Staying in touch is an illusion."

"Um, well, then—"

We shuffle our feet. Something isn't right.

"But our deal is different," he says, and we exchange addresses.

With the now goofy two-foot boomerang in hand, I walk Brigitte to her hostel. Low trees and shrubs across the street mark the edge of the dry riverbed, a black void. Only, it isn't a void. Raucous voices drift up. She unlocks the steel security door. We say a few words. Maybe she's expecting more, a romantic glint, a kiss—

Two guys materialize from obscurity between the trees across the street.

She slips through the door, clanks it shut, locks it umpteen times.

They're looking at me. They yell something. Their voices are drunk and aggressive.

What was I thinking, accompanying her down here? Now *I'm* alone. I walk back toward the corner, try to appear powerful, try to swagger, puff out my chest. They're ahead of me. They yell that I shouldn't carry a boomerang. They start crossing the street, barefoot and unsteady. They ask if I know how to use it. I have to reach the corner before they do. They shout things I don't understand. Maybe they want to show me how to throw the boomerang better. Other voices call out from behind them. I reach the corner, turn, hightail it up the street, away from them, away from the blackness of the Todd River, and I'm on the well-lit main drag. Two parallel worlds one block apart have briefly overlapped, and it has scared the bejesus out of me.

12

FATALIST UNDERTOW

Bleary-eyed backpackers mill around the minivan when Wouter strides up. We greet each other with the hoopla of ancient friends.

"Change your mind again?" I say.

"I came to see you off."

"At 5:50 a.m.?"

"Hey man, we're friends."

We awkwardly rehash our plans. He hugs me. It comes out of nowhere. And it doesn't last long.

"Very unusual for a Dutch guy," he says.

"What is?"

"Hugging a guy."

The van drives north on the Stuart Highway. Glowing orange sand and rocks everywhere. Sunrise on the right. I talk to the Japanese guy next to me, tell him I'm going to Japan, that I'll be studying Japanese in Tokyo, but he doesn't understand anything, doesn't speak English.

We stop at the Tropic of Capricorn sign and at the Devil's Marbles—teetering granite spheres, some of them fifteen feet in diameter—and take pictures. We have lunch in Tennant Creek. Vegetation becomes less sparse. We stop in Daly Waters, a town of fourteen people and a pub with rooms, five hundred miles north of Alice Springs. I share a bare air-conditioned room with the Japanese guy. We communicate by smiling, nodding, and gesturing, which works.

At the pub, I'm hunched over my beer among Aussie cadences and foreign accents, and I'm staring down the froth.

"The pub is the oldest in Northern Territory," says the bartender to some French guys. "Back in 1872, when the telegraph line reached Daly Waters, they promised us the Ghan. And, guess what, they're *still* bloody promising us the Ghan."

Actual green invades the scenery the next day. We buy sandwiches to go in Katherine, and people take pictures of the intersection with the Victoria Highway into Western Australia. People take pictures of the darnedest things. We picnic in Nitmiluk National Park, by a pool a few hundred feet across, fed by a cascading waterfall, surrounded by tropical verdure. So much green! So much water! I'm dying to go swimming.

"Are there any crocs in it?" I ask the driver.

"Might be some freshies in it. But they don't usually eat humans."

"*Usually?*"

"At least there shouldn't be any salties in it."

"*Shouldn't?*"

"Unless something has changed since last week."

The problem with Aussies is that you can't trust their pronouncements. And then he uses my question as a segue into telling gruesome stories about saltwater crocs that stalk humans for lunch. Nevertheless, I go swimming. It's sensational, if nerve-wracking. And as we're piling back into the van, a squall drenches the land.

In Darwin, 940 miles north of Alice Springs, the driver drops me off at a lodge on Mitchell Street where millions of frogs in the swamp across the street orchestrate a deafening welcome concerto. I deposit my duffle bag in my sweltering room and head out. I'm looking for the hostel that the guidebook says holds mail for travelers.

In my last letter to Izumi, I gave her the address so she could write me. I love her letters. The months before I left home, we sent letters and faxes across the Pacific at an ever faster rhythm. One day, I asked her what a Japanese-style toilet was; the dormitory of a language school I was considering was so equipped.

It resembles an oversized scuff, she wrote. *Its popularity is declining because it makes you tired.* She sketched one and indicated where to place your feet and which direction to face. *Squat above the basin and remember the round part is the front. Press the flush lever by foot. The water comes from the rear to the front, and everything is finished. See, it's simple.*

She can make you crack up at the most unexpected moments. But she didn't like the language school and its location. Instead, she proposed the school where she was doing her coursework to become a teacher of Japanese for foreign learners. It was in Takadanobaba, a perfect location, two stops from Shinjuku, five stops from Shibuya. Since they also taught Japanese to foreigners, she asked them to send me a brochure.

When I received a fax from the school, I filled out the application and faxed it back. Then I faxed Izumi to let her know.

I have my little trip notebook here, she faxed back. *The last entry is smeared with tears. It says, "I finally found such a nice guy, but why do I have to leave him without knowing him! He might be OK because he is grown up. But not me." You must understand how happy I am that you're coming! Billions of kisses (… is that too much?).*

The guy at the hostel puts a box of mail on the counter. I comb through letters and postcards from around the world. Nothing for me. Her letter will arrive in a day or two. My flight to Bali won't depart till the morning of April 3. No worries, mate.

Saturday, March 30.

At dawn, I try to call Don Colson from a pay phone on Mitchell Street, but the frogs are so loud I can't even hear the dial tone. I move to another pay phone, but I still hear the frogs. He's my friend and lawyer, and he offered to sort out any issues during my absence.

"Hey Don, what are you up to?"

"Honking and burning gas," he says. "Want to know the latest?"

"Sure."

"I ran into Ginger."

"How's she doing?"

"She was mountain biking with some dude."

"The one she invited to our going-away dinner party?"

"Yup."

"Denny Divine!"

"And they weren't just mountain biking."

Frog crescendo in the background.

I'm not prepared for this. I'm prepared to hear that a bill is past-due or that my condo has burned down, but not this, though I've known the logic of it all along. She has promoted her plan B to plan A.

"Other than that, your absentee life is in order," he says.

I call Visa and MasterCard to check balances. They'll be paid off automatically. I call Amex to trigger the payment. The amounts match the numbers in my travel book. On a mechanical level, I'm operational. I call my answering machine. Unimportant messages, clicks, static, and pauses. I call Ginger.

"What's that God-awful noise?" is her greeting. For her, phone calls start in the middle of a terse conversation.

"Frogs."

"Yuck. Where are you?"

"Darwin, Australia."

"When are you coming home?"

"Not sure. Not for a while."

"What's a while?"

"A couple of months."

"I can't do this forever."

"I know."

"It's already been too long."

The fatalist undertow of our lives has broken the surface. I inquire about her orchids. She lightens up. Two of them have started blooming. Her shop is fine. She's mountain biking again. "I was so out of shape when I came back it wasn't even funny," she says.

Listing, I have breakfast. I'm not even griping about Nescafé anymore. I've become inured to it. Ginger is separating herself from me, a process I've encouraged, a process that is necessary so she can pursue her dream. Yet, in its orderly and irreversible manner, it abrades me.

As the first drops splatter on the pavement of the Mall, I dive into the booking office and ask the girl about a tour to the tropical wilderness of Kakadu National Park.

"We're still in the wet," she says with a wave toward the watery hell outside. "Most tracks are impassable." She shows me a glossy flyer with a photo of a leaping crocodile. "This is the only Kakadu tour we offer right now. It departs on April 2 and returns on April 4."

April 3, I'll fly to Bali. Kakadu is out. A major miscalculation. That's what you get if you don't plan. Spontaneity my ass. And I find myself in Darwin with all sorts of time on my hands.

The sun turns the water on the pavement to steam, but the AC in my room is disabled during the day—to save energy, I'm told at the reception when I complain about it.

I seek refuge in a café and write Ginger a letter. Australia reminds me of the Southwest, I write, its vastness, its landscapes, its pioneer culture. I don't mention bush flies. You have to experience them. Anything less is a waste of ink. Writing these four pages is hard, and whatever I'm writing is moot. I don't even know why I'm writing, other than to wind down our relationship gracefully.

Tuesday, April 2.
Cyclone Tracy plowed into Darwin on Christmas Eve, 1974, killing 65 people, injuring hundreds, and leveling the town. No signs of the destruction remain, though a port-town spirit bleeds through the new polish here and there.

I buy Lonely Planet's *Bali* and *Japan*. I replenish my supplies, do laundry, and get a haircut. I'm good to go to Asia. What's missing is a letter from Izumi. I ask the guy at the hostel if he could have put it into a different box.

"Come back tomorrow, mate," he says.

Tomorrow, I'll be in Bali. Izumi hasn't written. Perhaps she no longer wants to see me. She might be in a relationship. Exigencies of life in Tokyo have prevailed. Wouter was right. Staying in touch is an illusion.

13

PRETTY TITS

The taxi driver honks his way from the airport through Denpasar's polluted, dusty chaos and drops me off at a walled compound in Kuta across the street from the beach. From the gate, I see a tropical garden, a bar-and-restaurant pavilion with a pointy ceramic-tile roof, a swimming pool, and two-story guest buildings farther back. A girl in red flowery sarong and sheer blouse checks me in. My room on the second floor is the size of an Aussie hostel dormitory for sixteen people. It has a king bed, rattan furniture, a sliding glass door to the garden, and an AC that isn't disabled during the day.

At the pavilion, another girl, also in red flowery sarong and sheer blouse, smiles at me when I show up to have lunch. I haven't been smiled at by a waitress in weeks. She recommends local dishes, which turn out to be excellent. Later, I recline in a chaise longue and sip a beer. A butterfly lands on my belly. Birds twitter. A woman massages the hirsute back of a guy on a mat in the grass. Hubbub percolates over the walls. And nearby, the gardener goes *snip-snip-snip,* trimming flowers.

Culture shock. It's the low price I'm paying for all this, compared to the prices I paid in Australia for dingy hostels, vapid food, and surly service.

Then restlessness sets in. This kind of experience is worthless unless you can share it. I think of Ginger, who is pursuing her dream, and of Izumi, who has become an illusion.

This is the mood I'm in when I cross the street to watch the sunset, a popular event, judging from the people along the beach. Sunsets are brief this close to the equator, and as the spectacle above the Indian Ocean wanes, a boy of maybe eight tugs on my sleeve.

"Where are you from?" he says.

"America."

"Where are you going?"

"Nowhere."

"You want girl?"

Stupid question. But I don't say that. I ignore him.

"I show you."

"No thanks."

"Many girls."

"No thanks."

"You choose girl."

"Go away."

"Two girls, same price."

I shake my head. His faceless shapeless girls don't inspire me.

He offers cigarettes, then wrinkled postcards. "Buy something," he pleads, now a street urchin struggling to stay alive.

Thursday, April 4.

Noises outside my back window wake me up. I stick my head out. It overlooks an alley and part of an intersection. Vendors set up cooking stands, clank with pots and utensils, and fan charcoal fires. Suzuki micro-trucks *put-put* between pedestrians and bicyclists. The air is redolent of spices, smoke, flowers, and oily fumes. And not a tourist in sight this early in the morning.

The next surprise comes at breakfast.

"Nescafé or *kopi Bali?*" the girl says with a smile. Gosh, being smiled at by a refined girl in a red flowery sarong and sheer blouse first thing in the morning makes your day.

"*Kopi Bali?*" I ask.

"Grown and roasted in Bali. Brewed the Bali way."

I'm skeptical after seven weeks in Nescafé purgatory.

"Best coffee in the world," she says.

I'll try anything she recommends.

She glides to a table by the wall, puts several spoons of coffee grounds and a lump of sugar into a carafe, adds hot water, brings it to a boil, and lets it settle. She's serious, precise. But when she serves it, she smiles again.

I sip.

She gauges my reaction.

"Awesome."

"It means you don't like?"

"It means I like a lot. Why do you offer Nescafé, when you have this?"

"Many foreigners don't like *kopi Bali*. They prefer Nescafé."

"Stupid foreigners."

She smiles. The warm breeze ruffles her sarong. I love Bali already.

By midday, streets are abuzz with tourists and with locals engaged in the tourist trade. Shops and restaurants are lively. Dancers in extravagant masks and costumes perform on a mini stage, their fingers in expressive configurations.

At a rental car agency, I haggle over an air-conditioned car for tomorrow. It's too expensive, and I'm making motions to leave in order to force the price down. But the price doesn't budge. I get up. He smiles. I'm halfway out the door. Having run a big car dealership for ten years, I know a thing or two about haggling. But his price is like the Rock of Gibraltar. Am I misreading his tells? What if I can't find a cheaper rental car anywhere else? I hesitate, wondering if it's time to blink—

"There's other option," he suddenly remembers.

"Ah."

"Cheaper option."

"How much cheaper?"

"I make you deal if you take car with driver."

I sit back down. More haggling. And the car with driver becomes cheaper than a car without driver. Go figure. The driver would also be my guide. "He knows everything," the man says. And that clinches the deal.

Street urchins swarm around you everywhere, except on the beach, which seems to be off limits to them. There, a curious spectacle is unfolding. Fully clothed Indonesians of all ages—men, women, and kids, some in sarongs and various kinds of shirts, others in pants and shirts, and quite a few women in headscarves and robes—stroll along the water, barefoot, sandals in hand, and peer unabashedly and with amused expressions at the copious reddish flesh of Western tourists roasting in the sun.

At a bar, I get into a conversation with the guy next to me, a fat Aussie with a sunburned face. He's a doctor. Inevitably, conversation swerves to Bali girls.

"They cost almost nothing, and they have pretty tits," he says.

"I haven't seen their tits yet," I admit sheepishly, now exposed as inexperienced and inconsequential. "I just got here." A lame excuse, but it's all I can think of. I don't tell him that I spent three weeks in his country and didn't see any Aussie tits, either. I'm too embarrassed. I stayed on the backpacker track, isolated from Aussies. The only Aussies I met—with the exception of Tammy and Travis, the two errand spirits on the Wayward Bus—were those in the tourist trade. And they didn't show me their tits.

"Have you seen the wood carvings?" he asks.

"Yes, I have. Awesome, aren't they?"

He nods.

"Such intricate detail." I feel important. I've seen something! And they've taken my breath away. In a gallery, I got tangled up with a carved doorposts-and-lintel set that in its crooked manner was so seductive I almost bought it, though I'd have to pay a fortune to ship it home, and then I'd have to pay another fortune to build a custom wall to accommodate it.

"Made by children in sweatshops," he says.

"By children?"

"Yeah, a bloody shame." He swigs his beer. "I'm buying a couple of biggies for my office."

14
THOUSAND-YEAR FESTIVAL

A bony kid with a big grin is the driver of my rental car. He's fifteen, at the most. His name is Komang. The vehicle is a diminutive Suzuki. I tell him the temples and historic sites I want to visit.

"Yes, yes," he says.

I show him on my map to make sure.

"Yes, yes," he says. "You need hotel in Ubud?"

"I might."

"I find hotel for you, no problem."

We climb in.

"Where are you from?" he says as he steers into the morning chaos.

"America."

"New York?"

"Dallas."

"Yes, yes. Dallas. I know. JR. Cowboys."

"Yes, yes. How do you know?"

"I see on TV."

Homes hide behind walls. You espy only their curvy, pointy ceramic-tile roofs. But as we're talking about JR, we pass an open gate. Beyond it are several small houses, a garden, religious statuary, and an altar with offerings and burning incense.

"You married?" he asks.

"Yes." I don't want to shock him.

"How many children?"

"None yet."

It saddens him.

"Are you married?"

"When finish school."

"How many children do you want?"

He thinks for a while. "Four."

At least he has a plan.

He provides commentary on life in Bali. It's the only place in the world with three rice harvests per year, he says with pride. People speak Bahasa Indonesia and Balinese. "I speak both, and English," he says. He switches off the AC when we get bogged down in traffic, which is most of the time, and when we go uphill. "Engine overheats," he explains.

The Suzuki strains up a road into the foothills of Mount Agung, a 10,300-foot volcano somewhere in the clouds. By now, the AC is off permanently. People with straw hats work the terraced rice paddies, whose grassy dikes draw asymmetric curvilinear patterns across the hillsides. He stops at some stone ruins that vegetation is in the process of reclaiming. I ask him what the site is called.

"Yes, yes," he says. "Very old."

Same story at the next ruins. He doesn't have a clue what it is, what it's called, where on my map it is, or whether it's one of the sites I requested to see.

"Yes, yes," he says.

I'm being too systematic with him. So I give up prodding for things he doesn't know, sit back, and enjoy the ride. We're behind a motorcycle: father in front, mother in back, two boys sandwiched between them. The mother's purple batik sarong and yellow blouse flutter in the wind. Every moment is a visual adventure.

Traffic becomes heavier. Our goal is Pura Besakih, Bali's most important Hindu temple. A line of cars, packed with families or with men, snakes up the road into the clouds—until it grinds to a standstill. I gaze for a while at the same rice paddies and at the same sacks of fertilizer and at the same old woman squatting in front of a door, flat basket between her feet, paring fruit.

"Why aren't the cars moving?" I say when she's finished.

"They go to festival."

"What festival?"

"Thousand-year festival at Pura Besakih." He explains it. Very sacred festivals are celebrated every ten years, the most sacred festivals every hundred years, and the most sacred of sacred festivals every thousand years. "Imagine, every *thousand* years!"

"How long will the festival last?"

"Several days."

"Will we have to sit here for several days?"

He doesn't know.

"Why didn't you mention it this morning when we were planning the tour? We could have adjusted our plans."

He looks at me quizzically.

"Your boss, when I discussed my plans with him yesterday, why didn't he mention it?"

Now I've annoyed him.

"Can we walk to the temple?"

"*Walk?*"

God, I feel ignorant. We wait in silence.

"Let's turn around and go to Mount Batur," I say, my other major goal.

He makes a U-turn, shuts off the engine, and coasts down in second gear against the solid line of cars. When the road flattens out, he steps on the clutch and lets the car roll. When he needs the motor on uphill stretches, he starts the engine by popping the clutch. "To save gas," he explains.

We have lunch at a patio restaurant built into the steep mountainside with views of the valley. It has a festive buffet of Balinese specialties. Everyone is dressed up: some men in elegant sarongs and Nehru shirts, others in slacks and shirts, women in flashy sarongs and tight, sheer blouses. Even the kids are dressed up. I feel woefully underdressed in khakis and a wrinkled shirt.

We eat with our hands, and it's heavenly—despite the aggravation of Komang's racket, as evidenced by his negotiations with the matron in Balinese and with me in English over the price for the two of us, which I whittle in half, and which is still so exorbitant that the matron smiles benignly at my naïveté. He must be raking in more in kickbacks than he's getting paid for driving me.

We continue downhill then turn into a different valley of terraced rice paddies and villages. Traffic tightens up. Soon we're mired in a motionless line of cars.

"What's the problem now?"

"The festival."

Ha, I knew that.

We try patience. It doesn't work. Skipping the discussions about waiting several days or walking, I ask him to take me to Ubud. "Yes, yes," he says, makes a U-turn, coasts downhill with the engine off, pops the clutch, etc.

In Ubud, he tries to sell me on bungalows built on stilts into the gorge of the Ayung River with sublime views from their back patios. Alas, there's no one to share this with, and it doesn't make sense to waste it on myself. "No problem," he says each time, and the places get cheaper as we go. At a hotel at the end of Monkey Forest Road, he haggles with the guys at the reception, and they make me a deal no one in his right mind could refuse.

Leaning on the balustrade by the pool, a sweating beer in hand, amid flower thickets and palms whose fronds chatter with each puff of air, I look down the slope and watch the people who, bent over from the hip, toil with hand tools or with bare hands in the terraced rice paddies beneath me. I wonder what they're thinking under their straw hats when they look up at me in this concrete monstrosity—but they don't look up at me.

What *I'm* thinking is how resplendent all this is, these endless curvilinear patterns of brown paddies and green lines, the stands of trees and banana plants and palms, the shrubs and flowers. And as the sun sets, crickets and frogs harmonize their orchestras.

Monday, April 8.

I while away the weekend in Ubud, advertised as the cultural capital of Bali. It's the kind of place a Westerner dreams of getting stuck in. Tropical flowery lushness and terraced slopes form the backdrop to restaurants, shops, massage parlors, spiritual healing places, galleries, and Westerners who've gotten stuck. Some of them are artists whose paintings are on sale next to paintings of Balinese artists. They're all waiting for a dreamy-eyed tourist with a loose wallet.

In the afternoon, I take a minibus to Kuta. Packed with locals, it costs so little it's ludicrous. The traffic chaos, noise, and airborne filth are insane. I get off at a prominent beach hotel and plunk into a chair on its beachside patio. I inhale the ocean breeze, sip a Coke, and listen to the waves breaking. Every day in Bali has been this way, a mix of chaos and tranquility.

When it's time, I take a taxi to the airport. At the duty-free shop, I buy a bottle of eighteen-year-old single-malt Glenfiddich for Izumi's father. Gifts, my guidebook says, pave the way for everything in Japan. And if Izumi is an illusion, I'll drink it myself.

15
CHERRY BLOSSOMS

Vibrating with irrational post-flight euphoria, I place my feet on size 24 yellow footprints painted on the floor at immigration and wait. Travel lore has it that Tokyo Narita is a congested and problematic airport. But at 8:25 a.m. I see no congestion and no problems—until an immigration officer waves me over. He studies my ticket, doesn't like it.

"How long stay in Japan?" he asks.

"Ninety days."

"Why come from Indonesia and not from America?"

"Long vacation."

He studies my onward ticket, doesn't like it either. "Why fly to Korea, not to America?"

"Very long vacation." I say.

It was the idea of the travel agent in Australia, the one who sold me the ticket to Bali and the onward ticket to Japan. To get into Japan on a ninety-day airport visa, she told me, you have to have a ticket out of Japan. And if I wanted to stay longer? Get a ticket from Tokyo to Seoul, she said. It's the cheapest way out of Japan. Stay a week in Korea and then fly back to Japan for another ninety days. Everyone's doing it, she said.

"What are doing in Japan?" the immigration officer asks.

"I want to get to know your country a little."

"How are you paying for your stay?" He's polite. "Japan is expensive. I need proof you have enough money."

I show him $2,300 in cash.

"Not enough for ninety days."

I show him my Amex, Visa, and MasterCard.

He grunts with distaste.

"It's a platinum," I explain about the Amex, which converts his distaste into ridicule.

"Hotel vouchers?"

"I don't have any."

He exhibits the tell-tale signs of official exasperation.

"I'll be studying Japanese." I scramble to dig out the language school's registration certificate, which seems to help.

"What you do for living?"

"Nothing."

"Where your money come from?"

"Investments."

My concise, truthful answers puzzle him. He thinks I'm flippant. He thinks I'm lying. He thinks I'm smuggling drugs into his sacred Japan.

Two customs officers spread my effects out on the counter. They ask the same questions, and other questions. They flip through my books and have me empty my pockets. They take the battery out of my flashlight and inspect my Zaurus ZR. "Sony," one of them mumbles with an appreciative nod. And when they don't find anything of interest, they say, "Welcome to Japan."

Welcome to Izumi's land, Izumi the illusion.

I need to get some yen to buy a phone card and pay for transportation into Tokyo, but I don't want to change dollars. That's my backup fund. So I stand in line at an ATM. It sports a Visa logo, a comforting sign. The text on the screen is in Japanese script, which is to be expected in Japan, but where the hell is the Union Jack icon? You press it, and English appears on screen. I've done it hundreds of times in other countries. But there's no Union Jack. How can they install an ATM without a Union Jack at an international airport?

With Teutonic persistence, I try to advance my cause by guessing, but the only thing I accomplish is holding up everyone else behind me. Several

Japanese, who pool their expertise to help me, can't get the ATM to work either, not with my card, though it works for everyone else. To get me out of the way and allow their compatriots to go about their business, the two who speak some English take me to a bank counter. They ask in Japanese, the clerk answers in Japanese, and they translate: upstairs on the third floor there's a foreigner ATM.

"A foreigner ATM?" I say, bewildered.

Discussions back and forth in Japanese.

"For foreign Visa cards," one of them translates.

I still don't get it, patently slow as I am. More discussions in Japanese.

"Japanese ATMs work only with Japanese Visa cards," he translates.

I'm having trouble wrapping my brains around this concept, and I'm worried about losing my English-speaking guides. So I ask them to ask the banker if he could give me a cash advance on my credit card.

This befuddles them. Long discussions back and forth.

"I'm sorry, no credit card," is their astonishing explanation, and even I see that I've exhausted their patience. Then everybody bows and says, "Thank you" and "I'm sorry" several times, and I do the same, instantly drawn into what must be a Japanese ritual translated into English.

But once on the third floor, I can't find the fucking foreigner ATM. It's absolutely nowhere. Instead, on a different floor, behind an escalator, I bump into a dedicated Amex ATM! Maybe the only Amex ATM in the world. Certainly, the first one I've ever seen. And the default language is English!

I want to withdraw the equivalent of $400, enough to get me through the first few days. It asks seemingly simple but ultimately confusing questions, like, cryptically, something about *multiples of 10,000*. I spent the night on the plane and at the airport in Jakarta, and instead of doing math, I'm dreaming about coffee. I type *40*. It accepts and spits out a stack of forty bills. When I look at them, I discover that they're 10,000-yen bills, worth $100 each. $4,000! Out of an ATM! Based on the fees and finance charges I'm paying on this, Amex will be able to increase its quarterly earnings guidance.

With one of the 10,000-yen bills, I purchase a phone card at a kiosk, and the girl doesn't flinch—try using a Franklin at a kiosk in the US! I'm making progress. I call the language school to find out what to do next. I'm transferred to Naoko.

"Take Airport Limousine to Shinjuku and wait for me," she says.

"How will I recognize you?"

"Don't worry. I recognize you."

"How? I didn't send you any photos."

"It's easy. You look ... American."

One more in what will be, I suspect, an endless series of mysteries.

The Airport Limousine turns out to be an ordinary bus. But it has seatbelts! Then I notice that people actually fasten them. And in case I didn't notice, a bilingual digital female voice exhorts me to fasten it.

It's a crisp, cloudless morning, full of promise. Tiny pink specks dot the naked branches of cherry trees here and there between airport installations. The bus rolls into a land of gentle hills, forests, rice fields, orchards, and villages. But soon, the bucolic fantasy transmogrifies into an endless cacophony of industrial buildings, dense neighborhoods, office buildings, buildings of all imaginable shapes and sizes with huge script on their roofs and walls. They alternate with dirty-gray noise-protection barriers, sooty tunnels, expressway interchanges, and canals with stagnant toxic water.

This isn't how Izumi described Tokyo. Where is the life, the glitter, the energy? Is it even possible to build uglier buildings? And from my perch on the bus on the elevated expressway, I notice something else. The sea of urban ugliness has no chimneys. None. What do they do with the fumes from their heating systems? Breathe them?

It takes two and a half hours to traverse this, and when I get off in Shinjuku, I find myself on a sidewalk, smack-dab in a stream of Japanese men and women in charcoal, navy, and earth-tone business attire. Some of them are weaving through it all on bicycles. Billboards I can't read pulsate from drab office buildings with exposed plumbing and helter-skelter wall-mounted air conditioners.

I'm the only guy in jeans and denim jacket loitering with an inane grin and too much luggage. God, I feel conspicuous. Naoko was right. She'll recognize me. I'm looking for her, and I see thousands of Japanese girls. But after thirty minutes, one of them stops in front of me.

"I'm Naoko," she says. She's wearing a blue blazer over a pink T-shirt. *Them are mine* it says distractingly in golden cursive across her chest.

"Hi," I say.

"We're lucky it's not rush hour."

"I like the writing on your T-shirt."

"Writing?" With panic in her eyes, she looks down at her barely visible curves. "It means something?"

"Oh no. But it's very pretty."

She smiles, relieved the gaijin has stopped saying stupid things. "First, we go to your room. You can—" She motions at my luggage. "Then we go to office."

At a traffic light, masses of people accumulate around us, and when there's a gap in the traffic, no one jaywalks. No one even thinks about it, though my feet get itchy, and I can't understand why they're just standing there.

"Japanese only cross when the light is blue," she explains the phenomenon.

"Blue?"

"Yes. Excuse me. My English is very bad. You say green."

In the train station, she shows me how to buy a ticket at a ticket machine, how to use the turnstile, and how to queue on the platform. After the train ride, we get on a bus. She had ten years of English in school, she says, but it isn't good enough for a job teaching Japanese at the language school. Now she's working with foreigners to improve her English. It takes her a long time to say this and me a long time to untangle it.

We get off on a four-lane street lined with dreary five-story buildings. *Mejiro-dōri* a street sign says in romaji, in addition to whatever it says in kanji.

"Where are we?" I wonder.

"In Ekoda."

"Not Tokyo?"

"Yes, Tokyo."

"Thanks."

Whatever. Down the street, just past an inexplicable five-foot heap of abandoned bicycles, we enter the external staircase of a concrete building finished with dirty brown tiles and climb to the third floor. She unlocks a door and hands me the key. We stand at the edge of a breakfast area with kitchenette. Vapors of grease and spices.

"Always take off your shoes at the entrance of a Japanese home," she says. Several pairs of men's shoes are lined up in the entrance area, whose floor is four inches lower than the rest of the apartment. Two pairs of slippers sit on the higher part of the floor. I deposit my duffle bag by the shoe rack against the wall.

She points at the kitchenette. "In Japan, water is, how you say—" She motions drinking from a glass.

"Potable."

"Yes, potable, unlike in other countries," she says proudly.

"It's potable in America."

Which puzzles her. Dirty pots and dishes in the kitchenette. Clothes, books, and bedding on the floor in the back.

"Two other foreigners live here," she says.

"Where do I sleep?"

"They tell you."

My new home for the next three months.

From Mejiro-dōri, we turn into a nameless alley. "Remember the way so you find back alone," she says. We turn into another nameless alley. I memorize landmarks—a cleaners in a shack of wood, rusting corrugated iron, and green corrugated plastic; a utility pole halfway in the street; a crumbling concrete planter without plants; a wall plaque I can't read.

She continues reciting her list of rules. Always have a lot of cash with you because credit cards are rarely accepted, she says. Ha! With 400,000 yen in my pocket, I'm way ahead of her on that one.

We turn this way and that way and enter a maze of even narrower alleys with tiny shops and restaurants. I recognize them as restaurants because they have appetizing replicas of noodle, tempura, and sushi dishes in their shopwindows. I'm getting hungry.

"It's easy to find something to eat in Japan," she comments relentlessly. Dissonant electronic jangles blare from a glitzy establishment. "Pachinko," she says. The barriers at the four-track crossing clang and beep. "The Seibu-Ikebukuro line," she says. People pile up on both sides. A passenger train rattles by.

We walk up the steps into Ekoda station, a formerly charming iron structure from a hundred years ago that looks as though it had been designed by an apprentice of Gustave Eiffel—now ruined by cheap add-ons. We buy tickets at a ticket machine, practice getting through the turnstile, and practice queuing at the platform, though it's mostly empty. We take a train, get off at the third stop, Ikebukuro, maneuver through a multilevel tunnel system, buy tickets again, more turnstiles and queuing, take another train, get off at the second stop, Takadanobaba, which she pronounces like a burst of machine gun fire, and walk to the language school, which is on the sixth floor of an eight-story office building.

The only thing I know for sure is that I'll never find my way back.

She introduces me to Kubo-san, a woman in her forties who greets me with a bittersweet smile. Naoko bows and backs out of the room. She has done her job, has indoctrinated another foreigner into the rules and rigors of life in Japan.

Kubo-san wants to interview me in Japanese to ascertain my skill level. I tell her it's zilch. She doesn't believe me. She says something in Japanese. I shake my head. She says something else in Japanese. I shake my head. And so on. She could have just believed me.

While I complete some forms, which are helpfully written in English, she types into her adding machine, tears off the tape, and shows it to me. It's a number. A big one. It's how much I owe her for a month at the apartment and for tuition. I pull out my Amex card.

"Cash," she says sternly.

"I'm just kidding," I say and produce a wad of 10,000-yen bills from the front pocket of my jeans. Did she just do a minor double take? I count.

She opens her desk drawer. It contains pencils, pens, erasers, Post-it pads, a receipt pad, and a substantial stack of 10,000-yen bills topped off with smaller bills. She carefully inserts the ones I handed her, counts out change, and hands me the bills with both hands. Then she fills out a receipt in Japanese and presses a seal on it.

"You brought cherry blossoms," she concludes with her bittersweet smile. "It's auspicious."

Only by a miracle do I find my way back to the apartment—where two Asian guys grin at me apprehensively from the breakfast area.

"I'm Mr. Kim," one of them says in English, visibly relieved I'm taking off my shoes in the entrance area. He's in his thirties. "Mr. Song," he says about the other guy, who is in his twenties. "We are from Korea."

"I'm Wolf. I'm from America."

We all shake hands. Mr. Song speaks no English, and we can't communicate.

"Welcome, Mr. Wolf," Mr. Kim says.

"Thank you. Just call me Wolf. No Mr."

Perplexed, he gives me the grand tour. The breakfast area sports a table for two, four chairs, and a TV on a stand, the only visible furniture in the apartment. He points at a sliding door of wood and torn rice paper on one side of the breakfast area. "My room," he says. On the opposite side is a small open space. A rail in the ceiling is all that remains of a partition. "Mr. Song's room," he says about the vinyl floor that makes up the right half of the open space. Clothes and textbooks are scattered around an inch-thick futon. "Your room," he says about the four-mat tatami floor that makes up the left half. It has a futon, a comforter, and a pile of filthy sheets. A pink pay phone on the floor by the edge of the tatami catches my attention. "Only for Tokyo," he says. "Only 10-yen coins."

Opposite the kitchenette is a plastic accordion door to a niche with a washer, a sink, and two doors: one to a toilet, the other to a moldy bathroom with a stainless-steel tub deep enough for a short guy to sit in, water up to his neck. A rubber hose with showerhead is slung around the faucet.

"Shower here," Mr. Kim says. In the corner, not in the tub. And there's a floor drain.

I dump the untouchable sheets into the washer. He loans me some of his detergent and helps me push the correct buttons. Then I walk back to the alleys around Ekoda station to buy the essentials that will allow me to live in that place—even find the supermarket Mr. Kim mentioned.

The produce section has all sorts of vegetables, leafy greens, roots, and mushrooms but only a few kinds of horridly expensive fruit. The fish section occupies a third of the store, and pickled vegetables a whole aisle. Jam is strawberry, two brands, two sizes. The smallest bag of rice weighs eleven pounds. Orange juice comes in bottles, one type with 10% of something, the other with 100% of something. If you blink, you miss the meat section. Bread is white and comes in bags of six thick slices or eight normal slices. Beer cans range in size from eight ounces to a gallon.

I buy a bag of ground coffee, detergent (color scheme of Tide), bananas, apples, bread (the eight-slices kind), a bottle of orange juice (the 100% kind), and strawberry jam. Items I recognize. I'm too tired to experiment. And the prices make me dizzy. At a small kitchenware shop, I buy a French press and a porcelain mug with a green and white foliate motif. The French press is so expensive that the lady at the cash register feels sorry for me and apologizes.

By now, night has set in. Lights blink and flash, showcases are illuminated, and everything looks a lot better, more festive, and millions of people try to get through the alleys and squeeze past one another. But my landmarks have become invisible, and everything is different.

Tokyo is a lovely place, I pray, *but please don't send me in the wrong direction. It's hard enough already. You don't have to add to it.*

Whether it's divine guidance or sheer luck doesn't matter to me, but when I see the gridlock of Mejiro-dōri at the end of an alley, I'm jubilant. I've jumped over another hurdle.

Mr. Kim assigns me a corner of the kitchen cabinet and agrees somewhat flummoxed to let me store fruit and bread on top of the fridge, the only unused space in the kitchenette. When I pull the sheets out of the washer, he suggests I drape them over the clothes rack and a chair by the heater. Then he asks if I want to go out and get some dinner with him.

I have the urge to hug him. I haven't eaten since breakfast on the plane, and he just saved me from having to grapple with the Japanese restaurant scene by myself.

He takes me to a ramen shop a block away. By the door is a vending-machine-type apparatus with faded photos of noodle dishes. He pushes the button under one of the photos and inserts some coins. I opt for a different dish. Any idiot can order this way, even I. The chef behind the counter reads our orders off a screen and gets busy.

We sit down at a chipped Formica table and wait. The only other customer is bent over his bowl. A thick tangle of noodles hangs unappetizingly from his mouth into the bowl. He sucks violently and repeatedly to coax them increment by increment into his mouth while controlling them with his chopsticks to prevent them from slinging broth on his shirt and tie. And when his mouth is so full he can't inhale any longer, he bites off the remaining noodles and lowers them with his chopsticks into the broth.

Unperturbed, Mr. Kim talks. He's an engineer. His company sent him. He arrived two months ago for advanced courses. Mr. Song arrived a week ago and is a beginner. And he teaches me Japanese, *bīru* for beer, *biru* for building. "English words," he says.

"They don't sound English."

"Yes. Japanese use many foreign words, Korean and Chinese mainly, and now English. But they change them."

The chef hollers something. We pick up our steaming bowls at the counter. Two slices of pork, some seaweed, a slice of fish cake, and bamboo shoots float on top of mine. After this kind of day, the salty tasty broth, al dente noodles, and sparse ingredients are perfect. Mr. Kim must have known instinctively what I needed the most. And he watches me with a subtle grin as I battle the noodles with my chopsticks.

Back at the apartment, there's one more thing I need to do. Call Izumi. I'm not sure how she'll react. I haven't heard from her in two months and haven't seen her in seven. I feed some 10-yen coins into our pink pay phone on the floor and dial her number.

"*Moshi-moshi?*"

Her voice? The pitch is too high. Have I forgotten what she sounds like? "Izumi?" I say tentatively.

"Wolf?"

"Hi."

"Where are you?"

"In Tokyo, I think."

"Have you been to the school?"

"Yes, everything's taken care of."

"That's good."

"Can we meet?"

"We can."

"Tomorrow after class, at 1 p.m.?"

"Shall we?"

"Where?"

"Maybe in the lunchroom, on the seventh floor?"

It's over in a minute.

When I come out of the shower, Mr. Kim has retreated behind his sliding door. Mr. Song is studying on his futon, forming silent Japanese words with his lips. I'm wiped out. Every little thing has been hard, or a surprise, or a lesson, or something to remember or figure out. For example, I can't figure out what the phone call means. Her voice was devoid of emotion. Is she looking forward to seeing me, or is she just fulfilling an obligation toward a visiting foreigner?

I can't figure out anything anymore. My overloaded circuits have shut down. I stretch the moist sheets on the futon and crawl in. The last thing I hear is a symphony of grinding sounds against my ear as my sandbag-like pillow, chock-full with buckwheat shells, shifts under the weight of my head.

16

TIME RAG

At 4:45 a.m., daylight already shines through the opaque windows. I slide one open. And there's my new neighborhood behind the house: sheds pieced together from rusting corrugated iron, green corrugated plastic, and weathered wood; tiny yards cluttered with junk; and concrete buildings finished with grey, beige, or brown tiles. Windows are opaque for a reason. You don't want to be confronted with this on a daily basis.

Then, on the way to the bathroom, at the little step to the utility niche—*BANG!* I see stars, brace myself against the wall, grope for what hit me. The fucking rail of the accordion door. What kind of country is this where a barefoot five-foot-eleven guy doesn't fit through the door?

But the motions of fixing coffee with my French press and the aroma rising from it infuse me with a sense of home. I slouch on my futon, drink coffee from my porcelain mug, and read a French novel.

Mr. Song is sleeping in a tracksuit on top of his blanket. At 6:45 a.m., he stirs. At 7:00 a.m., Mr. Kim, also dressed in a tracksuit, opens the sliding door and goes to the bathroom. At 7:15 a.m., Mr. Song pan-fries chunks of meat, fumigating the apartment with grease vapors. At 7:30 a.m.,

Mr. Song serves meat, rice, and kimchi to Mr. Kim, who's watching TV, and they both eat in front of the TV.

I leave at 8 a.m. The sun is already high. Mejiro-dōri is clogged with traffic. In the alleys, salarymen in suits and women in skirts and jackets ride by on unisex bicycles with wire baskets in front. They dodge random utility poles and pedestrians and file into the maze around the station. Oblivious to shops and restaurants and even to the dissonant pachinko parlor, they head to the fence along the railroad tracks to find slots for their bicycles, and there are already thousands of identical unisex bicycles lined up side by side as far as the eye can see. And then everybody converges at the station entrance.

As taught by Naoko, I queue at a ticket machine and at a turnstile and on the platform. Expresses and semi-expresses speed by. A local train stops. Inside, people are glued to the windowpanes. Doors open to a wall of dark suits with heads on top. Stoically, with a suggestion of an apologetic nod, people on the platform press themselves backward into the mass until the whole body is inside.

Oh Lord. The fast-paced chime announces the closing of the doors. It's my turn to press myself into the mass, and others press themselves on top of me, shoving me deeper into it. Doors close. As the train accelerates, lurches left and right, and brakes, my body is vised into position by other bodies. My eyes are above the uneven river of black hair. I feel tall for the second time in my life, the first time having been this morning at the accordion door. Faces are inches apart. Some people pretend to sleep. Others hold manga in front of their noses. No one says a word. At the next stop, the impossible happens: more people get on. Pressure radiates from the doors in waves of shuffles and body adjustments.

At Ikebukuro station, the terminus, I'm washed out of the train and sluiced into tunnels and up some stairways, a bizarre tall denim particle in a dark liquid that flows with slow shuffle-steps and inscrutable patience until it comes to a halt on the stairs. No one can move forward or backward, and there's no escape. We're stuck and don't know why, but no one speaks, shoves, or elbows. To them this panic-inducing situation is merely another boring event on the morning commute, and some pretend to be asleep.

Then, somehow, the pressure lightens, and soon the mass shuffles forward again, anonymous bodies without distinguishable marks, no longer male or female, merely particles of a tarry fluid. I'm worried about ending up in the wrong flow and getting irrevocably washed down a wrong corridor and up a different stairway to some other destination from which I won't find my way back.

But I make it to the queues for the Yamanote-line ticket machines, and I queue at the turnstile, and I queue on the platform, and I get packed into the train. In Takadanobaba, I squiggle my way out of the train and get swept along to the queues at the exit turnstiles. From there, it's five minutes on foot on congested sidewalks through which bicyclists wind their way somehow.

Fifty minutes from door to door, and I'm already a wreck. What materials are these people made of to be able to withstand this every day?

Of the eleven other students in my class, ten are Koreans in their late teens or early twenties. The eleventh is a busty German girl. We have to introduce ourselves in Japanese. Nothing makes sense, and memorizing these meaningless sounds is impossible. But the Koreans pick up everything at once. Even the German girl responds correctly. Only I don't get it.

During break, she comes at me like ferrous scrap to an industrial magnet.

"How long have you been in Tokyo?" she asks in English. Bigger than most Japanese guys, bigger than me, she must feel even more out of place.

"Since yesterday," I say. "And you?"

"Two weeks."

"Enjoying it?"

"It's hard. Where are you staying?"

"At an apartment in Ekoda, with two Korean guys."

"Where's Ekoda?"

"No idea. All I know is how to get there by train."

She chuckles.

It's not funny. I absolutely have to unearth a bilingual map of Tokyo, but you can't just walk into a bookstore and buy one. They don't carry them. You have to find a bookstore with a gaijin corner. According to my guidebook, there are a few. But finding them without a bilingual map is the hard part.

"Where are you staying?" I ask.

"At a gaijin house in Shinjuku."

"How is it?"

"Filthy. It stinks. Someone stole my shampoo. I'll rent something better once I start making money."

"Teaching German?"

"No, teaching doesn't pay. Hostessing. A friend of mine worked in a hostess bar and made a ton of money."

So we chat for most of the break.

"Why don't we hang out together tonight?" she says when the teacher returns.

"I can't. I have a date."

A date with an illusion.

After four hours of class, my brain and ego are pulverized. I wait for Izumi in the lunchroom, which is a bulge in the hallway in front of the elevator. It's overrun by young Koreans. I sip a Coke, the sole item I recognize in the vending machine. Its familiarity is a tonic.

I'm anxious. Izumi's face has faded from my memory. She could be among the Korean girls watching me, and I wouldn't know. I don't even know if she's still interested in me. Then I see her. Well, I don't see her. I see a girl getting off the elevator whose eyes light up when she sees me. She maneuvers around some Koreans and is in front of me.

I try to hug and kiss her. She stiffens. The Koreans gawk. The embrace withers. The kiss miscarries.

God, what a dolt I am. And so conspicuous.

"Let's get out of here," I say into the awkwardness.

We squeeze through the Koreans to the elevator. When the door closes, we're alone. We hug, mere seconds until the elevator slows down again, not nearly long enough to resolder the connections that have broken apart over time. But it's a start.

Outside on the sunny sidewalk, her eyes sparkle beneath the elegant curvature of her eyebrows. A dimple forms on her cheek. Her hair drapes over her shoulders. I imagine her breasts and her tiny waist and the scrumptious layer of fat on her belly and hips, and it's all coming back.

"Shall we go to the Imperial Palace for cherry blossom viewing?" she says.

"Awesome."

We start walking. I have no clue where what is or how to get there. I just tag along.

"Did you receive my letter from Australia?" I say.

"Yes. I loved it. Did you receive mine?"

"You sent a letter to Darwin?"

"Of course. Didn't you get it?"

"I went to the hostel so often the guy at the counter was getting tired of me."

"I'm so disappointed. I wanted you to have it. There must be a long time rag."

"Time rag?"

"L or R?"

Even that, I forgot about. "Time lag, with an L."

The subway is practically empty compared to the mayhem this morning, but she clams up. I say a few things. She doesn't respond. I say a few more things, and she responds reluctantly. School kids in uniform read or study. Some people doze. Others stare straight ahead. But no one talks. *Don't talk on the subway* must be a Japanese rule Naoko failed to mention, and I'm beginning to suspect that there are many more rules she failed to mention.

When we get off, Izumi recovers her bubbly personality and holds forth on partying last week with nameless ex-colleagues. We stroll along a moat with imposing curvilinear stone walls.

"Hirakawa-mon," she interrupts herself as we cross a bridge over the moat and head toward a monumental gate.

We ramble through the East Gardens. From the top of the stone foundation of what used to be Japan's highest keep, we gaze at the park and at office towers surrounding it. She names some of them and points out the National Diet Building in the distance, or rather its pyramidal roof, which is all you can see. We move on and admire wispy cherry blossoms that have barely started unfolding their petals, and we crunch across a gravel expanse hemmed in by Japanese black pines with artful tufts of needles on their branches. She talks about her trip to Würzburg, Germany.

"I was totally moved by Tilman Riemenschneider's sculptures," she says. "Though I'm not Christian, I felt comfort and peace when I looked at the warm expressions of his biblical figures. I think this is a feeling people all over the world can share."

And all I think about is what comes next, but I'm uncertain how to move forward in this land of rules. We stop at a bridge over an inner moat.

"The Niju-bashi bridge," I blurt out. I know something! "You sent me a postcard of it. On the back, you drew a map of the Imperial Palace."

"You remember my map?"

"It's so cute. You traced moats in blue, the cherry blossom area in pink, the rape blossom area in yellow, and you put a red dot on it for the Niju-bashi bridge." But something is odd. I don't remember seeing it on the postcard. "What are these baroque lampposts doing on a classic Japanese bridge?"

"They're famous. They were added during the Meiji Restoration."

She explains the Meiji Restoration and comments on the Emperor, whose bridge this is, and on his minimal role in modern Japan.

"Then why do you still have an emperor?" I wonder.

"We use him for birthdates. We say, for example, 'I was born in Showa 44.' In the forty-fourth year of Showa Emperor."

"Would that be Hirohito?"

"That's his foreigner name."

The melody of her words transcends their meaning. I ache for her body, ache to see it and touch it and smell it, and somewhere off to the side near some willows by a moat, I know what to do. I take her in my arms and kiss her. In Tours, at night on the street, she abandoned herself and sank into my arms. In Tokyo, she kisses with restraint. And I wonder what will be next. In Tours, her hotel room was next. In Tokyo, there's no discernible next.

Our fingers laced together, we mosey from the Imperial Palace through Hibiya Park to Ginza's shopping avenues. She picks a café on the second floor, and we settle into Viennese-coffeehouse armchairs by a floor-to-ceiling window. I'm the only male in the place. On the menu, only the prices are legible.

"What's this?" I ask about the cheapest item.

"Coffee."

"Irish coffee with a double shot of single-malt whisky?"

"Black coffee."

"For this much?"

"That's Ginza."

We order it. Well, she orders it. The waitress serves us two demitasse of coffee with utmost daintiness and angles the spoons on the saucers just so.

But the coffee itself is oxidized filter coffee, barely better than dealership coffee.

"I'm so glad you came to Japan," she says.

"Did you doubt I would?"

"People promise things all the time that never happen."

"I don't promise much, but when I do, I try to stick to it."

"I like that."

"I was worried you wouldn't want to see me."

"Not want to see you? Why?"

"You might have met someone, for example."

"Yes, that could have happened," she says.

We talk about her classes and about woodcarvings in Bali and about the Red Centre of Australia ("I've never been in a desert," she says), and there's still no discernable next.

I pay the cashier on the way out, which is what all the other customers have done. I don't count the change because it may be considered impolite, my guidebook says. I just shove it into my pocket. I want to be a good gai-jin. I want to follow the rules.

On the landing, the waitress catches up with us. She stretches out her right hand, palm facing up, and supports it with the fingertips of her left hand. On her palm is some money. She says something to Izumi, who nods. Something embarrassing has happened. They steal a glance at me. It's my fault. Maybe I didn't pay enough.

"It seems you forgot some money on the table," Izumi says to me.

"Oh that. It's her tip."

"We don't tip."

The waitress offers me her tip. I can feel myself flush.

"Arigato gozaimasu," I say as I take it off her palm, and I nod the way I've observed Japanese men nod. "Thank you very much" is the only phrase I remember from four hours of grueling class, but that may have been the wrong thing to say in this situation.

"Why didn't you tell me at the table?" I ask once we're outside.

"I didn't notice."

"You didn't see the tip in the middle of the table?"

"I didn't look."

It's dark already, and Ginza has been transformed into a sound-and-light show of brilliant billboards, signs, and storefronts. Pedestrians pulse through backstreets lined with restaurants, bars, and clubs. Touts bow and hand out cards to men, to Japanese men—not to me, and not to girls either.

Izumi chooses a dining bar. In Tours, I was in charge. Now she is. She translates the menu, and she orders. We drink wine and eat tapas-sized portions with knife and fork. She explains each dish. Familiar flavors are paired in surprising ways with exotic touches, and we *ooh* and *aah* with each bite. At some point, I suggest that I'd also enjoy eating Japanese food.

"This *is* Japanese food," she says. "Japanese-Western fusion. We eat it a lot."

"I mean the food you eat with chopsticks."

"We'll have plenty of opportunities," she laughs. She's happy to be here with me, happy with the status quo, with eating and drinking and laughing together, and nothing more. She doesn't ache for my body as I ache for hers.

We're back on the street. I want to peel off her clothes but can't figure out the logistics. My apartment has zero privacy. We have to find a love hotel. I've read about them in my guidebook. But I don't see any, don't even know what to look for. I'm hoping she'll suggest one, but she doesn't. I'm wondering if I should ask her, but it would probably violate a rule. And we're in Ginza station. It's midnight. It's over. There won't be a love hotel. She makes sure I buy a ticket for the right amount.

"Follow the red ring," she says at a fork in the corridor.

"Which red ring?" I don't see it because I'm still thinking about love hotels.

"That one." She points at a red ring half a foot in diameter painted on the wall. "Get on the train to Ikebukuro. From there, you know."

"Can we get together tomorrow?"

She considers it. "Three thirty at the lunchroom?"

"Perfect."

We kiss so lightly it isn't even a kiss. Then she melds into the flow of dark suits and outfits, some staggering, others holding on to each other in the midnight rush to catch the last train home

17

RULES

No telling how I survived another rush-hour commute and four hours of class, but I won't survive them again. So after class, I wander into Kubo-san's office and ask her to cancel my classes. "I'd like to sign up for private lessons," I add.

Seconds elapse.

"Private lessons?" she whispers.

"Yes, please."

"But they're *very* expensive."

"How expensive?"

"How many hours?"

"Same as the class, four hours a day."

She punches some numbers into her adding machine and shows me the result. In light of the price of a demitasse of oxidized dealership coffee at a café in Ginza, it's outright reasonable. I request to start at 10 a.m. to avoid the rush-hour commute. She says she'll line up five teachers, one for each day of the week, and will call me Monday morning to confirm.

This time in the lunchroom, I don't try to hug or kiss Izumi. On the train to Shibuya, I don't say a word. I heed rules. I want to be a good gaijin. At the big intersection outside Shibuya station, all traffic lights for pedestrians turn green at the same time due to a horrid miscalculation, and the masses lined up on all sides advance toward each other from every angle like Roman legionaries. It'll never work. They'll collide, block the intersection, and cause fatalities. But it works, without shoving, yelling, or cussing, a mathematical elegance to its randomness. Chaos theory at work.

"We call it a scramble intersection," she says.

Shibuya's streets palpitate with the young and fashionable. And love hotels are everywhere, my guidebook says. Yet they're nowhere. At a café, she orders cappuccino for herself and a double espresso for me. They're excellent, and far less costly than the stuff we had in Ginza.

"I finally know where I live," I say proudly. I pull out the bilingual pocket street atlas of Tokyo that I bought before our date, open it to the right page, and show her.

"Cool," she says about the atlas—not about Ekoda—and leafs through it.

"Can you show me where you live?"

She flips to the overview map of Tokyo. "Soka isn't on it," she says. "It's a suburb. It's that direction." She flicks her finger off the top of the map. "I just sleep there. I do everything else in Tokyo. Even my piano lessons."

"You play piano?"

"I started again. I used to play in school. At first, my fingers were like wood. Now it's better. I try to practice every day, depending on how much time I have, sometimes three hours, other times twenty minutes." She plays piano on the edge of the table, lists pieces she's working on, sips her cappuccino, licks away her milky mustache, smiles, and her eyes sparkle. Surely, we'll run into a love hotel. They have to be somewhere.

"Let's have dinner in Shibuya." I'm playing for time.

She becomes tense, looks at her watch.

"It doesn't have to be Shibuya," I say.

"I need to be somewhere at 6 p.m."

This is unanticipated. My love-hotel bubble deflates with a long but practically inaudible hiss. Someone else will take her to a love hotel. Who am I to butt into her life? To impose on her my corny expectations?

"Tomorrow?" I say, flailing.

"Tomorrow is good." She smiles again. "At 6 p.m.?"

"Deal."

Friday, April 12.

I scour the alleys and one-lane streets of the entertainment quarter of Takadanobaba for love hotels but still don't know what to look for. Instead, I find a normal hotel, not an international one with exorbitant rates, but a business hotel for the underlings of Japan Inc. I recognize it by the *HOTEL* in its name.

It's modern and impeccable. One of the counter clerks even speaks some English. The rate is reasonable, and when I book a room for tonight, he accepts my foreigner Visa card. But for reasons I can't figure out, he doesn't give me a key.

I'm elated, having accomplished something on my own. I'll spend the night with Izumi. The logistics are in place. Planning triumphs over spontaneity. It's a gamble. She might say *no*. She might say she has her period or a sore throat or that she needs to go home. But hey.

We meet in front of the school and head into the entertainment quarter. A myriad of lights, signs, and red lanterns lend splendor to buildings that are grungy during the day. Bowing touts encourage salarymen to enter. Bowing girls hand out tissue packs imprinted with phone numbers. Men and women rove in groups. Izumi translates some menus posted outside, and at one of them she says, "Shall we?"

When we walk in, the four chefs toiling in the open kitchen stop what they're doing and yell a greeting. We sit down at the counter that surrounds the kitchen on three sides. People are in their twenties and thirties. She translates the menu, item by item, four pages, from beginning to end. "Hmm," she says, or "Looks good," or "I'd love that."

We eventually pick three items for our initial order, but the chef doesn't glimpse at me when he takes the order from her, nor does he glimpse at me when he situates the dishes in front of us. I've become invisible.

She pours sake into my glass.

"Thanks."

"Your turn."

"To do what?"

"We pour each other."

She holds her glass with the fingertips of both hands. I pour. We say *kampai,* chink glasses. I've only had hot sake before and don't remember it too fondly. But this is chilled. It's dry, complex, with lingering nuances. It's delicious.

I study the way she controls her chopsticks: inside chopstick between thumb and ring finger, outside chopstick between thumb, index, and middle finger.

"It's needlessly complicated," I say.

"That's how we do."

"Why do you also use your ring finger?"

"It's easier."

It's the hardest part. You have to contort it up at an odd angle and press it forcefully against the inside chopstick. But the people around us are all holding their chopsticks the same complicated way.

She orders one or two dishes at a time, and we share. Each is a pleasure, but sake renders the Japanese way of chopsticks increasingly arduous. They keep rolling off my fingers, food keeps dropping from them, one of them pops out of my hand and falls to the floor—and she has to ask the chef for another set. *Conspicuous* is what comes to mind, and yet, the chef still manages not to notice me when he puts the fresh chopsticks in front of me.

My ring finger is cramping. She massages it. I pour the last drops of sake. She cuddles against my side.

"I've reserved a hotel room," I say.

Her head sinks on my shoulder. It means *yes*.

Outside, we take in the glow, the people. Static electricity of anticipation. I'm aching for her body, and this time, the logistics are in place. I've planned and prepared for it. I've been looking forward to it for so long. She clings to my arm. She doesn't seem eager, but she doesn't hesitate. Then she hesitates.

"I have to call my mother."

"About what?"

"I need to let her know."

"Isn't it a little late?"

She calls from a pay phone, the briefest of phone calls.

"What did you tell her?"

"That I'm not coming home tonight."

"That's all you said?"

"I said, 'I'm staying with a friend. And Chika-chan's apartment is in central Tokyo, so it's more practical at this hour.'"

"Who is Chika-chan?"

"A girlfriend."

"You lied to your mother? At your age?"

"I didn't lie," she laughs. "Both sentences are true. You're the friend I'm staying with. And Chika-chan does live in central Tokyo. If my mother wants to combine the two into one meaning, it's her interpretation and not what I said."

"And she didn't ask any questions?"

"No, why should she? She doesn't want to ply."

Ply? I've had too much sake to sort through her Ls and Rs. By now, I'm buying every word like a used car—as is, with all its faults and defects and without warranty, expressed or implied, of whatever kind. "But why not tell her you're staying with me?"

"My parents are traditional. I need to follow the rules."

Ha! I knew that. The rules. But I want some precision. "They told you that spending the night in a hotel with a gaijin is against the rules?"

She looks at me blankly.

"Did they tell you what any of the rules are?"

"Of course not."

"Why not?"

"It's not necessary."

"So how do you know what the rules are?"

"Everyone knows."

Everyone but me. We amble toward the hotel. My arm is draped around her back. Her waist is so narrow that my hand comes to rest on her belly. Her shoulder slips into my armpit. Familiar pieces fitting together like a puzzle. I know where to go. I'm leading her. I feel competent, practically manly.

The night clerk at the hotel, however, doesn't speak English. And instead of offering me the key on the palm of his hand with a gracious nod, he ignores me and speaks to Izumi. There's a snag. He looks askance at our luggage—my daypack and her purse.

"He asked us to sit down and wait," she translates his barrage of words.

We plop down on the couch. She tries not to let it show just how much I've loused it up, and I try to take it in stride, and we chat about whatever. He riffles through some papers, clicks around on his computer, discusses it with his colleague, gets on the phone, maybe wakes up the guy on the dayshift. After a while, he says something to Izumi, and we approach the counter like two guilty kids. With an icy nod, he gives me a key. Clearly, his hotel isn't for this type of sordid activity. I can read it on his face.

But the room is nice, if not much larger than its double bed. As I close the door, the nightmare clerk downstairs drifts off into oblivion, and the air crackles with anticipation of sordid activity. I switch off the light and open the window to the glow and hubbub of Tokyo. We kiss and she melts in my arms and abandons herself with a sigh. Soon she's naked and glorious, and her skin has the texture of compressed air and her breasts a hue of neon light.

Saturday, April 13.
Seconds before cutoff, we slip into the hotel's breakfast room and opt for Western breakfast—rather than Japanese breakfast—because it comes with coffee, which is what I need the most. It was Izumi who mentioned breakfast is included. I had no clue.

In certain other aspects, I'm no longer clueless. For instance, I find my way through Takadanobaba station without any problems, and when we take the Yamanote line to Shinjuku, I buy my own ticket for the correct amount with near-Japanese fluidity.

Yet I still stare at a homeless settlement of densely configured cardboard shacks in a pedestrian area under an office tower when we come out of Shinjuku station. With four million passengers a day, it's the busiest station in the world, no less, and I stare at shoes that are arrayed in front of ingeniously fashioned sliding cardboard doors. I stare at a guy who's sweeping out his dwelling with a three-inch paintbrush. I stare at a handful of guys who squat around a camping stove and sip tea. Another guy sits on the floor inside his cardboard box that is barely tall enough for that and reads a newspaper. There are no empty booze bottles or beer cans and no piles of trash. Everything is neat in its way, a fascinating microcosm.

For the people that bustle by, the homeless settlement isn't there. Izumi, too, focuses on something straight ahead and speeds up a notch.

Our first stop is Kinokuniya bookstore, the Japanese equivalent of a Barnes & Noble, only bigger. At the gaijin corner, I stand among people who are taller than me, skim titles I can read, linger over authors I recognize, and feel normal for the first time in days.

"This is my favorite Japanese novel," she says and hands me a boxed set of two paperbacks. "It's our most famous literary work. It was written by a woman a thousand years ago. I love how she describes court life during the Heian period in Kyoto, their clothes, their buildings, their music, their whole way of life."

The Tale of Genji. I leaf through the two paperbacks and do the math: 1,090 pages of dense, small print. "It's long," I lapse.

And inevitable.

In addition to *Genji*, I select two contemporary Japanese novels translated into English. She selects a Japanese book for herself. When I take it in my hands, she flips it over so that the spine is on the right, and the back is the front. In Japan, every little thing is different.

We head to Shinjuku Park. The areas under the blooming cherry trees are occupied blanket to blanket, so we stretch out in the grass a bit away but with a glorious view of the whitish-pink mass. Our heads are resting on my daypack that is filled with books. She is telling me episodes from *Genji*, and the more she's talking, the more I want to go to Kyoto with her.

"Let's go to Kyoto together," I say when she pauses.

"I'd love that. I've been dreaming about it."

"Can you get away for a few days?"

"During Golden Week I can."

She explains it. It isn't a week and has nothing to do with gold. It's a weekend and a series of holidays spaced apart by a few workdays. And that's when we decide to go.

"It makes me so happy to think we can be in Kyoto together," she says. "You should read *Genji* beforehand. You'll see Kyoto in a different light."

We kiss, hug, and murmur. After sunset, we migrate to an *izakaya*. We drink beer and order from a menu with photos—cucumber-seaweed salad, sashimi assortment, grilled eggplant, and octopus salad to start. I ask her to be my private teacher. I've been mulling it over for days. I'm paying the school a lot of money. I'd rather pay her, but less than I'm paying the school, and we'd both come out ahead.

"I'm not yet a qualified teacher," she says.

"You're qualified enough for me."

"And your lessons at the school?"

"I can cancel them."

"Where are we going to do this?"

"At the apartment. Or at a coffee shop."

"I don't know."

"If it doesn't work, we'll just forget about it."

"I'm not sure."

"We can try it and see how it goes before I cancel my lessons."

She doesn't like it, has objections, hems and haws, but leaves the door open. I drop it for the moment because I know her resistance will wither away quietly. Next time I bring it up, she'll acquiesce.

When her time is up, we join the midnight deluge that drains into the two-hundred entrances of Shinjuku station and kiss good-bye at a turnstile, our lips barely brushing.

18

CRAZY AMERICAN

I sit on my tatami, Japanese textbook in my lap. Mr. Song is starting his morning routine—cooking rice, chopping veggies, and frying meat. I get up at 5 a.m. every day to enjoy daylight for a couple of hours before he ruins it with his revolting grease vapors. Mr. Kim emerges from the toilet and turns on the TV. But before he sits down to watch it, which he does every morning to improve his listening comprehension, he makes one step toward my tatami and stops at the edge.

"Mr. Wolf, please eat breakfast with us," he says in English.

"Thank you, but I already ate."

He nods, and they have a brief exchange then continue with their routine: Mr. Song cooking, Mr. Kim watching TV. It's Sunday, and there's a soupçon of leisure in their movements. Mr. Song serves rice, meat, vegetables, and kimchi, and they eat and watch TV together.

"Do you understand?" I ask Mr. Song in Japanese and point at the TV.

"Not much," he says in Japanese.

It's our first complete conversation where each said something that the other actually understood, and we grin and are so proud of ourselves.

When they're done eating, Mr. Kim continues watching TV. Mr. Song clears the table and stacks the dirty bowls on top of the frying pan and saucepan in the sink. Then he joins Mr. Kim, and they both watch TV. It's all part of their hierarchy.

"I'm going running," I tell Mr. Kim in English. My Japanese is still insufficient to express anything of this complexity.

"Running?" he says, baffled.

And I know what he's thinking, from the way he looks at me. He's thinking, *Another crazy American!*

My plan is to run on Mejiro-dōri toward the suburbs for thirty minutes and then run back the same way to avoid getting lost in the tangle of nameless alleys on both sides of the street. Fifteen minutes into my run, a Ferris wheel and treetops appear above the low buildings to the right, signs of a possible oasis amid this urban ugliness.

I cut through the neighborhood toward the Ferris wheel, past houses with three-foot wide gardens, rusting fences, Japanese black pines that protrude above perimeter walls, and junk. A lot of junk. Every house has a collection of it stacked against a wall—don't they ever throw anything away? The Ferris wheel, however, has vanished.

Alleys curve, end in T-intersections, or split into Ys. Due to the thick cloud cover, I can't even orient myself by the sun. The Ferris wheel pops up again, behind me. I adjust my course, follow the alleys this way and that way. The Ferris wheel disappears. When it reappears, it's on the left, though it should be on the right.

Okay. I'm lost. I've been running in a circle.

And there isn't a soul on the street I can ask. Forget the fucking Ferris wheel. I just want to get back to Mejiro-dōri.

At an intersection, a middle-aged woman comes out of an alley. I slow down to an unthreatening walk. I'm humongous compared to her. I stop at a polite distance, excuse myself in Japanese, and ask where Mejiro-dōri is. It comes out very smoothly, almost flawlessly. All she has to do is point in the right direction.

Panic fills her eyes. She makes a strange gurgle, raises her forearms into an X in front of her face, and skedaddles. That's how advanced my Japanese communication skills are.

Monday, April 15.

Takano-sensei, my Monday teacher, is too small for his suit, and the collar of his shirt droops around his neck. His passion in life is to teach me to introduce myself to a salaryman, humbly offer him my business card with the fingertips of both hands, and reverently receive his business card in return. With unshakable seriousness, he teaches me how to bow from the hip, hands flat against my thighs—I must be a hilarious sight, but he doesn't even snicker. He attempts to teach me vocabulary and grammar. He gives his all to sustain a word-by-word practice conversation, during which he reveals that he's single, twenty-eight, and the only male teacher at the school.

At 4 p.m., I pick Izumi up at Ekoda station for our first lesson. When I introduce her to my roommates, Mr. Kim chats with her in fluent Japanese. Then he and Mr. Song grab some books and decamp—an act of mercy for which I'm immensely thankful.

She observes with fascination how I fix coffee with the French press. Every motion seems to be important to her, seems to astonish her. I pour some into one of the teacups that belong to the apartment and the rest into my foliate mug. She tastes it, likes it. Then she teaches me Japanese. She's professional and patient. She pronounces each word with utmost clarity. She encourages me and prods me for answers.

But I can't concentrate. My brain, fried from four hours of Takano-sensei, has become impervious to Japanese. I can't remember these random sounds from one minute to the next. I consider biting her nipples and bending her over the table, but I don't know when my roommates will return.

"This isn't working," she says after an hour.

"Maybe I lack the intellectual horsepower to learn Japanese."

"Nonsense. You'll learn it. It's just that I can't be your teacher."

So we give up. I want to pay her for the hour, but she refuses my money. While I rinse out the French press, I formulate a strategy that will lead to her body. I need to lure her near a love hotel, and they're truly everywhere in Shibuya—I verified that in my guidebook.

"Why don't we have dinner in Shibuya tonight?" I ask.

Her lips open slightly, but no sounds come out.

"It doesn't have to be in Shibuya," I backpedal. "We can go somewhere else."

"I can't."

"You can't?"

"I have to do other things with other people."

Other things with other people. This is normal. She has a life. Good for her. You can't let that get to you. I'm concentrating on scrubbing the French press, which doesn't need to be scrubbed.

"Tomorrow?" I say.

"Tomorrow is not available."

"Wednesday?"

"Wednesday is good."

I smile. She smiles. And everything is perfect. I accompany her to the station and see her off at the turnstile, knowing she'll do other things with other people tonight and tomorrow night. What did I expect, parachuting into her life like this? That she'd renounce everything to accommodate me?

Tuesday, April 16.

My Tuesday teacher, Chiba-sensei, reviews the material I'm supposed to remember from yesterday and attempts to make conversation. She sketches objects on the board with precise strokes and explains grammatical concepts in the simplest Japanese terms, which are gibberish to me. I beg for English, just a few words to let me find my bearings, please, but in vain.

"Only in Japanese," she says in Japanese, endlessly patient and falsely confident that some of it will eventually stick.

My lunch spot is a narrow park, or rather a fat part in the sidewalk with two trees, a bush, a bench, and a five-foot heap of abandoned bicycles—heaps of abandoned bicycles being a ubiquitous Tokyo phenomenon. It isn't exactly bucolic, but it's a respite from the claustrophobic classroom.

Lunch is a banana and two *onigiri* I bought at a 7-Eleven. Removing the ingenious plastic wrappers from the triangular rice balls requires a special skill set. You have to be able to read Japanese instructions that tell you how to pull on the three tabs in the proper sequence and direction, and you have to do it with the right amount of force and with a certain *je ne sais quoi*. If you screw up any part of it, you have moss-green shreds of roasted seaweed on your lap. But today, I look like I've been doing this all my life.

"Where are you from?" someone says in English.

I look up from my *Wall Street Journal Asia*. A thin short guy is standing in front of me. "America," I say, leery.

"May I sit down?"

"Sure."

I fold up the paper, and he sits down next to me. He's an engineering student at Waseda University. His name is Shige. His hobbies are tennis, karaoke, and getting drunk. And he needs to practice his English, he says. I should charge him for the lesson.

In the afternoon, I ask Mr. Kim and Mr. Song in Japanese if they'd like some coffee.

"I never drink coffee at home," Mr. Kim says. "Sometimes I drink coffee at a café."

"I never drink coffee," Mr. Song says.

"Try it." Then I switch to English. "If you don't like it, you don't need to drink it." Such intricate structures are way beyond my Japanese.

Mr. Kim explains the situation to Mr. Song in Korean, and they discuss it with short phrases and grunts. In the end, they aren't enthusiastic but accept. We huddle around the table. I work the French press. They monitor with trepidation the substance trickling into their cups. Its aroma has whacked them, and now they're reluctant to proceed to the next step.

"Do you have milk?" Mr. Kim asks.

"No, I'm sorry."

"Do you have sugar?"

"No, I'm very sorry."

They're waiting. Perhaps they want me to try it first. To reassure them, I take a sip. They look at me then at each other. Mr. Kim tries it. One slurplet.

"It's good," he says in English. "Very strong. I like lots of milk and sugar in coffee. I'm sorry." And he sets it back down on the table.

Mr. Song lifts the cup toward his lips but doesn't allow it to touch them and sets it back down with an apologetic grimace.

"I'm sorry," he says in Japanese.

Wednesday, April 17.

I wait for Izumi in front of First Kitchen, a hamburger chain whose orange sign across the storefront actually says *First Kitchen* so that even I can read it, though the entire menu is in Japanese, and I can't read anything.

It's near Takadanobaba station, and pedestrians amass at the curb and cross the street in waves. I scan the dozens of girls in each wave for Izumi. Most of them wear short skirts as if to encourage me to take a good look at their thighs.

They're nicely shaped thighs, though perhaps not in the Western sense. They're shorter than Western thighs, both in absolute terms and in proportion to the torso, and I wonder why they're so sexy. Suddenly, in a eureka moment I'll be proud of for years to come, I get it. Their sexiness is based on sheer math: If the hemline is six inches above the knee, as may be the case with their long-legged Western sisters, but the crotch is only eight inches above the knee—rather than, say, twelve inches—then it's a mere two inches from hem to paradise.

While I'm fine-tuning my theorem, two girls come to a halt in the middle of the sidewalk twenty feet away, talking. I calculate the sexiness of their thighs, but one of them is taller, and her legs—or rather her thighs— are longer, which complicates my calculation. She makes eye contact with me. Smiles. Izumi! And I only recognize her because she's smiling at me. Am I blind? Or does my facial recognition system not function in Japan?

They separate and wave at each other, and now beaming, Izumi approaches me. We don't kiss or hug or shake hands, but we do the Japanese thing and greet each other with a cropped nod, like distant acquaintances.

We go to Ueno Park for cherry-blossom viewing. Blankets are spread out under every cherry tree. People picnic and drink. Some blankets are guarded by a lone manga-reading salaryman. Cherry blossoms thrill us, and the white petals twirling to the ground sadden us. It's the beginning of the end. She shows me postcards of her mother's work. Dolls, she calls them. They're sculptures of older people of European appearance with expressive postures, and they're made entirely of cloth, even their faces and hands that seem to recount their lives.

We buy a bag of *takoyaki* from a guy behind a cart and eat the steaming octopus-filled dumplings with toothpicks.

"I should probably tell you," I venture. She might get angry and call it quits. She might use terms like *senseless* and *waste of time* and *spinning my wheels*. She might underscore them with *selfish* and similarly hackneyed vocabulary of the female canon. But I believe in laying the issues out up front, and having learned my lesson with Ginger, I deploy the nuclear option instead of leaving room for false hope. "I've had a vasectomy."

She doesn't know the word. I explain it. Circumflex across her forehead, she digs her Bible-paper dictionary out of her purse. We've stopped walking, and we've stopped eating the *takoyaki* still in the bag. Cherry blossom petals twirl past our eyes and gather on the pavement like snowflakes. One lands on her hair.

"Oh," she says.

"Does it bother you?"

"I haven't thought about having or not having children," she says. She aligns her words one by one. "Because I'm not ready to have children. But I've never excluded having children."

I have my reasons. When my father was born, there were a billion people on the planet, and it had taken us millions of years and a lot of failed efforts to get that far. When I was born, there were two billion people on the planet, and it was already a crowded, polluted place. Then, *wham*, we open the floodgates, and in the span of forty years we triple the population to six billion people.

Are we like totally nuts? If we triple it again over the next forty years, there'll be eighteen billion people on the planet. But it won't get that far. A natural or manmade cataclysm will see to it. To avoid that cataclysm, we as a population need to stop growing. And I'm simply doing my part. That's all there is to it.

People who want kids find this argument atrocious. They deny that the planet is overpopulated. Or they say, "Yes, there are too many of *them,* but there aren't enough of *us*"—an argument that makes me puke. And even if they admit that the planet is overpopulated and headed for ruin, they say, "What does that have to do with me? Why should I give up my dream just because *they* have too many kids?" I can't think of anything more selfish than that.

That save-the-planet theory isn't the only reason. There's another one. A personal one. I don't want to propagate the genes my parents passed on to me. I don't want to be able to do to my kids what my parents did to me. My brother and sister, they don't have kids either. We're cutting off our limb of the family tree.

Because people lose their appetite over this, I don't get into it anymore. When asked why I don't want to have kids, I say I don't feel like it. They might not understand, and they might still call me selfish, but they leave me alone and continue eating. And a girl who's looking for an inseminator knows what she has to do: find some other dude.

But Izumi doesn't ask why. She cups her hand around my hand that is holding the bag of *takoyaki*, and with the toothpick in the other hand, she pokes into a steaming dumpling, coaxes it out of the bag, and cautiously bites into it. Is that it? End of discussion?

Despite the *takoyaki*, which are filling, we have dinner at an *izakaya*. The subject doesn't crop up again. We rent a karaoke room. A waitress serves us cocktails. Izumi sings Japanese pop songs. You should never watch a girl sing. It'll do you in. She stands erect, chest out, mic close to her lips. The electronics make her voice full and reverberant.

I'm so in love with her. Pity the men who aren't in love at least once every now and then. It brightens our lives, gives us youth and vigor, and shakes off the doldrums. And if you're in love in Tokyo, you fall in love with Tokyo itself.

19

FILM NOIR

Mr. Song has already left. Mr. Kim is watching a garish talk show on TV. The kitchen sink is full of dirty bowls, utensils, pots, and pans. Vapors of grease and kimchi hang in the air.

"I'm going to walk to school," I tell Mr. Kim.

"Walk?"

Now he has what he has been looking for: incontrovertible proof that I'm crazy.

I walk down Mejiro-dōri toward Takadanobaba. At a gas station, a suicidal attendant steps into the heavy rush-hour traffic and bows so low that his upper body and arms are parallel to the pavement, head pointed at the oncoming car. Surprisingly, the car stops. And the cars behind it stop. Within seconds, the entire curb lane backs up a block. No one tries to get around. No one honks. Another attendant—less suicidal, this one—blocks the sidewalk with a bow, but not as deep. A customer pulls from the gas station into the street, and as he drives off, all five attendants holler long polite phrases after him. Now that's service!

A major intersection is covered with steel plates, the signature of subway construction. And wherever there's space, there's junk. For instance, the two-foot space between two houses is littered with a hot plate, rusting sheet metal, a bicycle frame, a chair, lumber, and flower pots with dead plants. A canal emerges from underneath a building, carrying on its water the flotsam of urban life. The scene is framed by run-down apartment buildings and narrow shoddy homes. But the commuter trains that burst every two minutes from the tunnel and run parallel to Mejiro-dōri are shiny and spotless.

More pedestrians appear on the sidewalk, and when I turn right to cross the tracks, I'm in a mass of people balling up at the clanging barrier. Train after train zooms by before the barrier opens for a few seconds. On the other side of the tracks are the alleys of Takadanobaba. People stream past restaurants, *izakaya*, and hostess bars without giving them a second look. Occasionally a car tries to inch through all this.

At my top walking speed, it takes forty-five minutes from door to door, five minutes faster than the commute by train. It's free, healthy, and agreeable, the biggest no-brainer in the history of mankind.

Shirai-sensei, my cute Thursday teacher, is blindly determined to teach me Japanese. Though I've studied for hours, I can't remember a thing, and nothing makes sense. We labor through a story in the textbook on the social importance of getting drunk with friends and colleagues after work.

"I want to get drunk *now*," I say in Japanese, peeved by her steadfast refusal to resort to English to shed even a glimmer of light on Japanese grammar.

"Me too," she laughs, and perhaps it's an invitation, or perhaps it's a practice conversation.

At any rate, driven to the limit of exasperation, I go to Ikebukuro after class and commit a forbidden act. In the gaijin corner of a bookstore, I purchase a Japanese grammar written in confidence-inspiring English. I study it at a Dotour's coffee shop and grasp more grammar over a cup of house blend than I have in all my lessons combined.

Night arrives early in Tokyo, and when I step outside, the street that was drab in daylight is a jarring, flashing orchestra. A guy in a hut at the edge of the sidewalk is baking fish-shaped pastries with sweet red-bean filling. I love these things. I buy one, and as I bite into it, I espy a cluster of strange buildings up on a side street. Tokyo is full of strange buildings you're better off not looking at, but these are decorated with fairy-tale European and Arabian motifs. Their entrances are concealed behind hedges and walls. Signs are in katakana and end with *hotel* in cursive pink. Love hotels! Hallelujah.

And I have a date with Izumi at 8 p.m.!

Our meeting point is the Café Renoir in Takadanobaba. Crackling with anticipation, I get there, buy a cup of coffee, and wait. She's twenty minutes late, a draining period of uncertainty. We greet each other with cropped nods and smiles, like other people around us greet each other, and all I think about is spending the night with her at my love hotel.

We end up at the counter of a basement dining bar. She has pizza and a salty dog. I have jambalaya and a margarita. She has another salty dog, I another margarita. The bar gets louder as alcohol slackens the Japanese rules of conduct, so we hold hands. After the third round, rules get tossed overboard, and convention allows you to do whatever you can't do otherwise. We kiss, and it becomes clear that this will be a night to be reckoned with. Feelings are welling up inside me, and random thoughts coagulate into words.

"I love you," I say.

She beams, but whatever she wants to say remains inside. She has another salty dog and I another margarita.

"Travel with me in France," I say.

She absorbs my words.

"Stay with me in the US."

She giggles and tells me how she once got caught cheating with her commuter-rail pass by riding much farther than allowed, which everyone was doing, and how she rescued herself with apologies and false tears.

When we climb the stairs up to the street, she grips my arm. Her legs are unsteady, her English slurred and sexy.

"Let's go to a love hotel in Ikebukuro," I suggest.

"You found them?"

"Sure."

"I'm amazed."

Amazed I've accomplished so much with so little.

It's the midnight rush to catch the last train home. The station is chaotic. Someone is barfing. Our train is packed with drunks in suits. Some are talking. Others can barely keep themselves upright. At Ikebukuro station, hundreds of girls queue at dozens of wall-mounted pay phones to tell lies to their mothers, and Izumi gets in line to do the same. I join the boyfriends cooling their heels off to the side. I've become an accessory to an ancient ritual.

My love hotel, however, is full. The next one is also full. The third one has two rooms available. I can tell by looking at the room selection board. Two photos are still illuminated, each with a different motif. I press the button under one of them. To pay, I turn toward a foot-wide hole in the wall catty-corner from the selection board and put a 10,000-yen bill on its mini-counter. An old woman's fingers remove the money and render change. That's it. No registration forms, no credit cards, no questions, no confusion, no icy nightmare clerk. Not everything is hard in Japan.

We kiss on the elevator and in the hallway, any applicable rules having been annulled by now. The room is larger than our hotel room was. It has everything: a queen-size bed, a firmament with stars, a tray with two disposable toothbrush kits and *one* condom, a box of Kleenex, a karaoke system, buttons in the headboard to adjust the lumens of the stars and the volume of the music, a coin-operated minibar, and an opaque window to an air gap between inside wall and outside wall of the building. Even with the window ajar, you're sealed off from the world. The bathroom has a tub for two and a separate shower, also for two. Everything is perfect.

"I have my period," she says.

But it doesn't bother me, and it doesn't bother her either. We bathe together, and when we make love, her juices gush out, and she arches her back and is ravishing, and above us is the firmament with stars, and her cries are shrill, and when we crater, sticky goo is gluing us together.

Friday, April 19.
Cacophonous cawing of crows weaves itself disconcertingly into my dreams until it wakes me up altogether. It's 5:45 a.m. Even the dual building walls fail to deaden the racket, and when you're half asleep, it's almost scary. But in front of my eyes is a tuft of black hair. She sleeps without sound, without movement, her arms contorted underneath her. I inhale her chemistry as if it were a controlled substance.

At 8 a.m. we bail out of a situation that looks as if we sacrificed a lamb in bed. Out on the street, crows are cawing and fighting over a bag of French fries in the gutter, big hideous Tokyo crows with huge black beaks. We detour leerily around them and lumber to the station. We're showered and groomed. We don't hold hands. No one can guess what kind of night we had. We say good-bye with a nod. Rush-hour rules apply. We're sober. There are no excuses. And she dissolves into the Japanese liquid of dark-suited people who pretend to ignore us.

I walk to Takadanobaba. My knees are shaking. My mind is fuzzy. I have coffee and a muffin at a coffee shop. I'm trying to get my brain to function. By the time I sit down in my closet-sized classroom, I'm operational on a basic level.

Asakura-sensei, my distractingly voluptuous Friday teacher, wrongly assumes and insistently believes that I remember certain things from my prior lessons, and she wants to review them and build on them. But everything is gone, and I don't know what keeps her from throwing in the towel. During break, I address her in English, which she graciously allows me to do and which she speaks surprisingly well. Turns out, she spent a year in the US teaching Japanese. She's factual, doesn't flirt, and isn't timid. A cold shower on a steamy day.

Odor of grease and kimchi greet me at the apartment. Mr. Kim and Mr. Song are gone. A greasy skillet and dirty bowls are stacked in the sink. A pot with rice burnt into it is on the stove. I abhor messy kitchens. The odor makes it impossible for me to make and enjoy my afternoon coffee. So I open the windows to let in some fresh air, which in itself is a contradiction in Tokyo, because what's out there in the afternoon isn't any fresher than what's already inside. But the idea of an open window and the illusion of fresh air make me feel better.

A van with speaker horns mounted on the roof creeps by and blasts the neighborhood with the aggressive verbiage of an over-amplified pissed-off man. Thank God, I don't understand Japanese. I do the dishes. The pot with rice burnt into it requires extra time and muscle, but I get it perfectly clean. I put everything away and wipe the counter. Only now can I enjoy brewing coffee.

Hours later, after finishing their dinner of fried meat, veggies, kimchi, and rice, Mr. Kim and Mr. Song position themselves side by side at the edge of my tatami, something they haven't done before.

"Mr. Wolf, thank you for doing the dishes," says Mr. Kim in English.

"You're welcome."

"In the future, please don't wash the rice pot."

Mr. Song shows me the pot with rice newly burnt into it from dinner.

"It's the best part," Mr. Kim says. "We make tea with it."

Mr. Song puts some water into the pot and lets it boil. After a while, he pours the light brown liquid into three cups and pours the remainder into the one-gallon screw-top Sapporo beer can on the counter that I've been wondering about. Then he offers Mr. Kim a cup, who takes it.

"Wolf-san, please, it's good," he says in Japanese as he offers me a cup. I take it, and we stand around and sip. It doesn't taste like burnt-rice tea. In fact, it's quite pleasant, and I tell them in Japanese.

"It's delicious," I actually say, which is an exaggeration, but I don't know how to say *quite pleasant* yet.

"We drink it hot or cold," Mr. Song says.

"You should visit Korea," Mr. Kim says.

"It's very different from Japan. You will like it."

"I'm going to Seoul in July."

They act surprised and pleased.

"How long?" Mr. Kim asks.

"A week. Then I come back to Tokyo."

"Hai," Mr. Kim says. Then he switches to English and invites me into his room, a hitherto unheard-of privilege, even for Mr. Song. It's a six-tatami room. The window faces Mejiro-dōri. His belongings and a folded futon spill from the closet—the only closet in the apartment. We sit down on the tatami by a low table and play with his laptop. He demonstrates Japanese Word. As he types on the QWERTY keyboard, letters appear on the screen and accumulate until they convert automatically into hiragana. Then he converts certain groups of hiragana into kanji via a pull-down menu. He shows me a document he has written. It's black with kanji, all typed on a normal QWERTY keyboard. The whole concept is so insane, it's almost cool.

"How long did it take you to learn this many kanji?" I ask, practically in awe of him.

"It's easy for me. Modern Korean is written in the Korean alphabet, but we learn Chinese script in school. It's part of our cultural heritage. And kanji is based on Chinese script."

He demonstrates some other features.

When he says a bit abruptly, "I have to study now," I retreat to my tatami. He slides his door shut behind me. Mr. Song is parked on his futon with a textbook on his knees, enunciating Japanese words in a whisper.

This isn't the kind of Friday night I've always wanted to have. It renders me philosophical. In love, especially if you've been drinking, the temptation is great to get carried away with words. But words make promises, and promises make commitments, and commitments make disappointments. Words don't satisfy anything. All they do is cause future problems. The words last night over salty dogs and margaritas, for instance. I wonder why I uttered them and if I'll ever repeat them. What I said in essence was this: I love you, let's travel together to France, come stay with me in the US. I meant it. And I might still mean it now. But will I mean it when the time comes to turn these words into reality? If not, how do I take these words back? Suck them in? Like ramen noodles? What havoc will they wreak?

The deeper question is whether to stay away from words when you're in love because your mind is in a state of drunkenness, or whether to use words temporarily to increase intensity and accept future havoc as a trade-off.

And how about words that have been omitted? For instance, what words has Izumi omitted? She omits certain words when she tells her mother where and with whom she's spending the night. In fact, she omits me altogether. To her family and friends, I don't exist. So, might she tell me whatever she believes I ought to know and omit the rest? Because I'm *traditional* or whatever?

You bet. For instance, she omitted to tell me why she couldn't see me tonight.

So I sit here on a Friday night, and instead of making love to her, I'm writing these lines. This is love in Tokyo. It differs from love in the rest of the world only in its details.

If I were a smoker, I'd pluck a cigarette from a silver case, tap it with the filter against the case, and stick it between my lips.

"Girls are the reason we exist," I'd say. "And during the pursuit, they're well worth the crap we have to put up with."

I'd light the cigarette with a Zippo and exhale a funnel of smoke toward a bare dim light bulb dangling from the ceiling by a twisted pair of wires.

"But the corollary is also true," I'd say. "When they're no longer worth the crap we have to put up with, it's time to move on."

I'd contemplate for long moments the smoke curling toward the light.

"In the end, it's always time to move on," I'd add, "because happiness lies in the pursuit."

I imagine myself in a film noir recounting with a husky voice my cynical perceptions, which I'd be compelled during the remainder of the film to surrender piece by piece.

20

QUITTER'S REMORSE

The phone rings in our love-hotel room. It's Sunday, 8:50 a.m. "What the fuck?" slips out of my mouth. No one knows we're here. At the reception, if you can call it that, they don't even know our names. But Izumi, undeterred, answers with a polite *moshi-moshi*, says a few words in a high subservient pitch, and hangs up.

"She reminded us that checkout time is 9 a.m.," she says in her normal voice to me.

Instant panic. We try to make it but overstay by six minutes and have to pay for two hours daytime rate, which practically doubles the cost of our stay. Such are the rigors of love in love hotels.

We step into the backstreet, circumnavigate the hideous crows agitating over some lumps in the gutter, and turn into the main drag that leads to Ikebukuro station, a few blocks away. At the first café we come to, we have the breakfast combo—espresso-type coffee, croissant, tuna salad, yogurt with jam, and a fried meat substance. Teensy-weensy everything, but good. It's a light breakfast for normal mornings, but after the kind of night we had, it's woefully inadequate. Nevertheless, it gets us going.

On the street, overlapping store jingles and company anthems assault our ears. Bowing girls chant polite phrases and hand out tissue packs imprinted with ads and phone numbers. Each pack contains eight tissues that are so flimsy they're practically useless, but they're free, and everyone takes them and stuffs them into their pockets or purses without looking at the ads. Pigeons dart between our feet. A teenage rock band plays on the plaza. A man holds up a placard with a list of services and a photo of a girl in lingerie. Base price is ¥5,000. Additional services range from ¥1,000 to ¥3,000. A 10% discount applies before 5 p.m. I can read the numbers. The rest I can guess. Izumi stops in her tracks. She can give you whiplash. She stares at a shopwindow.

"Can I have?" she begs.

Jewelry? No, rice crackers. A whole shop of them. Then she has to choose among dozens of types of rice crackers, a knotty and cumbersome process for her. She culls two bags: black-bean flavor and shrimp flavor. As soon as our feet hit the sidewalk, we tear open a bag and start munching.

Today's project is to buy a sports jacket to round out my wardrobe; there are times in Tokyo when my denim jacket leaves me feeling a tad underdressed. We head to the Seibu department store and up to the seventh floor where men's wear is.

You'd expect escalators to offer a brief period of calm, a form of respite from the relentless onslaught of disorienting and unnerving sales propaganda, mirrors, bra mannequins, and toxic perfume vapors you're bombarded with between the aisles. But here, at escalator after escalator, high-pitched female voices doggedly exhort you to do something incomprehensible while you're just standing there. By the third floor, it's getting on your nerves. By the fifth floor, you're ready to wring the lady's digital neck. When you get off at the seventh floor, you're numb.

The saleslady, however, panics when she sees me. The top of her head doesn't reach my shoulder. She bows and apologizes incessantly. Izumi translates my questions in a high subservient pitch, and they talk to each other as the saleslady leads us through the racks.

Brand names are important in Japan. It is said that the Japanese are not trained to make judgments but rely instead on brand names with big price tags. If it doesn't have a brand name with a big price tag, it's a high-risk purchase. Colleagues might not approve of it! Much better to stick with what's safe. Brand names with big price tags are always defensible. Which explains why Japan is the world's largest market for luxury brands. And brand names with big price tags are on display. Once you've been in Japan long enough, you might get inured to these kinds of numbers, but I haven't reached that level yet.

The saleslady stops and lifts a size LL Burberry's linen jacket from a rack. *Made under license in Japan*, the label says. She comments for several minutes on its style, materials, and workmanship.

"The largest jacket in the store" is how Izumi translates the avalanche of words.

The saleslady bows every time she looks at me. But when I try on the jacket, she stares at me, a monstrous curiosity with orangutan arms that stick grotesquely out of the sleeves of the largest jacket in the store. She asks Izumi if she can touch me.

"Please, go ahead," Izumi says with an encouraging gesture, quite amused.

Gingerly, hesitantly, the lady lays two fingers on my shoulder while holding her left hand in front of her mouth. Turns out, I'm truly some kind of miracle. And instead of helping me, they discuss me. They giggle and steal glances at me as they delve into the pros and cons of being with a man of my proportions.

As no more help is forthcoming, I wander off and circulate. When I return to them, the saleslady refocuses on me. She bows and apologizes for the shortness of the sleeves, and she bows and thanks me, and she bows and apologizes for the price, which deserves an apology, and she bows when she accepts my credit card.

Monday, April 22.

Takano-sensei is mysteriously pleased with my progress or has changed strategy and is using false positive reinforcement to motivate me to work harder. Either way, it emboldens me, and I'm in high spirits when I enter an Internet café and ask in Japanese if they have AOL. I want to access my email, which I haven't been able to look at since I left home. The attendant doesn't know what I'm talking about. I rephrase and repronounce it several times. No go. My Japanese is still useless for anything other than introducing myself to a salaryman.

I'm still stewing at Ikebukuro station, and I'm frustrated and stressed the way Tokyo makes you on a normal day, and I'm waiting for the English text to appear on the departure screen of the Seibu-Ikebukuro line, when I hear a female voice.

"Do you need help?" she says.

To be talked to in a station! By a Japanese woman! In English! I turn toward her. She's in her forties, has shoulder-length hair, and is dressed in an earth-tone pants suit.

"Thanks, I'm okay," I say.

"Where do you want to go?"

"Ekoda. I'm waiting for the local." On the screen, the line for my train scrolls into view. "Platform one," I read out loud as proof that I know what I'm doing.

"I'm waiting for the express. It leaves after the local." She tells me the name of the place she has to go to, but it means nothing to me.

"Do you live there?" I ask.

"Yes."

"How far is it?"

"One hour by express."

"That's a long commute."

"Yes, but I don't come to Tokyo often. Today I had an appointment."

"I've got to go to platform one or else I miss my train."

"I go with you. I can take the local."

"Isn't it too much trouble?"

"Not trouble. I can change to an express later."

As she cobbles together her words, and as I endeavor to make sense of them, it occurs to me that I'll never, ever speak Japanese as well as she speaks English. We wander to platform one and board the local.

"Japan can be lonesome for foreigners," she says, violating with apparent impunity the rule not to talk on the train. "We are not very welcoming." As the train jostles along, she scrawls her name and phone number into a little notebook, carefully separates out the page, and gives it to me. *Uehara Yasuyo.*

"Thank you," I say.

"You're welcome to visit me."

"That's very nice of you."

"It will be good for my sons."

She hands me her notebook and pen. I write down my name but don't remember the number of the pink pay phone in the apartment. I tell her that. *Pay phone in the apartment* puzzles her, but I don't have time to explain.

Ekoda is coming up. I apologize. The train is screeching to a halt. I give the notebook and pen back to her and get up.

"Can we make appointment?" she says as the doors are opening.

"Um, sure." But the fast-paced door chime puts on the pressure, and I can't come up with an actual appointment, like a day or a time, nor do I know what she means by *appointment*, and I need to think things through and understand them before I can agree to them.

"Call me if you need anything," she says.

"I will. Thank you." And I jump out.

"Call me if you want to talk," she says through the door.

She's so nice I'm stunned. And this in the same city where a hotel operator gave me a curt *no* and hung up on me when I asked her if she spoke English—that was before I discovered love hotels.

And I do want to talk. I have nothing else to do. I could have stayed on the train with her. We could have gone for a cup of tea or coffee at a station café somewhere. She could have explained what she meant by *appointment*, what it included and didn't include, for example. But I'm skeptical by nature. I need to evaluate risks and estimate outcomes. I want to know why she's so friendly and what her motives are. I'm systematic and lack spontaneity. To sort things out, I need time, not much time, a few minutes—but too much time.

Frustrated with my own iniquities, I promise myself to call her. And I promise myself to be more spontaneous next time. Wasn't that one of the goals of my trip, to learn to become more spontaneous? To learn to go with the flow?

Mr. Kim's sliding door is shut. Mr. Song is sitting on his futon, textbook on his knees, mumbling Japanese words under his breath. I lower myself on the tatami and open my textbook, but instead of studying Japanese, I think about Izumi. What's surprising is how much I want to be with her. It's the what-you-can't-have syndrome. And it's weird how I spend so much time thinking about her and so little time being with her. This is my fourteenth night in Japan, of which I've spent three with her.

Tuesday, April 23.

The Loyal Dog Hachikō, a bronze Akita, sits on a stone pedestal amid the after-work melee that reigns near the exits of Shibuya station. He's Japan's most famous dog, the subject of movies and books, held up to this day as an icon of total to-the-death loyalty to your master. The propaganda machine of Japan Inc. at work. And people buy it. Or at least, they buy the Hachiko trinkets that are for sale in Shibuya station.

The story goes back to 1925. Every morning, Hachiko accompanied his master to the station. In the evening, he'd return to the station at the time his master's train would arrive, and they'd walk home together. But in May of that year, his master died at work, and Hachiko waited in vain. The next evening, he returned to the station again and waited again. Evening after evening, he'd sit there, and commuters rushing by got to know him and fed him. Stories began to circulate, word spread, and soon people dropped by just to take a look at the loyal dog. In 1934, the government figured out a propaganda angle—total loyalty to your master—and erected a bronze statue at that spot, while Hachiko looked on, quietly thinking his own thoughts. A year later, he was found dead nearby.

Today, the statue of the sitting Akita is a popular meeting spot. Young people congregate around it, waiting for friends or lovers. But when you think about it, it's really not a propitious meeting spot. It's where you wait in vain till you die. And I'm thinking about that during the interminable period that I wait for Izumi.

"I miss my old colleagues," she says as we cross Shibuya station's scramble intersection, whose mathematical chaos continues to astound me. "It seems people in my courses aren't very motivated."

"You still want to become, as you said, a window through which others can see Japan?"

"I still want that. But my courses aren't challenging. Everything is kind of basic. Sometimes I think I should have kept my job."

Quitter's remorse. It also afflicts me periodically. With a difference. I quit a job at a frigging car dealership and have nothing to be remorseful about. She quit a job at the threshold to the antechamber of Japan Inc. Her loss is infinitely greater than mine. I don't say that, of course. But I do need to say something to make her feel better.

"I can't wait to go to Kyoto with you," I say.

She peeks up at me, confused, eyebrows ruffled.

"Visiting the temples with you will be awesome."

"I've been dreaming about it," she says and breaks into a smile. Kyoto, the panacea.

We take the elevator up to a chain *izakaya* in an eight-story building filled from top to bottom with eating and drinking establishments. Over dinner and beer, we plan our trip to Kyoto. Decisions made, we return to Shibuya station and buy Shinkansen tickets to Kyoto. Then she calls her mother to let her know she's spending the night in central Tokyo and her girlfriend's apartment is there, or something to that effect—as if her mother hadn't figured that one out long ago.

We're exuberant. Soon, we'll be in Kyoto together. We cruise through the streets that are thick with people. She urges me to read *Genji*. It'll deepen my experience, she says. I pull her out of the flow into a dark recess by a door and kiss her. Within seconds, an older woman darts out and shoos us away like rabid dogs.

We settle at the counter of a whiskey bar. The bartender chips with an ice pick at a chunk of ice until it's a sphere, and he does it without even once perforating his hand. He rolls the sphere into a glass, dribbles Knob Creek over it, slides the glass toward me, and says something that includes *"Nobu kuriku rokku."*

Knob Creek rock. Singular, there not being a distinct plural in Japanese. At this confluence of grammar, ice sphere, and Knob Creek, you can't help but love Japan. This sense of precision hiding behind all the vagueness.

"I'm thinking about renting an apartment," I muse.

"An apartment?" Her Cognac swaps over. A few drops spill on the counter.

"Mr. Kim and Mr. Song are conscientious roommates, and I'm fond of them. But I want a place where you and I can be together."

"Apartments are very expensive."

"It'll be more comfortable for us."

"Apartments are hard to rent."

"No more checkout time."

"Hmm, that would be nice."

"Can you help me deal with leasing agents and landlords?"

"N."

Japanese make that sound all the time when they're listening. It's deep, resonant, and nasal. It means "I heard you" or "I'm still here" or "I haven't dozed off yet." It means a slew of things. But the one thing it doesn't mean is agreement.

"I want to sign a lease before we leave for Kyoto."

"N."

Logistics stress her out, and she doubts it'll work, and she's worried about a million things. Yet the idea of lazing around together in an apartment appeals to her, and her resistance begins to soften.

People who have to catch the last train home scuttle out of the bar. Others straggle in. The ambiance changes. Now, no one looks at a watch anymore. And we too stay put because a cluster of love hotels is on a backstreet two blocks away.

21

CINDERELLA MOMENT

I scope out two apartments for rent. They're both in dingy buildings. Both consist of a four-and-a-half-tatami room, a kitchen corner, and something called *unit bath*. Maybe 120 square feet in total, with seven-foot ceilings. Getting a phone line hooked up takes several months. Rent is the same as my mortgage payment and association fees combined, though my condo is *fifteen* times larger and a *hundred* times nicer. Nonrefundable key money—upfront profit for the landlord—is three months' rent. Refundable deposit is two months' rent. Add to that the rent for the first month, and the amount due at signing of the lease is six months' rent. The numbers are just baffling. *Plus*, you must have a guarantor. There are financial institutions that offer that service, but you pay out of your nose for it. And then I have to buy a futon, sheets, towels, plates, bowls, utensils, pots, pans, and whatever I need to handle things that my Swiss Army knife can't handle. The ladies who show the apartments are unenthusiastic about leasing to a gaijin, and communicating with them is difficult.

"Welcome to Japan," I say in a deep funk on my tatami in Ekoda. I'm sitting on my heels the Japanese way, doing drills with my chopsticks— picking up erasers, pencils, pens, and coins. I've been doing this daily to master the Japanese way of chopsticks. My ring finger gets numb from having to tilt up at an odd angle. The chopsticks pop out of my fingers. The coins skid away. It's hopeless but therapeutic, requiring fine motor skills and meditation, a cure for the apartment malaise. I'm timing how long I can endure sitting on my heels. It's one of the most painful things you can do to your legs. Why would anyone ever invent such a position? To extract a confession.

Mr. Kim and Mr. Song are sitting on chairs at the table, watching TV, eating fried meat, kimchi, and rice. They're holding their stainless-steel chopsticks the more practical and simpler Korean way—without ring finger. They observe me out of their peripheral vision and mutter comments to each other, by now certain beyond doubt that I'm crazy.

Friday, April 26.
The problem is money. It dematerializes in multiples of 10,000-yen bills. There's even a word for ten thousand: *man*. Anything less is change. You pay two *man* yen for dinner and drinks, plus one *man* yen for a love hotel, plus one *man* yen for breakfast, lunch, and miscellaneous expenses. You've blown four *man* yen, or about $400, without having done anything fancy. *Man*-yen bills are always pristine. People remove them fastidiously from their wallets and hand them over with reverence. Cashiers accept them with humility and stash them away even more fastidiously. And when I wrest a crinkled, sweaty wad of these sacred bills from the front pocket of my jeans, they gasp, barely able to contain their horror and despair.

And now I need a refill. I stand at the pay phone on Mejiro-dōri and dial my broker. It's 4:00 a.m. A pink veil is floating above the roofs. The street is quiet, and half the block can listen to my side of the conversation. The brisk air invigorates my head, which is still smarting from having hit the rail of the accordion door. I've been hitting it every morning on the way to the bathroom. Ducking, like so many things in life, occurs to me only after it's too late.

I give a guy named Mark my account number, name, and social security number, hoping that no one in my neighborhood is taking notes. We go through my positions. Everything is up. Wall Street is funding my trip. Based on valuations and future potential, I pick one of my stocks and have him liquidate the position. Making these financial decisions in the quasi-dark at a pay phone on Mejiro-dōri is quite something.

In the afternoon, I meet Izumi at First Kitchen in Takadanobaba. We have coffee at the counter against the shopwindow and watch the street scene. I gripe about the apartment rip-off. She says *"N"* and nods every time I take a breath, and when I'm through, she says, "That's how it is in Japan."

"Renters are getting fucked."

"Maybe."

"They should revolt."

"Against what?"

"Against getting fucked."

"How?"

"I don't know." I stare at remnants of artificial *crema* in my cup.

She takes a folded magazine page out of her purse and flattens it out on the counter. "This is a Weekly Mansion ad," she says. "They rent rooms by the month. It's a chain. It's not fancy. They advertise everywhere." She hums their jingle.

We visit their two nearest properties. The Takadanobaba property is ten minutes on foot from the school. The room has a sliding glass door to a balcony that is big enough for the exterior AC unit and two pairs of Japanese-sized shoes. It has a view east over the roof of a school, which is nice, but the bed occupies most of the room.

The Ueno property isn't convenient, and the room has a window with view of a wall. But it has a Murphy bed, a big plus because you can move about the room during the day. Both are equipped with bedding, basic kitchen items, rice cooker, TV, phone, and mini-fridge. Sheets are provided. You bring your own towels, wash the sheets, and clean the room. A coin-operated washer and dryer are down the hall. Doorframes are high enough for me to fit through without hitting my head. Both are expensive.

"I can't live in a shoe box like this," I stammer as we leave the Ueno property.

"It's the size of a normal Tokyo apartment."

"How do you people survive?"

She doesn't know either.

Frustrated, we go to Asakusa. The hundreds of shops in the arcades around Sensō-ji temple sell everything from Edo crafts to postcards. It's the opposite of Ginza. It's low-rise, low-tech, run-down, and bazaar-like, exactly what we've been yearning for. In a kelp shop, an old guy with a scraggy face is shaving dried kelp. He offers Izumi a piece.

"May I try also?" I ask him in Japanese.

He holds a piece in my direction and says something to her. I've gotten used to being on the verge of nonexistence. The fact that people don't acknowledge me or don't talk to me when I address them doesn't bother me anymore. We move on, chewing kelp shavings.

"What did he tell you?" I ask.

She vacillates.

"He was talking about me, wasn't he?"

She doesn't respond.

"I recognized 'gaijin-san.'"

"He was unpleasant."

"Tell me what he said."

She hesitates. I prod her. The more she hesitates, the more I want to know. We're still chewing kelp shavings.

"He was wondering if gaijin-san could understand this taste," she says finally.

"I have to admit, he's right. I can't understand this taste."

"Me neither."

She zeroes in on a booth where a guy is baking rice crackers, and we buy a bag. Pepper flavor, and so hot they set my mouth on fire. We chase them with *daifuku*—rice dough stuffed with sweet red-bean paste. Inside Sensō-ji precinct, we buy our fortunes. It's one of the cheapest things you can buy in Tokyo, after the flimsy tissue packs they hand you on the street, which are free. I unfold mine. Columns of kanji on wispy paper. I give it to her. She scans it.

"And?"

"Category Good Luck, subcategory End of Good Luck."

"Is that good or bad?"

"It's above Bad Luck."

"Translate!"

"It says if you're humble and if you don't think stupid thoughts and if you work hard and if you have a lot of patience, your plans might come to fruition. If you're proud, disaster occurs. Your illnesses last a long time but can be cured. A good match may happen, but it takes a long time. It's a profitable time to buy and sell. If you try hard and wish very seriously, your wishes may come true. If you don't try hard, your wishes don't come true. It's better to think twice before traveling far. The person you're waiting for may come, but you have to wait a long time."

"Sounds like an uphill battle."

She unfolds hers. "Oh no!"

"What?"

"Big Bad Luck." She reads silently.

"What does it say?"

"It seems nothing works out regardless of how hard I try. Even if I'm humble, disaster occurs. My illnesses—" She doesn't finish. "This is not fun," she says.

We fold the fortunes and tie them to one of the racks to which thousands of other middling- to bad-luck fortunes have been tied so that the gods can take care of them.

Saturday, April 27.

We make an arch around the crows that are brawling and cawing on the sidewalk near the exit of our love hotel. We've come to hate these crows that are always there when we step outside. And the acoustics of the narrow backstreet amplifies their racket and renders their nasty black beaks even more threatening. It's a brutal confrontation with the real world after a night of passion and sweetness.

"Checkout time sucks," I say.

She doesn't know *sucks*. I explain it, which squashes the sensation of relief you feel when you hiss it loud enough.

"Yes, it would be nice to be able to relax in the morning," she says.

"I'd also like to be able to relax before dinner, then go out, then come back for the night."

"Hmm."

Love hotels aren't designed for that. They're designed for taking baths and fucking. The daytime limit is two or three hours. If you check in after 10 p.m., you can stay till checkout time in the morning. But if you leave your room, you can't get back in because your key works only once.

"I think I'm coming to grips with two facts of life in Tokyo. An apartment is going to be a shoebox, and it's going to be an expensive shoebox."

"Everybody has that problem. That's why we live with our parents."

"If you add the cost of love hotels to my Ekoda rent, it gets expensive, too."

"*N.*"

"Let's go to Takadanobaba and sign the lease."

The receptionist doesn't speak English. I ask Izumi to translate the lease documents. She studies the first page and after a while says, "It seems this is a lease." She studies another document, a list of some kind, furnishings probably, and says, "It seems this is a list." Having covered the essentials, I sign document after document, wherever the receptionist puts her index finger. At the sight of my credit card, she apologizes.

"Cash or wire transfer," she says.

I pull my wad of cash out of the front pocket of my jeans—she watches with the classic mix of shock and despair—and count out the deposit of five *man* yen. I'll wire the rent. I'll pay one *man* yen at move-in to activate the phone line. Move-in date is May 7, the day we return from Kyoto.

We're gleeful. Soon, we'll be in Kyoto, and after Kyoto, we'll have an apartment. To celebrate, we go to Yoyogi Park. Just past the entrance is a colony of tents fashioned of bright blue polyethylene-coated industrial tarps. Shaven and sort-of groomed men squat on a sheet of cardboard and slurp tea that they fixed over a camping stove. Their shoes are lined up at the edge of the cardboard. Order, even here. But people streaming into the park alongside us ignore these men in the Japanese manner.

"And where are the homeless women?" I ask.

She looks straight ahead.

"At home?"

She refuses to engage, refuses to look at the tents and at the men and at their shoes on the dirt. Therefore, they aren't there.

We select a spot in the grass far from everyone else, eat the *obento* we bought on the way, drink a bottle of wine, cuddle, read, and talk.

"I once had a Cinderella moment," she says. And in her way, she lays the groundwork for the story. She explains that getting into the semi-express during rush hour at Soka station is a community effort. Everybody knows what to do. Each person in line pushes the person in front to create a surge that packs people already on the train deeper into it.

"Otherwise, nobody can get in," she says.

"What about the people at the tail end of the surge? How do they get in?"

"Station employees push them in."

"Those poker-faced guys with white gloves?"

"Yes, they're a big help."

"That's worse than Ekoda."

"Only local trains stop in Ekoda. They're less crowded."

"N," I say for the first time. It comes in handy when you're speechless.

"One morning, someone stepped on my heel and knocked off my pump just as I was pushed into the train. I tried to stop and look for it but couldn't. Squeezed in between salarymen, I stood on one shoe and on tiptoe. I tried to get off at the next stop, but more people crushed into the train, and I couldn't get off. The second stop, Kita-Senju, is a big stop where people change trains, and a lot of people got off. I could look around, but there was no pump. I got off too and limped through the station, down the stairs and up the stairs to the other platform. I caught a train back to Soka and searched for my pump on the platform there. Nothing. So I went to the station office. The man was very polite. He asked me to have a seat. Then he left. Five minutes later, he was back with my pump. 'Could this be the shoe?' he asked. He was holding it in both hands, like a gift. I told him it was. He knelt down in front of me, like they do in a shoe store, and put the shoe on my foot to make sure it fit and was really my shoe. That was my Cinderella moment."

Tuesday, April 30.

The sun is up, there isn't a cloud in the sky, rush-hour traffic on Mejiro-dōri hasn't started yet, and the air is still fresh, if that concept can be applied to Tokyo air. It's 5:30 a.m., absolutely the best time to be on the streets. I'm dialing Ginger's work number. I need to give her an opportunity to ease out officially. I've tried several times to catch her at home in the evening—mid-morning, my time—but she's a busy girl.

"Where are you?" is her greeting.

"In Tokyo."

"What are you doing?"

"Basking in the sunshine on Mejiro-dōri."

"Is that a beach?"

"Almost."

"Why are you still in Japan?"

"I'm studying Japanese."

"What about me?"

"What do you mean?"

"It's not fair. I don't matter to you."

"That's not true."

"I can't do this any longer."

"I know."

"We need to break up."

"I understand."

She's eager to make babies, and I'll never make them. We both know it. Our words are mere window dressing. We wind down our conversation and wish each other the best. She didn't give me an ultimatum. She isn't waiting for me. She controls her life. She doesn't need me, has no use for me. And if Denny Divine doesn't work out, there'll be plenty of fertile dudes out there.

Her words sweep out any lingering illusions. I feel a lot. I feel intrigued by her spunk. I feel her levitating near me, a racy ghost. I feel confused. I feel the sun warming my back. I meander through my deserted neighborhood. I miss her. The world isn't binary, where everything is either on or off.

When I get back, Mr. Song is frying meat, and Mr. Kim is watching TV. In fact, nothing has changed.

Ekoda doesn't have a gaijin hangout, but Takadanobaba does. It's decorated with dark wainscot and brass rails. A guy can sit at the bar, peer philosophically at the bubbles pearling upward in his Guinness, and order a mediocre prime rib off a bilingual Anglo-American menu. Half the customers are gaijin this evening. The guy next to me is Darren from Nebraska. He teaches English at a school for adults and has the hots for one of his students, a girl in her mid-twenties, who spurns him. He takes off his Slickrock hat.

"My latest invention," he says with a proud smirk and shows me the padding affixed to the inside. "Softens the blow."

"What was this originally?" I'm fingering the black rubbery material.

"A do-it-yourself replacement shoe sole."

"I could use your hat in the morning for my trip to the bathroom."

"Man, I hit my head everywhere. In stations. On the sidewalk. I duck every time I walk through a door. People think I'm humble. They like that. Fact is, nothing in this place is built for a guy with a six-foot-eight frame."

"Lucky me."

Wednesday, May 1.

Mr. Kim is in his room, sliding door closed. Mr. Song, who never naps, is napping on his futon. My life with them will end tomorrow, and I'm taking some liberties. The plastic accordion door of the utility niche is shut behind us to the extent possible. Izumi sits on the Toshiba AW-42S7(H) washer. With its rounded corners and ideal height, it's perfect for fucking. Normally she screams, but with my hand cupped over her mouth, only a muffled squeal escapes. Then we walk through the rain to Ekoda Station. She has to go home to get ready for our trip. We're wet and chilled. Bicyclists weave unsteadily through the crowd, one hand on the handlebars, the other holding up an umbrella. We have sushi near the station. It's perfect. Everything is perfect. So be it if I don't see her often. When I do see her, it's perfect.

22

FAUX MAIKO

Izumi arrives on the platform for the Kyoto-bound Shinkansen with a purse and a small beige leather bag. Where did I get the idea that Japanese travel with gargantuan suitcases? I'm carrying my duffle bag and daypack because I didn't want to leave my belongings in the apartment for this long.

A businessman steps back from a group of salarymen and bows so lightly it's just a nod with a mild forward movement of his torso. The salarymen chant long phrases and bow low, torsos parallel to the platform, palms flat against their thighs. Even Takano-sensei never bent this low when he was teaching me to bow. The businessman turns away, boards the train. They remain in position until he's out of view. A baffling sight. And another element in the elusive distinction between the katakana words *sa-la-ri-ma-n*, a self-sacrificing and utterly loyal white-collar servant within a corporate structure, and *bi-ji-ne-su-ma-n,* who might still be a salaryman but is smart about business, reads the *Nikkei* on the subway instead of porn manga, and wears meticulously polished shoes.

On the Shinkansen, we act like a couple. We'll be together for five days and nights. There won't be other things she'll have to do with other people. We won't have to split at midnight by a turnstile in a jammed station. No one will call at 8:50 a.m. to invoke checkout time. We whoosh south on elevated tracks and eat the *obento* we bought at an *obento* shop on the platform. While eating on commuter trains is against the rules, and nobody does it, it's obviously de rigueur on the Shinkansen, and everybody does it.

I finally read the first pages of *Genji.* In between paragraphs, I try to catch a glimpse of Fuji-san, the ethereal volcano cone that adorns every brochure of Japan—often with this very Shinkansen I'm on in the foreground—but it's hiding behind low-hanging clouds. She raves about Kyoto, the epicenter of vegetarian Zen-Buddhist cuisine, where entire elaborate meals are conceived around tofu. Her mouth is watering as she describes the dishes, and her eyes become dreamy. "We must eat at a tofu restaurant," she concludes.

Kyoto has two thousand temples, shrines, and palaces. The most august ones are in every guidebook. And we go visit them. Others you stumble across as you walk down the street. For example, while a monk in robe, *tabi*, and *zori* peers at me sternly through his bifocals as he *put-puts* by on a scooter, I see to my right between two unsightly apartment buildings, and dwarfed by them, a wall with a decorative temple gate. Beyond it is a sumptuous garden with two buildings of the same sacred architecture as their famous brethren, only smaller. Surprised, we step inside. And there's no one because it isn't in the guidebooks.

At night, exhausted from Kyoto's aesthetic, spiritual, and culinary pleasures, we take a bath. Then, dressed in crisply pressed hotel yukata and disposable hotel slippers, she brews *ocha* on the electric toy hot plate that hotel rooms have instead of coffeemakers. Her skin is moist, her cheeks are radiant with heat, and her eyes sparkle when she offers me the handleless hot cup with the fingertips of both hands. I adore her so.

There are minor complications in our idyllic life as a couple, however. In the morning, we get up early to maximize our sightseeing, but I can't restrain myself. Consequently, we're two hours behind schedule as we slither into the breakfast room a hair before cutoff. We opt for Western breakfast because it comes with coffee, which is what I need the most. Instead of bringing our coffee right away, the waitress disappears for an eternity then returns with scrambled eggs, bacon, roasted potatoes, buttered toast, strawberry jam, and salad. Beautiful everything, but where the heck is our coffee?

"Could you ask her about the coffee," I ask Izumi.

"Coffee might come after breakfast."

"I'd like coffee now, not after breakfast."

"It's not a good idea to ask."

"I'm not even hungry until after I've had some coffee."

"You should be patient."

"It doesn't hurt to ask."

She resists, her lips become hard, and she acts as if asking for coffee were an insult or violated some rule.

"Ask her!" I say to break the logjam.

And she does. The waitress simply acknowledges the order, disappears, and reappears with two demitasses of coffee. When my demitasse is empty, I speak to the waitress in Japanese, first excusing myself, then asking for more coffee. She ignores me. I ask Izumi to repeat my request, but she refuses.

"Ask her!"

"Only one cup is included."

"I don't mind paying for it."

"Breakfast is decided by the hotel. You should accept it the way it comes."

"Coffee is on the menu. Even I can read that much. What's so complicated?"

The waitress bolted long ago. When I prevail at last, and Izumi does ask for coffee, the waitress confirms that it's à la carte and serves it right away. There's an unfathomable rigidity in the system, and bending that rigidity to obtain two demitasses of coffee before some rule allows it has exhausted me. What I can't figure out is whether the rigidity lies in some rules that no one has defined and everyone has to adhere to, or whether it lies in Izumi's imagination of those rules.

Excitement supplants all this when we enter the Nanzen-ji temple precinct. The first major building is San-mon, a freestanding intricate wooden gate within the walls. It isn't a physical entry point that can be locked like a castle gate but is more of a spiritual entry point. We pay—ah yes, money everywhere—take off our shoes—also everywhere—and climb the stairs to an exterior gallery around a lavish prayer hall with views of the precinct, forested slopes, and parts of Kyoto. Most fascinating is the enormously complex, elegantly curved and layered roof with its interlocking brackets, pillars, projecting beams, cantilevers, and rafters. You can lose yourself looking at it.

We visit building after building. All have these incredible roofs that float on wooden posts and beams instead of walls. In Western architecture, a wall is a wall and a door is a door, and there's never any question as to which is which. In fact, the question itself is stupid. But in classic Japanese architecture, posts and beams are the structural elements, while doors and walls are fluid concepts. Walls are made of thin wood and often paper. Some are ink-brush paintings. They can be slid aside or flipped up or folded away to open the room to a garden, the scenery outside, or another room. And when you move enough walls, everything is open, and the outside is part of the inside, and you realize that a wall is a door and a window and a painting or nothing at all.

The airy architecture amid these gardens makes you dream of spending the rest of your life in such a place. But the illusion lasts only a moment before the next wave of visitors moves you forward, this being Golden Week, when all Japanese trek to Kyoto simultaneously.

"What's *that* thing doing here?" I ask as we stroll to the next building. A Romanesque red-brick aqueduct cuts across the temple precinct. Japan is full of visually incongruous structures, but this? In a temple precinct?

She doesn't know either. "I've never looked at it," she says.

"You've been here several times before, and you've never seen it, this huge thing?"

"I've seen it but never wanted to look at it." She looks at it. "It's too ugly to look at." And she averts her eyes.

I approach it, study it, and as I walk underneath it, I see the bilingual plaque. It's a remnant from the Meiji Restoration, it says, when Japan tried to imitate all things Western.

In the treed garden of a less overrun sub-temple, we sit down and have *matcha* tea and minuscule pieces of sweets. It's peaceful, and I can't think of a place where I'd rather be than in this garden, drinking *matcha* with Izumi to the slow resonant *toc-toc-toc* of the *shishiodoshi*, the deer scarer. It's an ingenious device, a pivot-mounted bamboo tube whose down end sits on a rock while the other end, cut open to form a bowl, juts up into a trickle of water. After a while, the weight of the water forces that end down—and the other end up—until the water gushes out. Now empty, it pops back up, while the down end hits the rock. *Toc.* It's hypnotic.

"I'm so happy this touches you," she says.

"I could stay forever."

"Not forever. I'm hungry."

"Tofu time?"

And so we put our plan into action. At the entrance to one of the tofu restaurants that line the street to the temple precinct, we exchange our shoes for one-size-fits-all-Japanese slippers and plod behind a hostess in kimono up the narrow stairs to the second floor. Negotiating the steps is a bit tricky with these slippers; my toes don't fit into the toe-caps, my heels extend two inches off the ends, and with every step, my slippers threaten to fall off. But I make it without drawing attention to myself.

Once upstairs, we leave our slippers next to dozens of identical slippers at the edge of the dining area and continue in socks across the tatami to a low table. Two thin cushions serve as chairs. We sit on our heels. Having practiced that excruciatingly painful position every day while doing chopstick exercises, I can hold out for a few minutes. Izumi translates the menu, but even she has trouble reading the bold cursive columns of kanji. A *yudōfu* set catches our fancy.

A waitress in kimono hefts a pot of broth and tofu cubes on a hot plate in the center of our table. Next to it, she places a platter of tempura-fried lotus root, eggplant, yam, and pumpkin. Then she covers the rest of the table with a variety of bowls—rice, bonito broth, pickled mountain vegetables, bite-sized rolls of soymilk skin, a paste of ground sesame and kudzu starch, and a variety of condiments.

When there's no more room left on the table, she gives her spiel about each item. Izumi says, *"Hai, hai, hai."* I nod knowingly. As soon as she's gone, I straighten out my tortured legs in a direction where my soles don't point at anyone. Which isn't easy in a crowded place. But pointing your soles at people is against the rules, my guidebook says. Or maybe not anymore. I ask Izumi.

"No problem," she says. "You can do it."

"Would you point your soles at people?"

"I might not."

"So, it's a rule?"

"Not rule," she says, forehead rumpled into a quizzical frown.

I've run into this before. She denies there's a rule but follows it anyway. I want to follow these rules, whether they exist or not, because I want to be a good gaijin, but learning about a rule that doesn't exist and then following it is hard.

Izumi adds condiments of grated daikon, green onions, bonito flakes, raw ground ginger, dried seaweed, and ground pepper to her bowl of bonito broth. I do the same. Into this, we dip pieces of what honest folks admit under their breath is bland tofu. But it absorbs the sauce and resurfaces piquant.

"The secret of tofu is the dipping sauce," she says between bites.

"That's the way to eat toffff—"

The piece I'm holding near my mouth disintegrates between my chopsticks, splashes into my dipping sauce, and splatters a brown Rorschach test with condiments on my white shirt.

Izumi freezes.

I have the urge to cuss. But in Japan you don't cuss. Not even between your teeth. One of the rules. I do damage control with my napkin, which is ludicrous. The stain stretches from my belt to my sternum. Patrons pretend it hasn't happened and try not to snicker. Waitresses dissipate politely into thin air.

"Happens to everyone," Izumi says when the shock subsides.

"Happens only to newbie gaijin," I grunt.

With her chopsticks, she tears the *shiso* leaf that decorates one of the dishes into two neat halves. I didn't know you could even do that with chopsticks. It's ultra-cool, and I put it on my to-learn list. *"Dōzo,"* she says with the sweetest smile and places one of the halves on my plate. Her consolation gift.

In the evening, on our way back from Ginkaku-ji Temple, we run into a guy she knows. He is with a girl. Izumi and the guy palaver. The girl and I stand behind and off to the side of our respective partners. Neither the guy nor the girl glances at my Rorschach test, though it's the most glaring feature in the land. Heck, they don't even glance at me. I've been blotted out.

"Friend of yours?" I ask on the bus.

"My college *sempai*."

I don't know what that is. She outlines the concept. A *sempai* is someone who joins the organization a year ahead of you and is therefore above you in the hierarchy and deserves your respect, like an older brother. Turns out, you have to be Japanese for this to make any sense whatsoever.

"You could have introduced us," I say.

"We don't do that."

Against the rules? Ha, I've learned my lesson and know better than to ask.

One morning, we hike up the alleys to Kiyomizu-dera Temple. They're lined with noodle shops, cafés, snack shops, and souvenir shops in wooden buildings, some with multilayered curved and pointy roofs and patinated copper gutters. Guys in traditional or maybe fantasy outfits wait by their rickshaws and invite us with a bow. Random utility poles with spaghettiesque cables, a standard Japanese urban feature, dominate the sky even here. Two geisha hobble arm in arm out of a side alley. Their flamboyant kimonos, theatrical makeup, and dramatic hairdos attract giddy onlookers who yank out cameras and shoot photogenic geisha-in-alley pictures. My guidebook says Kyoto is the only city in Japan where you can still chance upon them.

"They're *maiko*, not geisha," Izumi says.

"What's the difference?"

"*Maiko* are apprentice geisha."

"How can you tell?"

"By their hairdo and makeup."

The *maiko* try to get away, but their high geta are ill-suited for speed, or for normal walking, or for anything else other than standing in four inches of muck without getting your feet dirty.

"They're faux *maiko*," she says. "They're girls who purchased a *maiko* package. Ads are all over Kyoto. A day package with makeup and accessories costs one *man* five-thousand yen."

"Why would anyone do that?"

"Lots of girls dream of being maiko for a day."

Inside Kiyomizu-dera precinct, we purify ourselves by ladling water over our fingers at a bronze dragon fountain. The main hall, built on stilts against the steep slope, overlooks the hazy sea of mid-rise buildings hemmed in by mountains. Incense wafts by. People await their turn in the prayer area. When it's their turn, they cast some coins into the coin box, put their hands together in front of their chests, and lower their heads for a few seconds. They can't be long-winded in their prayers. Two or three things. Sentence fragments, probably. Maybe bullet points. Other people wait in line to kneel on a hemp cushion and tap a bonze bell with a baton.

I gaze up at the curvilinear roof, at the thousands of wooden brackets, projecting beams, cantilevers, and rafters joined together without nails or bolts, defying gravity, defying rational thought, and it becomes a spiritual event. I wonder if this interlocking artificial complexity with its hypnotic beauty isn't the model by which Izumi thinks and decides. There has to be a link. They're too similar to be coincidental.

But no one else looks up at it. Izumi doesn't either. "For me," she says after her prayers, "this is a pilgrimage to a world a modern Tokyoite can easily lose contact with."

Our last night in Kyoto, weary from being on our feet all day, we have drinks at the black granite counter of a somber bar, a respite from so much classic Japanese culture. I'm a fulfilled sloppy mess, and saccharine words bubble to the surface.

"I love you," I say.

"Why?" she says.

"Um, I have a long list of reasons." I'm unprepared for her *why*. There's no list. I don't need reasons.

"For example?"

"Oh man. I can't choose."

"Choose at landom."

"At random? Okay. Let's see. Because of your looks."

"That's it?"

"Because of the way you make love."

"And?"

"That's enough."

"There must be more."

"Because you're a tough cookie." That one came out of nowhere.

"Tough cookie sounds stale and old. You might break your teeth."

"It's a compliment."

"I don't want to be tough cookie."

I explain it, and the more I explain it, the more I know it's correct. This sweet girl whose smile can melt me from the inside out is a tough cookie.

23

BIG LIKE

It's raining when the Shinkansen eases into Tokyo Station. It has been a phenomenal getaway. We even resolved the coffee-before-breakfast dilemma. The second morning, we chose Japanese breakfast, which came with *ocha* instead of coffee. So we had to order coffee up front, which Izumi did only after an intense back-and-forth. But the waitress simply confirmed it was à la carte and brought it right away. Then breakfast arrived. A lacquerware tray for each of us with miso soup, grilled salmon, sour plum, fermented soybeans, roasted seaweed, pickled eggplant, wasabi, freshly ground ginger, fish cake, and rice. Delicious as it looked, it exuded an amalgam of powerful scents that annihilated any desire to drink whatever remained of my coffee. Lesson learned: finish coffee before the food shows up. The next morning, Izumi voluntarily ordered coffee before our Japanese breakfast. And the morning after that, the waitress didn't even bother to confirm it was à la carte. The rules that no one admitted existed were bent successfully, and harmony ensued. A victory of sorts.

At Tokyo Station, we change to the Yamanote line. The train is packed, and we're standing. We aren't talking. Against the rules on commuter trains. Ikebukuro is announced. My stop.

"Can we go out tomorrow?" I ask in crass violation of the rules. "We can have dinner in Takadanobaba and spend the night at my new apartment."

"I can't."

It knocks the wind out of me.

"Thursday?" Hollow syllables echoing off walls in an empty cavern.

"I'm not available."

"Friday?"

"Friday is available."

"At the apartment?"

She nods. We say *bai-bai.* I get off and wave. But she doesn't see me. She faces the other direction. Our Kyoto romance has ended, and her mind has wandered off to other things she'll be doing with other people.

When I get back to the apartment in Ekoda, I'm dripping wet. But Mr. Kim and Mr. Song stand by the table in the breakfast area and greet me with broad smiles.

"Mr. Wolf, we were waiting for you," Mr. Kim says as I'm taking off my shoes. "We wanted to be here to say good-bye."

"That's very nice of you."

"How was Kyoto?"

"Beautiful. You should visit it someday."

"I hope I have time."

"Wolf-san, try Korean food," Mr. Song says in Japanese. He defers to Mr. Kim on everything and never speaks first. "Tokyo has many Korean restaurants."

"Mr. Song knows," Mr. Kim says, now also in Japanese. "He is a good cook."

"No, no." Mr. Song vigorously shakes his head and waves his hands, though he smiles broadly. He has mastered the Japanese way of accepting compliments by rejecting them. His Japanese is already functional, whereas mine is still near zilch.

"Call me when you are in Seoul," Mr. Kim says in English and writes down his number.

The move is easy. I pack my French press, coffee mugs, tea set, and books into my duffle bag, now a huge bulging monster, and head back out into the rain. At the Weekly Mansion, I hang up my clothes, stack my books on the floor, put my kitchen items into the cupboard, and deposit the bottle of Glenfiddich in the closet. I bought it at the duty-free shop in Bali as a gift for Izumi's dad. Even if he doesn't drink scotch, he'll welcome it because it's a brand-name item he can regift. I read that in my guidebook.

When the rain abates, I go to the supermarket on Waseda-dōri, the only two-lane street in my neighborhood of alleys. I've come a long way in my shopping skills. For instance, I no longer gape at price tags. But I still embarrass myself by holding a box the wrong way while trying to figure out what the label says. Then I discover in my so-called apartment that there's no space other than the floor to set down two bags of groceries. And when I set them on the floor, I have to crawl over the bed to get around them.

At night, in the ample time that Izumi's unknown activities leave me, I sit on the bed with the never-ending *Genji*. Instead of reading, I'm wondering how I'll make it through the next few days without her. In Kyoto, I became addicted to her chemicals, and now I have withdrawal symptoms. Behind the thin wall, someone clanks with kitchenware. The TV comes on. Channels get flipped to a talk show. Japanese talk shows have their own cadences of male and female voices with breezy ups and downs, not unpleasant to listen to, even if you don't understand a word. I put down *Genji* and engage in my newest form of meditation: The *shiso* leaves I bought earlier, I spread them out on the bedside cabinet, whose fold-up leaf is my table, and practice tearing them in two with chopsticks.

Wednesday, May 8.
Cantankerous crows wake me up. Bundles of sun rays angle from slits and holes in the metal accordion blinds. I open the sliding glass door and shove the blinds back. The air is humid and warm. The sun has cleared the roof of the school. Children's paintings are taped to the windows. Crows are altercating in the school yard. It's 5:30 a.m. I fix coffee and study Japanese— only to find out that I've forgotten everything. Takano-sensei will discover once again that his relentless efforts to teach me how to engage a salaryman in conversation have come to naught.

At 9:45 a.m., I walk to school. I pass a produce shop, a carpenter shop, a noodle shop, and a guy who sells vegetables from a plastic sheet spread out on the pavement. The alley merges with other alleys and with the entertainment street. Doors of restaurants and hostess bars are open, and clean-up crews are mopping up. A young couple slinks out of a love hotel. Now that I no longer need love hotels, I see them everywhere.

The entertainment street feeds into Waseda-dōri, whose sidewalk is congested with pedestrians and bicyclists coming from or going to the JR underpass. The elevated JR tracks cut Takadanobaba in two, and the underpass is a bottleneck. As a freight train thunders by on the steel structure above, a head of short blond hair bobs on the waves of black hair toward me, and in seconds she's within reach. Her chest bounces under a ruby tank top. Her belly spills ever so slightly over the waistband of her jeans. We smile with an instant sense of familiarity, each surprised to run into another gaijin at the JR underpass. And she's gone. A vision, perhaps.

Friday, May 10.
A long juicy kiss replaces the cropped nod with which I greet Izumi in public.

"Ah, nice," she says, probably about the kiss, not the apartment—because there's nothing nice about the apartment. She's looking for a place to put her purse. I point at the floor near the door, and she reluctantly sets it there. Then she's looking for a place to sit.

"Try the bed. Coffee?"

"I'd love some."

"You'll be a lot more comfortable if you take off your skirt and pantyhose."

"I'm fine." But she isn't fine. She's sweating.

"It'll keep your skirt from getting wrinkled."

She pouts but takes off her skirt and pantyhose, sighs with relief, and drapes them over the TV. She watches me intensely as I work the French press. I pour coffee into the mug I bought for her and hand it to her. I pour coffee into my mug, and we sit side by side on the bed, our backs against the headboard. The room with its bare white walls so close to our faces is awful, but it's *our* room, and we lounge around in our underwear, and we are so happy.

Later, we go to Akihabara—*Electric Town,* my bilingual street atlas labels it—a mid-rise bazaar for electrical appliances, computers, gadgets, digital kerosene heaters, adaptors, spy gear, motherboards, you name it. The amplified voices of sidewalk girls that tout cell phones mix with store announcements, jingles, and video games into a potent cocktail.

At the same Internet café I tried earlier, I persuade Izumi to ask the attendant if they have AOL—I still haven't been able to get to my email.

After an elaborate discussion between them, she says he has heard of AOL but doesn't have it. We click around for options. But she isn't familiar with Windows, and her translation of Japanese Windows lingo into English makes no sense to me, which flusters both of us.

Food and wine being the best way to overcome these impenetrable quirks of life, we settle into a dining bar in Takadanobaba and have *mentaiko* spaghetti and a bottle of Côte du Rhône. The noodles are al dente. The main ingredient of the sauce is spicy cod roe. Roasted seaweed, instead of parmesan, is sprinkled on top. Italian pasta reinvented the Japanese way. And it does the job.

Traipsing from love hotel to love hotel belongs to our past. She calls her mother from the pay phone in the quiet alley in front of the Weekly Mansion. The lies are the same, but an easier episode of our lives has commenced. The only problem is sound insulation. Love-hotel rooms are soundproof. You can make all kinds of noises, and no one can hear you. Here, my neighbors hear everything. She's trying to keep the volume down by holding her breath, but it only produces a brief period of dense silence interrupted by a piercing scream when she exhales, followed by more silence when she holds her breath again, followed by another piercing scream. Clearly, we have some work to do on our sound-control techniques.

Saturday, May 11.
Neither the obnoxiously cawing crows nor the brilliant beams of light angling through the metal accordion blinds wake her up. She can sleep regardless of what's going on around her.

"*Ohayō* my love," I coo into her ear and brush the curtain of hair from her face.

"*Ohayō*," she purrs.

"Ready for coffee?"

"Hmmm."

I help her sit up. She gropes for her glasses, puts them on, discovers her nakedness.

"Can I have something to wear?"

I toss her the white dress shirt I wore yesterday. She puts it on, laughs. "It's huge," she says and rolls up the sleeves until her fingertips poke out. She tiptoes to the bathroom, shirttails past her knees, and shoots me a coy smile over her shoulder. She's so irresistible.

We drink coffee in bed. We do all the things we couldn't do in love hotels. I fix breakfast—orange juice, bananas, bread, butter, and strawberry jam. Dressed only in my shirt, she sits on the edge of the bed. I sit on the chair. Between us is the leaf of the bedside cabinet, with no room for our legs underneath or our hands on top.

"I love this leisurely morning with you," she says.

"You can have it whenever you want."

"Really?"

"Every day."

When she comes out of the shower, the dress shirt is translucent with moisture and clings to her curves, and the white towel I bought for her is done up into a turban. She's crooning the melody of "If I Were a Rich Man."

When I come out of the shower, she's slouching on the bed. A Post-it note is stuck on the TV screen. It's in Japanese. The three katakana for *u-ru-fu*, the kanji for *big*, and the two hiragana *su-ki*. *Wolf big like.* Japanese works that way. Western names are unrecognizable in katakana. You just have to learn them like new words. Plus, avoid personal pronouns. They're too precise and direct and have a tendency to swerve into the impolite or crass. You must keep it vague. And *love* doesn't exist in Japanese. The very concept used to be forbidden and may still be frowned upon. To get around it, you say *big like*. But she added two hearts to confer the precision Japanese lacks: *I love Wolf*. She slips farther down on the bed. Her hormones are raging. Her body is in agony. I rub lotion on my torso, arms, and legs, delaying the inevitable to increase her agony.

"Lotion?" I offer when I'm done.

She writhes out of the shirt without unbuttoning it. I drip lotion on her, and each glob of cold lotion spattering on her superheated skin elicits a gasp, and when I begin to spread the globs, she moans, and my neighbor turns up the TV.

24
BOMB INCIDENT

The tall blonde sashays toward me from the JR underpass. She's wearing tight jeans and a cropped pink T-shirt under which her breasts bounce provocatively with every step. I want to say something to her to get a conversation going. Something simple. She's looking at me. I want to come up with something she can respond to. She seems to slow down. Even *hello* would do. We cross. I wonder where she's coming from and where she's going and what she's doing in Takadanobaba, and I wonder if she's wondering where I'm going and what I'm doing, but nothing comes out of my mouth. And she's gone. An unlikely apparition at the JR underpass of Takadanobaba. So I name her Takadanobaba Girl.

One of the newsstands inside the station carries the *Wall Street Journal Asia*. Before 8 a.m., the wrinkled prewar archetype has two copies. By 8:45 a.m., he's down to one. By 9 a.m., he's out. And now that I live a few minutes away, I get there in time to grab the last copy. Surely, the same two guys have been buying them for years, and now I come along and muck up their system. I feel like a thief. Yet one of the pleasures of living in Takadanobaba—as opposed to Ekoda—is being able to buy this paper in my own neighborhood and read it in a coffee shop on the way to class. Just seeing the familiar layout and sheer mass of English is a pleasure. I begin with the stock listings. Everything is up. Wall Street is funding my trip. My strategy is working. I feel smart. A rare feeling in Japan.

This is the mood I'm in when I enter the closet-like classroom for my lessons with Shirai-sensei. If it weren't for Japanese, she'd be a lot of fun. And during our second hour, as part of our practice conversation, I ask her to have lunch with me.

"I know a good *soba-ya*," she replies.

And that's where we go. Around us, guys are bent over their bowls, sucking noodles with fanfare. Others hold up their bowls with both hands and slurp the broth. But there are a few girls, too, and they're less noisy. Handicapped by the limitations of my Japanese, our conversation is basic.

"How old are you?" she asks.

I tell her. She acts surprised.

"How old are you?" I ask.

"Thirty-three."

I act surprised.

She asks what I did last night. She's asking in order to get me to practice past tense and topic-particle sentence structure. But gradually we drift away from grammar-driven sentences. She tells me she teaches courses for future teachers of Japanese. I already know that because Izumi is one of her students, but I don't mention Izumi due to the clandestine nature of our relationship. She asks in which state I live.

"Oklahoma."

"Yes," she says and tries to remember something. "Oh yes, I saw it on TV, the bomb incident."

I nod. The bomb incident, as she says, is all we're known for these days. A sad manifestation of our importance in the world.

Our conversation stumbles forward in its laborious and exhausting manner. If I did this more often, I might actually learn Japanese. But I want a human conversation, not a practice conversation, and switch to English.

"We should speak Japanese," she says in English, and when I don't get excited about that, she adds, "but I enjoy speaking English. Maybe we can compromise."

"You speak English very well."

"No, no, I have a long way to go."

"Did you learn it in America?" I say because of her faint American intonation.

"In China."

I guffaw. I like her sense of humor.

"I spent two years in China," she says. "I taught Japanese under a Chinese government program. My roommate was an American girl who taught English. At first, we tried to speak Chinese with each other, but—" She chuckles. "Let's just say that my English improved a lot more in China than my Chinese."

And so the conversation hopscotches along.

"We should have dinner together," she says as we finish our *soba*. "We can take turns, English an hour, Japanese an hour. And so on. We can get drunk together."

"If I drink, my Japanese goes to hell entirely."

"Opposite. Your Japanese improves with each drink. I know because my English becomes fluent after the third drink." She laughs while I imagine the sound of my Japanese after three drinks. When the check comes, she doesn't let me pick it up but insists with gentle authority on going Dutch.

"I bought a house two years ago," she says. "I like foreigners in my house. A Korean student stayed with me for three months. He left two weeks ago."

"Aren't you afraid the school might find out?"

"Afraid of the school? We Japanese are afraid of only four things: *jishin, kaminari, kaji, oyaji*—you know, earthquake, thunder, fire, and father. But no one is afraid of their father anymore."

"I was afraid of my father."

She laughs. "Actually, the school encourages it," she says more seriously. "Where do you live?"

"At the Weekly Mansion."

"When your lease is up, you can stay with me." She writes a phone number into my textbook. "Call me when you're ready."

At night, alone at my apartment, I grapple with the nuances of the conversation. Is she only interested in renting out a room and practicing English? Or is she interested in *me*? She never exerted any pressure. I never had to say yes or no to anything. I can follow up or not follow up. She's helpful without being maternal. She's flirtatious without being aggressive. She's cute without being gorgeous. She's the kind of girl gaijin guys get all starry-eyed about when they return home.

Friday, May 17.

Izumi came by Wednesday afternoon for a couple of hours but then had to go do something. Yesterday she was busy. But today she's mine. We sit on the bed, lean against the headboard, drink coffee, and watch a sumo match on TV. During a commercial break, she picks up the three plums on the TV shelf—the only spot available for them—and starts juggling. I wince because I paid dearly for them, but I let her because I love watching her.

"Where did you learn to juggle?"

"My mother learned it in school," she says, her eyes following the plums, "like all Japanese girls of her generation. And she taught me—" *Thud, thud.*

And I have to retrieve them from the dust under the bed.

We have dinner at a Tex-Mex in the Nogizaka Station area. I've been craving huge margaritas, free all-you-can-eat chips and salsa, massive portions of black beans, guacamole, jalapeños, corn tortillas, tamales, and ceviche. Our waitress is American. The menu is bilingual. I order, a rare pleasure for both of us. Our margaritas are minuscule but strong. Our order of chips for ¥800 comes in the form of five chips on a saucer with a thimble of salsa in the middle—at an average cost of $1.50 per chip. The beef fajitas are three well-marbled, paper-thin strips of beef. The guacamole was prepared minutes earlier from a fragment of a ripe avocado. The three slices of jalapeños make my ears ring. The small portions, however, encourage us to order more portions, and we manage to overeat. In Tokyo, there's nothing like a Tex-Mex to reset your spirits, though I'll need a rally in the stock market to pay for it.

We stroll to Roppongi and end up at some bar. She tells me how she and some unnamed tennis friends of unspecifiable gender—her *hes* and *shes* remain as fungible as ever—were going from bar to bar, doing *hashigo*, the ladder.

"I get bubbly when I drink, and people think I'm alright," she says, "but I don't remember anything afterward." Early in the morning, as they took a taxi to a friend's apartment, Izumi was in the rear, leaning against the door, sleeping. When they got there, the door opened automatically, as doors do in Japanese taxis, and she tumbled out and hit her head on the sidewalk. "But I can't remember any of it," she says. "My friends told me the next morning when I asked them how I got the bruise on my head." Monday was a holiday, and by Tuesday her bruise had spread around her right eye. "At the office, no one said anything about it. In the afternoon, I had an important meeting with a client, and even he pretended nothing was wrong, though I looked like a monster."

How she can tell this story with all its get-drunk details and funny embellishments without mentioning a single name is beyond me.

Wednesday, May 22.

I feel privileged; Izumi has shoehorned me into her schedule. We attend a Bunraku play at the Tokyo National Theater. The audience is composed mostly of older people. Everyone is dressed up: a lot of suits and dresses, but also kimonos—black, charcoal, or navy for men, colors of spring for women. Audio guide against my ear, I listen to the English translation and doubt I'll be able to sit through it.

Each of the lavish, near life-size puppets is handled by three puppeteers dressed entirely in black. Hoods over their heads, black veils over their faces, they trail behind the puppets like multi-limbed ominous specters. Only the head puppeteers, stars of the show, expose their faces. They move their puppet's head, eyes, and right hand. The left-hand puppeteers move the left hand. The foot puppeteers move the feet. The puppets seem to walk on solid ground, though their feet are in the air. They're alive and act out of passion. A chanter to the right of the stage tells the story, describes the scenery, and recites dialogues. His voice fluctuates from chant to narration, rising and falling whole octaves in a single breath. A samisen player accompanies the chanter. Other instruments are played offstage. Soon, I'm absorbed in the bizarre reality, and there are times when shivers run down my spine.

Afterward, we browse for a dining bar.

"This is where I used to go with my colleagues," she says at some stairs to a basement entrance. "Are you interested?"

"Sure, I'd love to meet them."

"Please wait here."

She canters down the stairs and disappears into the bar. I loiter inanely in front of a sign I can't read. My relationship with her exhibits all the characteristics of the one-sided trade relationship between the US and Japan. I pay a fortune to be in her country. Though I'm learning Japanese, she refuses to speak it with me. She has seen every aspect of my life in Japan, and I've told her whatever she wants to know about the rest of my life.

But I'm not allowed near her house, and her parents don't know I exist. I haven't met any of her friends, don't even know their names. And when we run into her *sempai* in Kyoto, she doesn't introduce me and doesn't mention his name.

Japan benefits from the openness of the US market and from our eagerness to surrender our hard-earned money in exchange for their baubles. But we're not invited to the party and not welcome in their homes. We're gaijin and always will be—outsiders to be kept outside. What are they afraid of? That we talk loudly or forget to take off our slippers when we step on the national tatami floor? That we sneeze or blow our nose in public and infect everyone with our crazy ideas? That we muck up their harmony and traditions with our harebrained insistence on using personal pronouns?

Okay, I get it. It's their country, and that's how they do it. I respect that. But is this the way you treat your lover?

She reappears at the bottom of the stairs and nods. The coast is clear.

It's a narrow, busy bar, but two barstools are still available at the counter against the wall. We order margaritas and some dishes. I make a few subtle efforts to find out what the deal was, but she doesn't respond. When I ask her directly, she says only that she wanted to make sure her former colleagues wouldn't be here.

"Why are all the puppeteers male?" I ask to change the subject.

"It's our tradition."

"Only in Japan would it occur to anyone to replace an actress with a puppet, three male puppeteers, and a male chanter."

That gets her going. Bunraku is important to her. Her chest swells with each sentence. She struggles with English words to express Japanese concepts. With her chopsticks, she holds a cube of grilled beef in front of her mouth. But as she continues talking, she sets it back down on her plate, only to lift it again to her mouth moments later. But she can't find the right spot to stop talking, sets it back down, tries again, misses another opportunity—and the cube never makes it into her mouth. When she's talking, she's talking, and she can do nothing else at the same time. I eat cubed beef and slimy mushrooms and finger-sized whole fried fish and grilled eggplant in sesame sauce.

"Eat," I interrupt her after a while.

It confuses her.

"Eat," I say and point at the cube of meat between her chopsticks.

She looks at it.

"Eat, or you'll leave hungry."

And the piece of meat completes its journey.

Friday, May 24.

It's another Friday night without Izumi, who is busy doing other things with other people. I decide to have ramen. Nightlife is in full swing. Bowing touts in black suits hand out cards to guys that mill around, but every time I get near a tout, he refuses to bow, and his right hand with the card between his fingers hangs down by his thigh. I know what this means. Whatever is going on in that establishment is for Japanese guys only. Gaijin guys are excluded. It doesn't bother me anymore. It's one of the first things you get used to in Tokyo, even before you get used to the prices. But why be so visual about it?

I'm passing a ramen shop of the type where you shout your order across the counter. I can't do that. I have to find one with a vending-machine apparatus by the entrance where you push a button under a photo, which any idiot can do. I duck into one with a potted bamboo outside, make my selection at the machine and pay. Then I squeeze in at the counter between salarymen in dark suits who accept my presence—denim jacket, jeans, and all—with surprised nods. I'm one of them. Dateless guys on a Friday night.

The chef is already working on my order. Deep lines descend from sides of his nose past his mouth to his chin. A rolled white cloth is tied around his head just above his eyebrows. His apron is splattered with brown stains. He dips a ladle into a vat of simmering broth and pours it into a bowl, on top of a dark brown sauce. With his two-foot chopsticks, he lifts a load of steaming noodles out of a sieve and eases them into the bowl. He adds half a boiled egg, seaweed, slices of bamboo shoots, chopped green onions, two slices of pork, and a slice of fish cake.

He sets the bowl on the counter with a few gravel-crunching words. I nod and grunt. It's all very manly. Tangled up in he-man thoughts, we're bent over our bowls and suck noodles. No one talks. All you hear are bursts of sucking and slurping, an occasional deep hum of appreciation, and from a corner of the kitchen, the perky ups and downs of a radio talk show. The noodles are *shiko-shiko*, the Japanese version of al dente. The broth is rich and pungent. The ingredients are a bit sparse, but good. When the guy next to me is done, he chants *gochisosamadeshita* and leaves. When I'm done,

I do the same, *gochisosamadeshita* being one of the few things I know how to say with some authority, and I delude myself into thinking that I might sound vaguely Japanese.

I get home, so to speak, exhausted from grappling with every little thing and drained from looking at all the kanji I can't read and beat up from maneuvering through the masses—and what's the first thing I do after having looked at Japanese faces all day? I double-check my own features in the mirror. And I'm shocked by how angular, chiseled, and harsh they are and by how long and narrow my face is. How come I've never noticed this before? Another mystery. I turn on the TV. Iron Chef is on. My neighbor is also watching Iron Chef. The dynamics of the cooking teams and the facial expressions and utterances of the jury as they taste the creations are priceless, even if you don't understand a word. And that summarizes better than anything else how my day has been.

25

BLUES

Izumi comes by in the afternoon, complains about the heat, and with a sigh of relief peels off her jeans. It's Saturday, and she has time. We drink coffee on the bed and flip through *Tokyo Walker*, an entertainment weekly whose text, despite the deceptively English title, is entirely in Japanese. We're in the mood for a movie. It has to be in English, French, or German with Japanese subtitles so we both can understand it. *Manneken Pis* catches our fancy. A bittersweet French romance, or something to that effect, the description says in Japanese.

During the first dialogue, a murmur permeates the theater. About half the people in the audience are gaijin, presumably Francophone, and they're all having the same problem I'm having. Izumi, however, is stoically reading subtitles.

"I have no clue what language this is," I whisper into her ear.

"What do you mean?"

"It's not French."

I recognize fragmentary German and bits of French, which I piece together the best I can. I get maybe 40 percent. The rest I fill in with my imagination.

We head to Takadanobaba for dinner so we can walk back to the apartment instead of having to worry about catching the last train. A trattoria with a handwritten bilingual menu—in Italian and katakana rendition of Italian—appeals to us. I've never studied Italian, but I have no trouble reading the Italian menu; and the waitress, who's Japanese, understands my Italian when I order. But after six weeks of Japanese lessons and endless hours of hard work, I still stumble badly when ordering the simplest things in Japanese, and I'll never be able to read a Japanese menu. It simply isn't a learnable language.

Knowing better than to confront an aspiring teacher of Japanese with this fact, I keep it to myself. Instead, we discuss the movie. Turns out, the 40 percent I understood was unrelated to the plot, which was centered on the other 60 percent. But its insufferable dreariness has infected both of us. It wasn't a bittersweet French romance, we conclude, but a bitter Flemish nightmare.

On the way back, when we pass the pay phone near the Weekly Mansion, she doesn't stop.

"Don't you need to call your mother?" I remind her.

"No."

"Why not?"

"She knows something is going on. She told me to inform her in advance, instead of calling late at night and waking everyone up."

"Did you tell her you'd be with me?"

"Of course not."

If she doesn't tell anyone of my existence, so be it. Why should it concern me? It doesn't matter. I can't allow myself to get bogged down in these details. What matters is tonight, and tonight she's mine.

The next morning, blinding sun rays punch through holes and joints of the metal accordion blinds. The AC is humming. The crows in the school yard have moved on. Izumi is lying naked on her back, arms raised into two columns, fingers dangling limply off her hands.

"My fingers are numb," she says.

It doesn't count unless she has a minimum of three violent orgasms. Except the day before her period. Then she's insatiable. And yet, I doubt she's addicted to me the way I'm addicted to her. When she's not with me, I suffer from withdrawal. Does she suffer from withdrawal? Probably not. Two nights a week and occasionally after class is enough sex for her. If she wanted more, she could have more, but she doesn't want more. She likes sex with me but doesn't have to have it. That's the nature of things. Where women are vulnerable, if anywhere, is in lifestyle and emotional comfort. Not sex. In that respect, she'll be freer than me. For her, it'll be easier to walk away, though she might cry a little. Which is also the nature of things.

She slips on my white shirt, sits up against the headboard, opens a book. I scour my guidebook for excursions.

"How about a weekend in the mountains?" I suggest. "It would be nice to get some fresh air, see some green, and do some hiking."

She likes the idea. We consider different options, elevate Nikko National Park to the top of our list, and decide to go next weekend. Then she buries herself in her book. I leaf through *Japan* backward, musing, reading, until I reach "Getting There & Away," subsection "Trans-Siberian Railway."

Russia! Wouter the Dutch guy raved about it. I leapfrog from section to section, piecing together a route through Japan to Russia. "I could hitchhike north along the Sea of Japan," I think out loud, dreaming, playing with concepts, my finger on the map. "I could cross over to Hokkaido, hitchhike to its northernmost town, Wakkanai, and take a ferry to Sakhalin."

"Sakhalin?" she says and looks up from her book.

"From there, it should be possible to get a ferry to mainland Russia and hook up with the Trans-Siberian Railroad."

"Siberian Railroad?" She lowers her book into her lap.

"I could go to France that way, from Tokyo to Marseille overland."

The white of my shirt brings out her features. She's ravishing in white. But she prefers earth tones and soft colors, and I only see her in white when she's wearing my shirt. So I'm sitting next to this girl I just made love to and can't spend enough time with and never want to leave, not even for a single day—and I'm thinking about traveling overland from the eastern edge of Asia to the western edge of Europe, halfway around the globe. An astounding collision of thoughts.

"We could go together," I say to bring some semblance of cohesion to all this.

She doesn't respond. She likes foreign countries. Such a journey should excite her.

"When my ninety-day visa expires, I can apply for a long-term visa, or I can visit Korea for a week and come back for another ninety days, or we can travel together."

She stiffens.

I talk of vast lands and exotic cultures to pump her up. A tear rolls down her cheek, drips off her jaw, makes a spot on the shirt. I pull her to me. She resists, then yields.

"What's the matter?"

She doesn't respond.

"Come on, tell me."

She breathes through her open lips, unwinds, and after a while she wipes her cheeks. "I'm fine," she says. "I just haven't thought about these things. They give me the blues."

It passes, and we talk about other things.

Later, she emerges from the bathroom in my white shirt and sits down on the edge of the bed in front of the mirror. Her hair is stringy and clingy and pitch-black with moisture. Her face is flushed from the heat of the bath. Tiny pearls of sweat accumulate on her forehead that slants backward from her eyebrows, and there doesn't seem to be enough room in there for a big brain, when compared to my enormous forehead. Yet she has a brain with four times the processing power and ten times the memory of mine. She drapes the white towel over her hair and twists it up into a turban that makes her look stern and seductive at the same time, and I wonder what I've done to deserve this spectacle.

This is the same girl who told me thirty minutes ago in her inimitable English, "Tuesday and Wednesday is not available." Nothing further needed to be said, apparently. A subtle brutality tints these statements. Or at least it seems that way to me because we've spent an incredible weekend together, nineteen hours of happiness. I'm not sure if the problem is a matter of language in that she hasn't fully grasped the nuances of English, or if the problem is in my own mind. Why can't she round off her statements with tidbits about what she'll be doing? A name, for instance, or something like "people I used to work with"? And if she's seeing someone else, so be it. I'm a big boy. But I don't think she's seeing anyone else. More likely, it's a categorical refusal to grant me access to her Japanese life. I don't fit into it. I only fit into her Western life, limited as it is. And her Japanese life remains hermetically sealed off to me.

26
VIOLENCE AND CRIME

When Izumi and I go to a restaurant, the staff talk only to her. Often they don't acknowledge me, not even with a glance or a nod, though I greet them in Japanese. They pretend the gaijin at the table doesn't exist. This way, they won't have to deal with the dreadful things they might otherwise have to deal with, and the disturbing concept of *gaijin* disappears from view, though I'm sitting right in front of them. When I eat out by myself, however, they don't have that option. So they get up their courage and deal with me, and it normally turns into a pleasant experience for everyone.

Based on Mr. Kim's and Mr. Song's encouragement, I'm trying out a Korean restaurant for lunch, a *bibimbap* place. I order by pointing at a photo on the menu and add in Japanese, "Yes, this please, and iced oolong tea please." The waitress repeats my order, or repeats something I didn't order, or says something unrelated to my order. I confirm. I can't be too picky. And when she brings out an iced oolong tea, I know at least that part of it worked.

"Excuse me, are you American?" says an older guy at the next table.

I grunt with a cropped nod in his direction, a Japanese affirmation between guys, but I never know if my version is authentic or ridiculous.

"It's hot today," he says. He's talking to me in English, though this is exactly the kind of crap I can say fluently in Japanese. He has finished his meal and is slurping *ocha*. He has thick salt-and-pepper hair and wears a tone-on-tone gray sports coat, shirt, and tie.

"It's very hot. Please be careful," the waitress says in Japanese. She sets down a charred wooden tray with a steaming and sizzling stone bowl. Octopus, vegetables, and an egg sunny-side up are on top of the rice. She mixes it together, rousing steam and sizzle to a frenzied climax.

"I used to work with foreigners during parts of my career," he says when she's gone. "Doctors tell us older people to exercise our brain. So I practice English."

Each word seems to involve a Byzantine thought process, and he packages and repackages every sentence several times. Meanwhile, the stone bowl has baked some of the rice into a crust that augments the textures and flavors exploding in my mouth.

"I work part-time. It keeps me, how do you say, nimble."

"Nimble! Wow, your vocabulary is excellent."

"Oh no, I have a long way to go. After I retired, I was at home every day. But my wife was used to having the house to herself. She got impatient and told me to find something to do during the daytime." His eyes twinkle each time he successfully reaches the end of a sentence. He introduces himself. His name is Satoru. He had a nearby appointment earlier today.

"I can show you some special places in Tokyo," he says. "Are you free on Monday, June 11, at 6 p.m.?"

"Sure."

"Can you meet me at the Nishi-Azabu intersection?"

I hand him my pocket atlas. He flips through it, finds the right page, and puts his finger on the intersection.

Then he has to leave for another appointment, and I finish my meal in silence, wondering why he started talking to me, if he had an ulterior motive, and what the next meeting would lead to.

Izumi drops by the apartment in the early evening to plan our weekend excursion to Nikko National Park. From my guidebook, we select a *pension*—Japanese never ceases to surprise me—by Lake Chūzenji-ko, and she calls to reserve a room for Saturday night. We drink wine, but she evades my advances. Knowing she'll be doing other things with other people on

Tuesday and Wednesday, I angle for a date on Thursday, but she edges away. Which renders our conversation a bit stiff.

"Can I make a phone call?" she says.

She makes two. While I'm hunched over my grammar, she speaks in extra-rapid Japanese and doesn't include names. But I've been studying Japanese like a maniac, and while I understand very little of such a conversation, I understand some. I understand, for instance, that in her first call she's finalizing an appointment for Thursday at 7 p.m., and in her second call she confirms something for Wednesday.

She hangs up and says, "Friday is available."

"Awesome."

And she has to scoot.

None of this matters. Except that she intended for her extra-rapid Japanese to exclude me from her conversation. And she didn't tell me whom she talked to or what she talked about. Without too much pain, she could have said something like "Oh, that was so-and-so, my tennis buddy, and we're getting together on Thursday with our tennis group." I assume sex isn't part of the deal. Even if it were, who am I to preach? And I know she loves me because I can touch, smell, and taste her body, and her body tells me she loves me, and her body can't lie. But her body is all I know. Everything else is a secret.

Tuesday, May 28.

Japan, the country of unlimited hassles! It's after 9 a.m., and I'm on the phone with Izumi to ask her about some Japanese grammar item, when the line goes dead in mid-sentence. I run down to the receptionist and ask why, or try to ask, and she seems to understand, nods, and replies. This is so beyond the silly situations in my textbook. It seems my phone calls, few and short as they were, used up my one-*man*-yen phone deposit, and the machine cut me off. So I run up to my room, get a *man*-yen note, run back down to the receptionist, offer her the wrinkled note with some sort of humility, and wait for her to write out a receipt and press her seal on it. But when I finally return to my room, it's too late to call Izumi back because now I have to rush to school.

And the much-touted sensitivity of the Japanese! How they can *sense* their conversation partner's wishes without having to communicate with words. Bullshit. In many indirect ways, I've suggested to Izumi that I would like to meet some of her friends and family. And as Japanese do, she ignores the issue, rather than sense it, and refuses to talk about it. *Therefore,* the issue doesn't exist. Japanese do the same thing with homeless settlements. Heck, they do it to each other on rush-hour trains when they're squeezed together for long periods of time, sweating, feeling other people's body parts, inhaling other people's breath. It's their way of bearing the unbearable. So I don't know if the Japanese are better than other people when it comes to sensitivity, but I know they're masters at pointedly ignoring things. And Izumi is no exception.

Ruminating darkly on these and similar concepts, I rush through the entertainment street, and as I turn into Waseda-dōri, like so many times in Japan, something surprising happens that pulls me out of a funk: Takadanobaba Girl sashays out of the shadow of the JR underpass. We smile at each other. She has the body of a goddess. We approach. I say "hello." She says "hello," slows down. Her cleavage glistens with sweat, her breasts sway, and her belly that bulges deliciously over the waistband of her jeans jiggles. I ransack my brain for words, phrases, ideas, anything, an open-ended question if possible, something that could start a conversation, something like "What's your favorite *onigiri* filling?" which I abandon because it's too obvious. Thus I fribble away the moment, and she's gone.

Thursday, May 30.
At the immigration office in Otemachi, I'm asked to write my request in English on a piece of paper and submit it. After a wait, I'm directed to an office. A middle-aged white woman with puffy cheeks and a gray-blond perm thrones behind a desk.

"So, you want to stay in Japan longer," she says with an icy British accent.

"Yes, ma'am."

"Your ninety-day visa isn't renewable."

"I know. I'd like to apply for a long-term visa."

"Do you work here?"

"No, ma'am."

"What kind of job have you got in the US?"

"I don't have a job."

"How do you support yourself?"

"I live off my investments."

She glares at me over the rim of her glasses. She doesn't approve of my stratospherically priced linen jacket whose shoulders are too narrow and whose sleeves are too short.

"You have to have a company that sponsors you," she says.

"I didn't come to Japan to make money. I came to spend money."

That doesn't sit well with her. Not at all. Her lipless orifice contorts into an expression of disdain. "If you try the ticket-to-Seoul caper, immigration will deny you reentry and send you back to Seoul. At your expense."

"Of course."

"*We* limit immigration. *We* don't want to become like *you*. Look at your country."

"What's wrong with my country?"

"Poverty, violence, and crime."

"Poverty—"

"Because you're swamped with foreigners from all over the world."

I feel my face redden with anger. Presumably, *we* means Japan, and *you* means the US. With a few words, she has succeeded in insulting me personally, denigrating the US, and conveying just how unwanted I am in Japan. Being fat in a country of thin people has to be really upsetting.

Somehow, possibly by divine intervention, I manage to keep that comment to myself. I go to Shibuya and bathe in its voltage. I'm not in search of anything. I'm drifting. But at 11:45 p.m., the juice is draining out of Shibuya into the entrances of Shibuya Station. Daytime rules have been annulled. People are inebriated. They laugh, barf, have trouble with locomotion—a welcome contrast to the reverential silence that reigns during the day.

On the train, I hold on to one of the stainless-steel overhead bars rather than the straps that dangle from it and that everyone else holds on to, my solitary act of outright rebellion. Two girls behind me rub against my back, butt, and thighs to the swaying of the train. Body heat bleeds through my clothes. The train isn't that packed, and they could avoid body contact if they wanted to, but they chitchat with each other, pretend it isn't happening, switch places, take turns. I don't cede territory either, though I could. I'm part of the Japanese liquid, or at least a foreign particle in it, neither shunned nor kept at a distance but integrated into it, sought out perhaps.

It has been one of those interminably frustrating Japanese days. And what's my first reaction back at the apartment after hosing off Tokyo grit and sweat? I miss Ginger! Not in the sense that I'm used to her and don't have her anymore but in the sense that I appreciate how she accepted me and shared essential parts of her life with me and didn't constantly lock me out of everything. I didn't even know people could do that—until I came to Japan. And so I miss Ginger, and I can never even let her know.

I open the bottle of Glenfiddich I bought for Izumi's dad at the duty-free shop in Bali. I no longer have any illusions. I'll never meet him. And he won't mind if I drink his eighteen-year-old scotch so long as I drink to his health, from man to man. It won't cross any more oceans and landmasses. It won't be gifted and regifted. It has reached the end of its road.

27

DEER SASHIMI

fter an awesome Friday night together—by definition, all Friday nights with Izumi are awesome—we get up early and take the Tobu line north to Nikko. Gradually, the sea of urban ugliness makes room for rusting industrial hulks and towns interspersed with rice paddies that old people tend by hand, quaint and hobbyesque at the fringe of the largest conurbation in the world.

The town of Nikko, jammed against the foot of the mountains, is famous for its historic shrines and temples. But we skip them and take a bus up a road of hairpin turns and landslide fortifications to Lake Chūzenji-ko. From the bus stop, we walk along the shore to our pension, a prefab log-cabin-style building where a woman in tight jeans and a boy hugging her thigh welcome us at the door. As they show us to our room, she recites a long list of rules. Dinner is served at 6 p.m., I get that much. And from our window, we have a view of the lake, the surrounding mountains, and ... a swan. One big ugly swan, so big and so ugly you can see it from miles away. A boat, actually, that ferries tourists across the lake.

"I mean, come on," I mutter. Does the urge to create pandemic ugliness know no bounds?

"What?" Izumi says.

"Look at that thing."

She looks at it then averts her eyes. "That's what I like about Switzerland," she says. "They don't have things like that on every lake."

We also skip Kegon Falls, a popular suicide spot and tourist attraction with concrete and steel infrastructure. Instead, we hike to Ryuzu Falls, where water cascades down between trees, bushes, and ferns. Birds twitter. A man behind a tripod-mounted camera with a 500 mm telephoto lens flicks a twig into a pool so that it'll float into his camera angle. When a piece of wrapper wobbles along, he fishes it out with a long stick. This is the antidote to the swan.

We make it back in time for a bath in the shared family-style bathroom downstairs. There is, Izumi says, the way to do. The way to do, *yarikata*, is an omnipresent concept that governs even mundane things, like taking a bath.

Step one: in the dry area, take off clothes.

Step two: proceed to shower area and scrub and fondle each other with soapy hands—the fondling part may be my extrapolation, but she likes it.

Step three: rinse off thoroughly.

Step four: proceed to hinoki tub filled with steaming water used by others before you and to be used by others after you.

Step five: get in. Whoa, it's hot! She sinks into it with a deep sigh that tapers into a whistling sound. My left leg is in it up to the knee. My skin is turning lobster red. I inch in farther, one leg, then the other, and the immersed parts go into a state of total relaxation. When my chest sinks into it, water slaps luxuriously over the sides, splashes on the tiles, and gurgles out the floor drain. Near-boiling water up to my shoulders, I pet her floating breasts with my toes, and she curls hers around my johnson. But fearing that heatstroke will knock us out before we get anywhere, we abandon our games.

Dinner is served in a rustic dining room. The joys of eating cement us together even more tightly, and the harmony between us emboldens me. We finish the fifth course, sautéed almond trout, and as I'm pouring the remainder of our bottle of wine, I broach the subject that has been on my mind for weeks and that I've broached in subtle ways before without getting a response. Now I want to violate *yarikata*. I want to communicate with her clearly and directly, with personal pronouns and all.

"I'd like you to speak Japanese with me," I say.

Her smile withers.

"I know my Japanese isn't good enough for a real conversation, but speaking it with you would help me improve."

Her fingers tighten around the stem of her wineglass.

"It would make it easier for me to participate in your Japanese life."

She stops breathing.

"And I'd like to meet some of your friends."

She rigidifies.

"At least, I'd like you to tell me who your friends are," I backpedal.

A double circumflex appears on her brow.

"You talk about episodes from your past and about trips to Europe and about all sorts of other things you did, and I enjoy that, yet you don't tell me who you hang out with, and I don't know a single name. It makes me feel excluded."

Her eyes, deeper and blacker yet, seize mine. They want to talk to me, these eyes, and there's magic in them, and they sparkle and charge up with energy. She opens her mouth slightly, inhales barely, prepares to speak, and there's a moment of suspenseful silence. But then her lips close again, her eyes shift, the magic dims, and whatever she's thinking and whatever her eyes wanted to say has been brought under control, remains inside, unsaid, maybe even unthought.

And then she does speak.

"There's a Doisneau photo show in Shinjuku," she says. "It includes the Kiss series. I'd like to go see it with you on Wednesday."

"Sounds great," I say. "I've always wanted to see his stuff."

Things don't bog her down for long. The woman in tight jeans who showed us to our room, who has been serving dinner, who opened our wine bottle, and who has been doing everything we've seen anybody do, comes around with dessert. She's proud of her creation and explains it in detail.

"What is it?" I ask Izumi after the woman has departed.

"Bluebelly mousse."

In the morning, we take a bus to a marshland that borders the lake and walk on a meandering boardwalk through the reeds. Rainy season hasn't started yet, and the swamp is mostly dry. Hence, there are only a few hikers, plus a lady photographer and some birders with binoculars. Then we climb a trail up the mountain, through woods and along mirror-like ponds. We sweat and breathe and put foot before foot in unison. Each step adds to the physical harmony between us and cements us together, and it's inconceivable we might ever be split apart. When we crest the pass, fit older hikers with brand-name hiking gear come our way and greet us with hearty *konnichiwa* and surprised double takes.

"What shall we eat in Nikko?" she asks as we descend on the other side. We had a solid breakfast at the pension but only an *onigiri* each for lunch, and after hours of hiking, we're getting hungry.

"I'm open to anything," I say.

"Hmm, ramen with lots of ingredients on top?"

"That would hit the spot. Preceded by a big piece of watermelon?"

"Followed by sashimi assortment." She lists the kinds of fish she wants in it.

"Or a dry-aged filet, rare, with mashed potatoes and cooked carrots."

"Or shabu-shabu." She mimes picking up a slice of beef and dipping it into boiling broth.

"Arugula salad with grape tomatoes and olive oil."

"Sukiyaki with lots of veggies."

"*Mentaiko* spaghetti."

"A ham-and-butter baguette sandwich like we had in Amboise for our first lunch together."

We descend the mountain, reveling in the idea of food. From the trail-head, we catch a bus down to the tin chalet that is Nikko Station. With forty minutes to spare before the departure of our train, we make a bee-line for the restaurant, a boisterous Formica-steel-and-plastic kind of place. Izumi orders mountain-vegetable pilaf. I order deer sashimi, a mountain specialty. The thin slices of raw deer are served with raw onion rings, fresh garlic, fresh ground ginger, and a vinegar-soy sauce. Possibly the best meat dish I've ever eaten.

But I shouldn't have eaten it. On the train, we face each other—and every time I speak, she dodges my breath. She rummages in her daypack. "Here," she says, stick of gum in her hand. The weekend has been full of harmony and intimacy, but now she hardly talks to me and refuses to hold my hand, constrained also by the two ladies in hiking boots next to us who pay scrupulous attention to everything we do and say.

"A limited express!" she suddenly exclaims at some station, springs up, grabs her daypack, says, *Bai-bai*, see you Wednesday," squeezes through between the knees of the startled ladies, and is out the door.

She dashes with a lot of other people across the platform to a waiting train. It's logical, certainly, but it wasn't planned. Her plan was to stay on the train with me until we got to Kita-Senju in Tokyo, the first stop after Soka, because our express would blow through Soka without stopping. In Kita-Senju, she'd get off and take a limited express back to Soka. That was the plan. Now obviated by events. And the two ladies in hiking boots are inventing their own explanations for all this.

How can the sense of eternal harmony evaporate so fast? How can the cement between us crack so soon? Something inside me got off the train with her and left behind a gaping hole. In Asakusa, I change to the Ginza line. I'm in a daze, groping my way around a vacuum. In Nihombashi, I change to the Tōzai line. How could she be so intimate one minute and so standoffish the next? The upcoming stop should be Ōtemachi. But the sign says something else. It catapults me out of my daze. I'm going the wrong direction. I've gotten on the wrong fucking train.

28

SCRAGGLY RED LINE

pproximately half of Tokyo shuffles in micro steps past the small black-and-white photos at the Robert Doisneau exhibit spread over three average-sized rooms with low ceilings in an office tower. You can't linger in front of a photo because the stream moves you along at a constant speed. You can't discuss what you see or ponder effects. It's stuffy, and the air has been depleted of oxygen. But Izumi soldiers on, oblivious to the situation.

"It's hard to enjoy the photos under these conditions," I whisper.

"What conditions?"

"The crowd, the air, the whole thing."

"That's how it is in Tokyo."

"Unlike Rembrandts, small black-and-white photos look the same in a book."

This puzzles her, and my logic doesn't sink in initially. But when it does, she buckles, and we forsake the masses and go to Kinokunya bookstore nearby and leaf through a Doisneau coffee-table book. The photos are the same as in the gallery, only larger, and we look at them page after page in total leisure and in what seems like a vast space with high ceilings and functioning ventilation. And looking at these photos is free, whereas I paid a good chunk of money for our tickets to the show.

We browse in the gaijin corner. I select two American novels for her and a Japanese novel translated into English for me. She selects *The Makioka Sisters* for me. *Japan's greatest postwar novel,* it says as sort of a subtitle.

"It takes place in prewar Osaka and Kyoto," she says. "It describes in exquisite nuances the pressures that girls had to deal with."

"What kinds of pressures?"

"All kinds. Arranged marriages, for example."

"But that disappeared after the war, didn't it?" I'm leery. This isn't a conversation about a book. She's trying to tell me something.

"People who grew up under the system are still around and pressure girls."

"You mean your parents?"

"My parents aren't that way. They were too young before the war. And I have little contact with older members of my family. Other girls aren't so lucky."

False alarm, possibly.

We end up at a tapas bar. The token Spaniard behind the counter yells greetings and repeats orders in Spanish to parallel the Japanese exclamations of his colleagues. A guy carves uneven slices from a cradle-mounted leg of a pig. We order some portions and a bottle of Rioja.

"Have you ever been to Spain?" I ask.

"Never."

"I haven't either."

"I thought you've been everywhere in Western Europe."

"Except Spain and Portugal."

"Oh."

"Let's go to Spain together someday."

Her eyes sparkle. It means *yes*. I come around the table and sit on the bench with her. She rests her head on my shoulder. And I'm wondering what *The Makioka Sisters* has to do with us.

"I cancelled my Friday appointment so we can be together," she says.

"You did?"

"I did."

I can't believe it. Our relationship is evolving.

Thursday, June 6.

Wouter the Dutch guy's words course through my head like a refrain in a traveler ballad: *You've got to go to Russia, you've got to go see Inga in Irkutsk.* And I'm researching the first steps in that direction at the Maruzen Bookstore in Ochanomizu, which has a gaijin corner with a Lonely Planet shelf. I pull out *Russia*. But next to it are other evocative titles, like *Vietnam, China,* and *Mongolia.* I expand my research. These countries are linked by rail. In theory, you can go by train from Ho Chi Minh City via China, Mongolia, and Russia to Marseille. It's one heck of a distance, it's crazy, but it's doable. Only South Korea—where my ticket is to—isn't linked to anything.

Getting visas will be a nightmare. Then there are the different languages, an even greater nightmare. And there will be risks. It might take two months. But why shouldn't I? I'm not permitted to stay in Japan, and I'm not permitted to enter Izumi's life. Wall Street is underwriting my expenses. I'm forty, and there's no better time than now to draw a scraggly red line halfway around the globe.

Feverish, I step into the swelter outside. The transformation of Tokyo from drab daytime city to nighttime center of energy has already occurred. A flotilla of girls with a whole spectrum of highlights clogs up the sidewalk, while salarymen and *OL* (pronounced *o-eru,* for Office Lady, the latest addition to my vocabulary) try to get around them. I get some iced coffee at a coffee shop and open the *Herald Tribune* to the stock listings to find out how much money I've made.

Biogen. Whoa! Dell. Oh my God! I go through stock after stock. My portfolio has crashed. Those scammers on Wall Street. I hate them! They've stopped hyping their worthless crap. And now they're dumping it to get out of their Ponzi scheme, and I'm left holding the bag. If they keep it up, my broker will issue a margin call and liquidate my portfolio at the worst possible time. It'll ruin everything. I'll have to start over. I'll have to go back and sell cars.

It haunts me, still, hours later, as I peer at my brewski at the gaijin bar in Takadanobaba. Fiasco is staring me in the face.

Darren, wearing his rubber-padded Slickrock hat, sits down next to me, orders a Guinness, and produces a photo of a Japanese girl in a miniskirt.

"She the one you told me about?" I ask.

"Yup. Got a date with her."

"No fucking way! When?"

"Monday."

"I'll be darned. Where are you going to take her?"

"Omotesando."

"What are you going to do?"

"She wants to go shopping."

"Cheers!"

We chink our glasses. He smiles because he thinks he has a date with a hot chick, and I smile because I'm not the only one whom fiasco is staring in the face.

Friday, June 7.

The receptionist at the Weekly Mansion hands me a postcard on my way out. It's from Izumi. On the front is a Botero painting—a fat woman in stockings and bodysuit, sitting on a bed, legs spread apart, banana upright in her hand. It's from the Botero exhibition we attended the other day. Postmarked Shinjuku, June 6. She must have mailed it yesterday morning after leaving my apartment.

My Dear Wolf, you can't imagine how much influence you've had on me!! I love you, every part of you, the way you love me, your sincerity, open-mindedness, active-ness—everything. Every moment we share is valuable for me, and I'd like to share much more time with you. Am I still a tough cookie? Try me. I'm chewable, and your teeth won't break. Thank you for finding me and coming here to see me. All my love.

While I'm waiting for her at a café in Jiyūgaoka, I reread these words for the umpteenth time in an effort to resolve their irresoluble contradictions. For instance, how can she write this and refuse to spend more than a couple of nights a week with me?

She blows in, dabbing her forehead with a folded handkerchief.

"Rainy season starts soon," she says as we greet each other with cropped nods. "It'll be a relief." She helps herself to a gulp of my iced coffee, gives it a second look, and finishes it.

"Can I bite into my tough cookie tonight?"

"You got my postcard?"

"I love it."

We go see the French film *Le Zebre,* and afterward at a dining bar we discuss it, how great it is, how French love stories have a special charm, how they're more honest because they don't have happy endings but French endings that leave you confused and searching for answers. Our lips are moving on autopilot while our hearts are communicating via our fingers that are intertwined across the table. We make the last train back to Takadanobaba and stroll arm in arm to the apartment. While I fiddle with the remote to turn on the AC, she drapes her skirt, pantyhose, and blouse over the TV and writhes into my dress shirt, which she never bothers to unbutton.

"Would you like some scotch?" I ask.

She makes a sound of agreement as she contorts her upper body to wrestle off her bra underneath the shirt.

"It's supposed to be a gift for your dad." I pour two glasses. "It's eighteen years old."

She pulls her bra out of a sleeve. She never tries to provoke me or turn me on or distract me by showing off her assets. If it were up to her, I wouldn't see her body at all, or at least not until we're in the first stages of having sex. But for me foreplay is visual, and I want to enjoy the sublime beauty and seductiveness of her body long before we get serious. Maybe time will allow. Of course, time is precisely what we don't have.

"But I can't give it to him because I won't ever meet him," I say. "So offering you a glass is as close as I'm going to get."

She puts a pillow against the headboard, leans back. I take off my khakis and socks, sit down with her, and hand her a glass. The AC purrs on max. The mood is sweet and intimate. People are getting slashed one by one to the guttural shouts of a very pissed-off samurai next door.

"*Kampai.*" We chink our glasses and take a sip.

"To our future." I sip again.

She looks at me without lifting her glass. A shadow flits over her face.

"We should probably talk about our future," I say.

"Future?"

"Future for us. I need to make some decisions about my travel plans."

"Travel plans?"

"I went to the immigration office last week. A fat white noodle with a British accent told me that Japan doesn't want to be overrun by people like me from all over the world. At any rate, I won't be able to extend my visa."

She holds her glass with lifeless fingers at an oblique angle.

"I have to leave when my visa expires on July 7."

"July 7?"

"Why does that bother you? I don't even know if I'm important to you."

"How can you say such a thing?" Her voice is barely audible.

"How can I? Well, I know nothing about your life. I haven't met any of your friends. I don't know a single name. I haven't met your parents. None of the people in your life know I exist. I'm nothing more than your secret gaijin lover two nights a week."

She seems forlorn, almost spilling her scotch, almost crying, with an element of shock on her face. I take the precariously tilting glass out of her hand and set it on the cabinet next to me.

"Japan doesn't want me, and the girl I love doesn't allow me into her life. It's hard to envision any kind of future for me in Japan."

A tear gains critical mass.

"Reverse the picture. You come to the US to see me. You stay at a motel. I spend two nights a week and an occasional afternoon with you. I never invite you to my place. You never meet my friends. None of them knows you exist. It's the definition of a secret lover."

She's crying because the temporariness of my visit is exacting its toll or because she can't elude the Japanese rules or because of some other reason. I can only speculate why she's crying. In reality, I have no clue.

"In Japan, that's how it is," she says after a while. "We don't introduce people until the relationship is established. Even then we might not."

"Have you considered a future for us outside Japan, since we can't have it in Japan?"

"I can't jump into it." Moments pass. "I wouldn't exclude it."

She has come to the end of what she's going to say. I've run out of words, too, and we sit there in our underwear and shirts. I sip her dad's scotch—my glass, then her glass, and I'm thinking about refills when she straightens up. Her eyes charge up with energy and magic, her lips separate slightly, she inhales barely, prepares to speak. There's a moment of suspenseful silence, and I assume she'll once again keep it all bottled up inside. But something pops.

"I wanted you to stay longer," she says with long pauses between her words, carefully weighing them, not wanting to give away too much. "You were right when you said I don't allow you into my life. I've been thinking about it ever since you brought it up. So I was hoping you could meet my mother during her exhibition on September 20 at the gallery in Ginza. But now you won't be here anymore."

Wow, that's exciting news. I'd get to meet one person in her life, and it would be at a public function where she might only have a few seconds for me, all well-orchestrated to avoid disruption and collateral damage. And the propitious date is three and a half months away.

With that, she has said everything about the subject she's going to say, the subject being the inclusion of me in some fractional part of her Japanese life. Nevertheless, it's an effort. I hug her. She lets herself be hugged, arms hanging down, and then she hugs me back and we kiss. She cries again when we make love, not tears of sadness but tears of pleasure and intensity, or so I speculate. In reality, I have no clue why she's crying again.

29

DNA

Even the normally maniacal crows in the school yard are subdued by the hazy humidity. I'm studying Japanese, which is like peeling the notorious onion. You peel layer after layer in search of some core, something that underlies everything else—something like subject, verb, object in English. Once you figure that out and add a few words, you can speak, not perfectly, but you can communicate. Not so in Japanese. You peel layer after layer in search of that core upon which to construct some basic communication, but no such core lies beneath these layers. And you peel that onion, and you peel and peel until the juice gets into your eyes, and you just want to cry.

The bulge under the covers stirs.

"*Ohayō,*" I whisper into her ear and help her sit up. It's Saturday, and we have time. I fix coffee for her; I finished drinking mine an hour ago. She no longer watches me when I work the French press but leafs through a magazine. Then we sit side by side on the bed, she in my white shirt that brings out her features, and we read and chat.

"I have an idea," I say.

"Idea?" She looks up from her magazine.

"Why don't we go to Vietnam?" I've been thinking about it for a while. July 7, the day I have to leave Japan, is only a month away, and I'm trying to include her in my plans.

"I'd love that. I've always wanted to go to Vietnam."

I show her my Vietnam guidebook, flip to the photos, exotic and alluring each one of them. "We could go in July."

"I can't. My piano recital is on July 23."

"We could go for two weeks and be back by the twenty-first."

"I can't. I need to practice."

"We could meet in Ho Chi Minh City after your recital."

"I have to check my calendar."

"N." Is this a Japanese way of saying no?

"I think it might be possible," she says. It infuses hope. We muse about the trip, whether we should do the south, the north, the highlands, or a combination.

We make it out of the apartment by late morning. Our plan is to picnic at Otomeyama Park. It's another one of my famous ideas. The humidity is so thick you can chew it, and we're sweating instantly. At a 7-Eleven, we buy *onigiri*, *maki-zushi*, seaweed salad, pickled eggplant, and two bottles of chilled *ocha*. Then I lead. I discovered the park on one of my runs. She has never heard of it. I turn this way and that way. I feel practically manly.

The park isn't big—a treed hill with a ravine—but this much dense wild greenery in Tokyo is impressive. We walk down the little trail to the creek. We're alone under the foliage, except for birds and bugs. Legend has it that it's the last area in Tokyo where fireflies can still be seen at night. But before we make it to the creek, a swarm of mosquitoes converges on us. We slap at them, but the more we slap, the more there are. We flee to the top of the hill where vegetation has been cleared around a couple of benches. The spot has views over the neighborhood. Surely, mosquitoes won't come up here. We settle down, dripping with sweat. The humidity is just insane. We unpack our lunch. Suddenly, mosquitoes. Angry, frustrated, hungry mosquitoes in attack mode. And they don't dillydally. They dive-bomb in formation. We scramble our lunch together and flee for good.

Lesson: If you're alone at a seemingly likable spot in Tokyo, you'll soon figure out why.

We sit down on a rusty guardrail that separates a small parking lot from a canal with a trickle of foul water. It's not the most idyllic spot for a picnic. But it's a spot. Then raindrops splatter on the pavement.

Lesson: If you're stupid enough to picnic on the first day of rainy season, at least bring an umbrella.

And this is how my days go. Lessons all day long. Izumi, however, is getting less and less impressed with my ideas.

Monday, June 10.

Satoru-san, wearing a chocolate blazer, cinnamon shirt, and hazel tie, is already at the Nishi-Azabu intersection though I arrive a few minutes before 6 p.m. Taxis barrel into the intersection, discharge passengers, and block the ramps that swoop down from the elevated expressway where traffic has come to a standstill. He greets me with a handshake and a nod amid a stream of pedestrians.

"I'm sorry I'm early," he says. Is this a translation of something that makes sense in Japanese? Or is it one more aspect of the Japanese art of turning apologies into subtle accusations?

"No problem," I say.

"My last appointment—" he waves up Roppongi-dōri. "It finished early."

"You're working a lot for a retired guy."

"It makes my wife happy."

"N."

"Today, I show you Aoyama Cemetery." And he turns around and starts walking.

Unisex bicycles with wire baskets in front, some with baby seats in the rear—*mamachari* they're called—clutter the narrow sidewalk that's already encumbered by random utility poles and signposts, and by scooters here and there, and people thread through it all the best they can. I stay behind him, he stays behind the person in front of him, and we advance in single file until the congestion clears up. Near the cemetery, there's hardly anyone.

When you enter the cemetery, the first thing you see on the left—and you see it first because it's visually so discordant—is a colony of tents made of bright blue industrial tarps strung up between trees, graves, and utility poles. Barefoot guys with craggy faces squat on flattened-out cardboard boxes around a teakettle on a camping stove. Their shoes are lined up neatly on the dirt next to the cardboard.

Satoru-san doesn't see the homeless guys. He peers up the street that runs through the cemetery. "I'm Buddhist," he continues his narration. "But for daily things, I go to Shinto shrine."

"What kind of daily things?"

"I thank the gods, for example, or I ask for good fortune, health, and other things."

We turn into a weedy gravel path. He says he worked for five years in Nagoya as branch chief. "It was the only time in my career when people treated me with respect. I felt like a real boss." With a sheepish grin, he combs his fingers through his hair. "They were the best years in my career."

He stops at a grave. Maybe someone he knew. After a few moments, he moves on. The cemetery covers a gentle hill with surprising views of Tokyo between the trees. It has been raining off and on, and the trees are dripping on us.

"I came to Tokyo once a month for meetings and to visit my wife and two boys."

"Didn't they move with you?"

"It's only two hours by Shinkansen, and we didn't want to disrupt their schooling." He mounts slippery mossy steps.

"My first New Year in Nagoya, I went to Ise Shrine on the other side of the bay. It's one of the oldest, most important Shinto shrines. During the New Year holidays, which last three days, the shrine sells wooden plaques. It was the Year of the Dragon, so the plaques were decorated with a dragon. I bought one, but instead of writing my request on it and hanging it up at the shrine, I kept it as a souvenir." Near the top of the hill, he stops. "Old Christian graves," he says. Indeed: crosses, gaijin names, and inscriptions I can read. "I went to Ise Shrine every New Year's while I was in Nagoya. During those years, I never had an accident and never got sick."

"Because of the shrine visits?"

"I don't think so. I was just careful."

The setting sun breaches a hole in the clouds near the horizon behind distant high-rises, and the underside of the morose cloud cover catches fire—an astonishing sight.

"Did you know this would happen?" I ask.

"Not know."

Moments later, the show is over, and we meander away from the Christian graves.

"The first New Year's back in Tokyo, I didn't go to Ise Shrine," he goes on. "It was too far and troublesome. On day one, I felt fine. On day two, I felt fine. But the morning of day three, my gut was churning, and I felt miserable. So I took the Shinkansen to Nagoya and went to Ise Shrine. Immediately, I felt better. Now I go to Ise Shrine every New Year, usually with my wife, and a few times with the boys. I have a stack like this of wooden plaques." He holds up his hands about a foot apart. "One for each year."

"Why Ise Shrine? Can't you go to a major shrine in Tokyo?"

"It's in my DNA."

Wednesday, June 12.

Amazing how much I want to be with Izumi. She can't, she says, stay away from home more than two nights a week, though I see her more often. Occasionally, she turns up at the apartment after class, and we make love. Or we meet somewhere and eat or go to exhibitions, museums, and movies. But only twice a week can we be together overnight.

Today she comes by in the afternoon. I fix coffee. We lounge on the bed and thumb through her new Japanese guidebook for Vietnam. Typical for Japanese guidebooks, it contains a large food section whose mouthwatering photos of beautifully arranged dishes make us *ooh* and *aah,* and soon we're kissing. Her mere presence makes me desperate. Afterward we're lying on top of the sheets, naked, cooling off. Four pages of the food section have gotten creased somehow. She pouts and blames me as she's trying to flatten them out, and we talk about Vietnam and our trip, and we try to plan it a little, when bad omens appear in her eyes.

That worries me. To get her to open up, I tell her three stories about girlfriends I took on trips, years apart, and after each trip, the relationship—surprise, surprise—was over. I maintain a jocular tone, though inside I'm serious because the bad omens in her eyes are palpable. One girl refused to sleep with me after our return though she assured me that everything was hunky-dory, that she just didn't feel like it. After six weeks of no sex, even I acknowledged that it was over. Another girl called me two days after we got back and told me she was getting married to her next-door neighbor, and I had to listen to her discourse on why, in a marriage, friendship was more important than love, something she knew a lot about and had experience with because she'd been married twice already. And so on. But Izumi doesn't think my stories are very funny, and neither do I.

"So, are you too going to drop me after our trip?" I continue in my jocular tone.

"Drop you?"

"Is our Vietnam trip a test that I will invariably fail?"

Moisture fills her eyes.

"What's wrong?"

She clams up, can't speak.

"Why are you crying?"

She rigidifies. Something is going on in her mind, something burdens her, and she isn't telling me. I hold her, and eventually she wipes her cheeks with her fingertips and asks something unrelated, like whether to spend more time in Hanoi and skip the highlands or whatever, and she never replies, and I don't pursue it. The shadow passes. We chat about different things and plan our weekend getaway to Bōsō-hantō, the peninsula that separates Tokyo Bay from the Pacific. She calls the pension we've picked out of my guidebook and makes a reservation. Then she looks at her watch.

"I need to get ready," she says.

"Cancel your appointment and stay with me."

"I can't."

I knew that. I didn't have to ask. It's getting dark outside, and the unlimited possibilities of Tokyo at night are calling her.

"*Mendokusai,*" she says, pronouncing the expression like a regretful sigh. It means "too much hassle" or "not worth the trouble." She always says it when she has to get up. But she does get up. She rinses off, gets dressed, puts on makeup, and wafts out. What lingers are her faint smells, the imprint of her body on the bed, a few long black hairs curving over the sheets, and the bad omens.

30

GAIJIN FLING

U ntil today, *tetrapod* didn't mean a heck of a lot to me. Creepy four-limbed bugs came to mind, but not much more. Today, we take a train to the Pacific coast of the Bōsō-hantō peninsula and hike along the coast. Deserted beach resorts alternate with cliffs and forgotten fishing villages where fish is drying on racks. But the vile stench of fermenting fish—some Japanese are said to appreciate it—is merely a background detail in the face of the tetrapods.

They're giant four-limbed ferroconcrete structures, and they're jumbled into an endless upside-down millipede that snakes along the edge of the water up and down the coast as far as the eye can see. The purpose is to break the force of a tsunami before it slams into dreary beach hotels, villages, and reeking fish racks. I didn't expect a pristine coast, but I did hope for a strip of nature where the ocean meets the land. Along designated beaches, the tetrapods are a few hundred feet out at sea. In theory, you can swim in the protected waters between them and the beach.

In theory—because in reality, Izumi and I are having a conversation.

"Let's go swimming," I suggest after dipping my hand into the water.

"The water is too cold," she says.

"No, it's perfect."

"You shouldn't go swimming now."

"Why not?"

"The season hasn't started yet."

"When does it start?"

"In July."

"The Pacific looks pretty full to me. It has plenty of water to go swimming in. I don't see any need to wait till July."

"We don't go swimming before the season starts."

And it's true. There isn't a soul in sight, and the hotel behind us is boarded up.

"I have to wait two weeks before I can get in?"

"It's better."

"But we're going back to Tokyo tomorrow."

"That's how it is in Japan."

As there are no witnesses, I rebel against the incomprehensible regimen of rules, the *yarikata* that govern every goddamn thing you do in Japan, and I dash into the glorious illicit water while Izumi pretends she doesn't know me. When I come up for air and look toward the horizon of the Pacific, all I see are, um, tetrapods.

Even the dining room of our pension has a tetrapod view, though dinner, served at 6 p.m., is a heavenly sequence of clam chowder, sea snails, sashimi assortment, sole meunière, baby octopus and cucumber salad, grated daikon with salmon roe, and so on. We eat with knife and fork, spoon, and chopsticks, however we see fit.

We go for a romantic moonlight stroll along the concrete seawall in front of our pension. Emboldened by alcohol and the cloak of darkness, I get her to violate a rule: we climb from the seawall onto one of the limbs of the adjacent tangle of tetrapods. We sit down on the limb and listen to the water splash and resonate beneath us. Soon we're necking and petting like high school kids because we're afraid of falling off and breaking our necks if we make love.

In the morning, we hike through the coastal hills. Midafternoon, starving, we land at a tiny sushi bar in a fishing village. The chef welcomes us loudly. The only other patrons are three guys slouching at the counter, who stir when they see me. I'm quite the attraction. One of them touches my arm.

"Kebin Kosunā," he says.

I don't get it.

He talks to Izumi, and they both laugh.

"He says you look like Kebin Kosunā," she says to me.

Mired in the tar pit of gaijin ignorance, I still don't get it.

"The American actor," she says.

"Oh, Kevin Costner." Now I also have to laugh because Kevin Costner doesn't look at all like me, other than that he's white and taller than anyone else in the sushi bar.

"Ānorudo Shuwarutsunegā," the chef says.

I don't get it either.

"The big actor," Izumi says.

"Oh, Arnold Schwarzenegger. Not him! He's twice my size," I say in Japanese.

It's hilarious to them, the fact that I can say something in Japanese.

"Richādo Gia," a guy at the counter blurts out. They applaud and laugh, even the chef. "Richādo Gia," they shout.

But alas, the American actor that does resemble me isn't famous for his handsome features but for his villainous roles.

Soon I'm the center of a vivid conversation between the three guys, the chef, and Izumi. They laugh, and I laugh too because their laughs are infectious.

"What are they saying?" I ask her after a while.

"They want to know how it is with a gaijin."

"How what is?"

"You know."

"No, I don't know."

"They want to know if, um, if you, um, if your ... is as big as they say."

"What did you tell them?"

"I just laughed."

Monday, June 17.

At 9 a.m. I call Izumi. I've been calling her in the mornings when I have trouble with my Japanese-only textbook. I can ask her in English, and she replies in English, which my teachers refuse to do. Plus, she has the same textbook, so it's easy for her to help me figure things out over the phone. As several times before, her mother, Yoshioka-san, answers the phone, and we exchange fixed expressions. I ask in Japanese how she's doing, comment with tag questions on the heat and humidity and on how much it rained last night, and wonder if it might rain again today.

She calls me Urufu-san but doesn't know the role I'm playing in Izumi's life. I assume she thinks I'm some foreign student who needs help. She plays along, however, and when I add two fixed expressions that I learned yesterday, she thinks I can understand real Japanese and chatters a hundred miles an hour. I enjoy talking with her. It seems she enjoys it too, and we've bonded in a vague manner. Maybe she senses something more complex is going on, and just maybe, she's giving me her tacit support.

When it becomes clear to her that I don't understand a word, we both chuckle, and I ask for Izumi.

In the background, feet pitter-patter down the stairs. Whispering in Japanese.

"One moment," Izumi says. Rapid steps, a door. *"Yoisho,"* she breathes into the phone, which means she's settled down someplace comfortable.

"Where are you?"

"Back in bed."

I tell her the page number and ask her to translate the instructions, which she does. Then I ask her about some kanji I can't read. The phone beeps.

"I'm getting another call," she says and puts me on hold.

But I'm not on hold for long.

"I have an important call on the other line," she says, confused and stressed, unable to separate English from Japanese.

"No problem. Thanks for your help—"

But she has already hung up.

Without doubt, whoever called her is infinitely more important than her secret gaijin lover. I need to remember that. I need to be prepared for the moment when the bad omens turn into reality. I need to steel myself for it. Because, in her overall scheme of things, I don't count. That much is clear. I don't need to know who counts, but I will need to remind myself when the time comes that it isn't me.

Tuesday, June 18.

Ji is the word for "hemorrhoid." I looked it up. The sound is identical to *chi,* which means "blood," and only the Japanese can distinguish between them. My problem is that I've run out of hemorrhoid ointment. Hemorrhoids only get worse, and ointments don't work. They're merely one more way for big pharma to transfer wealth from you to them. And to keep that stream of wealth flowing in the right direction, they brainwash you with their ads. It's called marketing.

Hemorrhoid ointments have one positive side effect, however: they give you the illusory satisfaction of doing something. Thus, they help your mind more than your anus. Like plain Vaseline, they also make it easier to stuff your hemorrhoids back in after you get off the john. And so I've looked up the vocabulary necessary to buy ointment for *ji*, and I've practiced my phrases for several hours.

A wiry lady in a lab coat, the only person in the small pharmacy, greets me apprehensively. I greet her in my best Japanese.

"I'm sorry to trouble you," I add, a fixed expression used in front of a question. It comes out smoothly, and I feel more confident.

Her apprehension grows.

"Do you have ointment for *ji*?"

Instead of bustling off to get it, she asks me something in return.

I apologize. Did I just ask for ointment for blood, and it didn't make sense to her? Or maybe she has ointment for blood and wants to know which brand I want? Or which size? I repeat my question, slightly changing the sound of *ji*, hoping to get it right. She asks me something different in return. God, I wish I understood real Japanese. I apologize and repeat my question. Now *she* apologizes and says several long sentences.

This isn't what I expected. I scratch my head. She looks at my hair, thinks I have lice. I stop scratching my head. I have three options. I can continue until one of us runs out of patience. I can put my finger on the spot where the ointment for *ji* is to be applied and hope for the best. Or, I can come back with Izumi. I select option three, though it poses its own set of challenges—the very challenges I specifically wanted to avoid. I smile, apologize, bow, and humbly back out the door.

When I meet Izumi in the evening, I don't mention the episode. It'll be a daytime conversation. Dinner and hemorrhoids don't go together. We eat at an *izakaya* in Takadanobaba and mull over our plans for Vietnam. Portions arrive one after the other, cucumber and seaweed salad, sliced duck breast, boiled spinach in sesame sauce, and slimy noodles that turn out to be seaweed. Each bite is delectable, even at a low-key *izakaya* like this.

"Eating with you is so much fun," she says, eyes sparkling, cheeks flush with pleasure as we pick the fatty, practically gooey, incredibly tasty meat out of a grilled salmon head that has been cut in half. Chopsticks are perfect for that. I order another round of draft beer, one of the few items I can order with aplomb. I'm in a philosophical mood and want to explore the unexplorable.

"I've been laboring over some thoughts," I begin.

"Thoughts?"

"I understand you need to keep me out of your Japanese life, so I appreciate every morsel that you tell me about your friends, though I certainly don't need to know any details."

Her chopsticks with a lump of fatty salmon between them halt in midair.

"And I know I can't have a monopoly over you. That's not what I want anyway. I'm immensely happy when we're together, which is what matters the most. The fact that we aren't together much is the price I have to pay, and I'm willing to pay it."

She puts the fatty lump down on her plate.

"For the time being, I'm willing to share you with whoever else is in your life."

She lays down her chopsticks. My comments have stimulated something in her.

I drink my beer.

"Actually—" she says.

Actually is unexpected. It fibrillates my heart. I try to drink my beer, try to appear casual.

"There is—" She searches for the right words, controls each syllable.

I wipe beer off my chin.

"Another option."

It's happening. This is it. The very moment when shit hits the fan.

"Two weeks before you came, a college friend told me he'd broken up with his girlfriend." She's choosing words, lining them up, rearranging them. "When I asked him why, he confessed his feelings."

"Confessed his feelings?"

"Yes."

"About what?"

"Me."

"Oh."

"He's trustworthy and reliable. I've known him for years. He's thirty. He wants to build a relationship that leads to marriage. He isn't interested in any other kind of relationship at this stage in his life. This systematic approach is meaningful to me. I respect it. I have to take it seriously. I can't dismiss it. I'm twenty-six. I have to think about these things."

"What's his name?"

"Watanabe-san."

"Watanabe-san." Articulating the most ordinary name in Japan, the outright symbol of inoffensive commonness, has a peculiar effect on me.

"I told him a foreign friend would come to Tokyo. I told him we'd planned this for half a year, and I asked him for time. He suggested a month. I told him it wouldn't be enough. So he said he'd wait for three months."

I need clarity before I can talk. I need to get out of the fog. In summary, her trustworthy, reliable future husband has been waiting in the wings all along. They agreed on a three-month moratorium while I'm in town. In addition to being trustworthy and reliable, he's also magnanimous.

"The three months are going to be up," she says.

"N."

"I'm not in love with him. Being in love doesn't happen often."

"N."

"I'm in love with you."

"N."

"I like him a lot."

"N."

"Actually, I'm not sure how I feel about him."

"You desire him?"

"Desire?"

"Physically."

"*Physically?*" She glares at me.

I order two more draft beers, and when I'm finished with the waitress, I've come to grips with Watanabe-san.

"Obviously, Watanabe-san is a trustworthy, reliable friend you respect. Those are crucial elements in marriage. Don't judge him by the initial sexual relationship. Allow him to grow into it. Give him a chance." Never before in my life have I said so much horseshit.

"What are you talking about?" she says.

We let this ferment. I stare alternately at my beer and at Izumi, who now is upset too. She has attempted to prepare me for this, not only with *The Makioka Sisters* but in oblique ways with references, bad omens, *N*s, and silences. And yet, inexplicably, I'm still not prepared.

"It's like an arranged marriage," I say. "It's logical. It makes sense."

"Yes, but we arrange it ourselves. Many young people do it that way."

I go to the restroom, insert myself sideways through the door. I'm not sure what a bigger guy has to do to get in. Go head first? And carefully. And let people know where you're going so they can find you and pry you out. All I want is some fucking clarity. I don't remember whether I've come to pee or to vomit. My three months with her are almost up. It won't be a disaster for her. She has a good option. Beyond doubt, he's the reason she has kept me away from her friends. They know him, and she doesn't want her two parallel men to have vicarious cross contact. I respect that. Her life will switch back to the Japanese track. Till then, I'm her gaijin fling. I respect that too. There's nothing wrong with being a fling.

By the time I return to the table, I've regained perspective.

"I'm comfortable with what you told me," I say. "It explains a lot. And you have a good option. It makes me feel better." The amount of horseshit coming out of my mouth astonishes even me.

For us, everything will come to a logical conclusion, a conclusion that doesn't have *us* in it. I wonder what will be next. How do you move on from here? How do you get out of this hole?

She opens the menu and says, "Hmm, what else shall we eat?" She has moved on. She orders chopped horse mackerel. She talks about practicing for her recital. Her words pass through me. I respond, possibly in a normal way. And by the time we sprint hand in hand through the rain to the apartment, a fatalistic lightheadedness has set in. I know my three months with her will be up soon. I know I can't stay. I know I can't let go of her. I know without her I'll lose my moorings. And I know I can never reconcile any of this.

31

KING OF TAKADANOBABA

I ask Izumi to help me with buying hemorrhoid ointment. She's bent over the TV to get closer to the mirror on the wall. She doesn't know *hemorrhoid*. I explain it. It doesn't make sense to her.

"*Ji* in Japanese," I say.

"What?"

"*Ji.*"

"How do you spell it?"

"J-I."

"No, the hemmolloid thing." She puts her mascara brush down.

I spell it. She pulls her 1,340-page Bible-paper dictionary out of her purse and looks it up.

"Oh, *ji*!" she exclaims.

"That's what I said."

"No, you said *ji*."

"Anyway, you know what it is?"

"I've heard of it. Something old people get." And that launches a thought process that is so intense it permeates her skull and becomes visible as micro-wrinkles across her forehead. She's grasping something. Until this very moment, I've been able to masquerade as a physically flawless male specimen. But now the truth has been revealed: I'm a man of a certain age with a mounting tab for having been alive this long. Not a pleasant thought for a girl her age.

"I tried to buy some, but the pharmacist kept asking me questions I didn't understand."

"I can tell you what to say."

"It won't work. She'll ask me to death again. Can't you come with me?"

"Is it really necessary?"

At lunchtime, we meet for a quick bite to eat then scurry to the pharmacy. The pharmacist is relieved I've summoned competent help. Instead of requesting ointment for *ji*, as I did, Izumi embarks on a long-winded discourse. Her voice is high-pitched and subservient from twenty-six years of training and hundreds of years of breeding. The pharmacist whispers several sentences. Izumi responds, also in a whisper. *Yarikata,* the way to do. Back and forth. They nod with increasing intensity. A consensus develops. The pharmacist disappears between the shelves and reappears with three products. I choose a box based on its familiar color scheme. She wraps it in plain paper, Scotch-tapes the paper, slips it into a paper bag, folds and tapes the bag, and slips it into a plastic bag. In her normal voice, now that the offending object has been concealed, she names the price. I pay, and all of us are thrilled the situation has been successfully brought behind us.

Outside, when Izumi switches back to English, her voice drops an octave. That she'll marry Watanabe-san hasn't cropped up again, though there isn't much else on my mind. He's presentable, responsible, reliable, trustworthy, etc. And magnanimous. She'll introduce him to friends and family. He fits into the Japanese fabric. He can read menus and order even difficult items with aplomb. He can buy ointment for *ji* on his own. He's perfect. Neither love nor passion, two forbidden fruits in Japan, will mar the acceptability of their relationship. They'll make a baby. It's all governed by *yarikata*.

She'll be busy with the orderly integration of their offspring into Japanese society, while he'll purchase his sex at the ubiquitous establishments set up for that very purpose. He'll turn over his paycheck to her, and she'll manage the household finances. For the next thirty-five years, she'll see him only briefly in the mornings and at night. Their marriage will be harmonious on the surface, as prescribed by *yarikata*, and sexless. She'll be buried at home. Cemetery of life, they call it.

I can never offer her any of this. As gaijin, even if I wanted to, I wouldn't have a chance. And love—that dippy notion we Westerners trip over so frequently—doesn't mean squat in the Japanese scheme of things. They don't even have a word for it. But being accepted by society means everything. Yet she's of the generation that's supposed to be free from these strictures and have options previous generations didn't have.

However, grudging respect is due Watanabe-san who graciously granted his future wife three months to finish her dalliance with a gaijin. How much self-confidence must he have to endure this? How much trust in the system must he have to believe he'll win? Does he think he's gambling? Or does he think it's a done deal? For sure, the man has balls. Or he's naïve. Or he knows what he's doing and doesn't need balls.

Thursday, June 20.
I call Izumi to get help with my Japanese. Yoshioka-san answers the phone, and we exchange fixed expressions. My mastery of them encourages her to sally forth into unscripted territory. I say *"Hai, hai, hai,"* which encourages her even more, though I don't understand a word because I don't understand real Japanese. Clearly, she enjoys talking to me. And unlike Izumi, she makes an effort to speak Japanese with me. I've come to look forward to these conversations. When she catches on to the fact that she's talking to someone dumber than a motor mount, she laughs, and I laugh too, and then I ask for Izumi.

"Wait a short while please," she says, which is a fixed expression. Once again, we're on familiar territory.

Izumi is still in bed, apparently, and Yoshioka-san carries the phone up to her.

"Hello?" Her voice is sweet and thick with sleep. We chat a little. With each word, her process of waking up advances, and her voice becomes firmer and clearer. She helps me with the Japanese instructions in my textbook and solves a grammatical enigma. When we're done, and when we're at the point where we normally say *bai-bai*, she says instead, "I can't go to Vietnam."

"You can't? Why?"

"I have a scheduling conflict."

"N."

She seems upset and apologizes a million times.

"It's alright," I say mechanically. "Don't worry about it." I've been studying Japanese since 6 a.m. I'm prepared to handle grammar and vocabulary issues, but not this.

"I'm sorry," she says again.

But the thing she doesn't say is what her scheduling conflict entails. Nor does she offer alternate dates—a week later, a month later, a shorter stay. You can get around a scheduling conflict if you want to, but she doesn't want to. She has decided that there won't be an extension to my three months with her, that they'll be up once and for all on July 7. Maybe Watanabe-san has become nervous after all and has given her an ultimatum.

"I'm a big boy," I say. "I can handle it."

Friday, June 21.

Should Tokyoites ever be overcome by an urge to live in a city that is aesthetically pleasing during daylight, they'll have to plow Tokyo under and start over. Walk down any street. Pandemic ugliness. And it's not for lack of money. The Japanese deserve better. But they're programmed to bear what they're dealt so that their sacrifice can benefit the greater good, namely Japan Inc. They're also programmed to avoid conflict and confrontation, so they close their eyes to the ugliness around them; thus, it ceases to exist.

Exhibit A: the buildings on Waseda-dōri. The sidewalk is congested with people, and no one looks up to see what's above them because they know they're better off not looking. Are architects required by law to design buildings that are this drab?

This is what I'm thinking when I wander into a hair salon situated on the ground floor of Exhibit A. The three male stylists, including the one who has a client, holler a long greeting. The one in the back ushers me into his chair. Having crammed haircut vocabulary beforehand, I describe in Japanese what kind of cut I want. Nonplussed, he asks me something. I repeat my description. He asks me another incomprehensible thing. I do the male thing: I grunt and nod. He asks something else. I grunt and nod. And off we go.

He hands me a hot wet towel—somewhat larger than the *oshibori* you get in every restaurant. What am I supposed to do with it? Clean my hands? But this is a hair salon. Put it on my face? That's what I do, and it feels awesome, opulent even—until he takes it away from me. And so it goes, from one mystery to the next.

The procedure includes a double wash, a scalp massage, a precision cut, a shave with a straight razor, a blow-dry, and a neck and shoulder massage executed with fists and elbows. Throughout, he puckers his face in fierce concentration. I'm so dazzled by this treatment and by the expression on his face that I forget to look at my haircut. I pay, and it doesn't sink in how much. And when I leave, the three stylists bow low and holler long polite phrases after me, king of Takadanobaba.

Monday, June 24.
Satoru-san is already at the *izakaya* near Mita Station when I get there, and I'm early. Despite the swelter, he's unflinchingly dapper in his charcoal blazer, gray shirt, and silver tie. "I'm sorry I'm early," he says, perhaps his standard greeting when he isn't late, which he probably never is.

Unlike Izumi, he doesn't dither over a menu. He doesn't have to unravel the whole damn thing before making up his mind. He orders faster than the waitress can write.

"Dark draft beer?" he asks me.

"Sure."

"I benefit from my freedom," he says with his sheepish grin. "My wife doesn't allow me to drink. Like many Japanese, I lack the enzyme that breaks down alcohol."

And we talk. Or rather, he talks. And when he asks me to, I help him with vocabulary. He swerves into health issues. He and his wife are walking three times a week because the government has been promoting it.

"Recently, they started promoting weight lifting for older people. So I've joined a gym for retirees." He flexes his bicep, but nothing visible happens under his jacket. "At any rate, one man in our group always tries to push the maximum weight, and he grunts and makes this face." He makes an ukiyo-e grimace of bulging eyes and contorted lips. "He tries to be, how do you say, macho. He forgets we're old men. Last week, he grunted and made this face, when—" He gestures breaking a stick with his hands.

"He broke the weight?"

"No, a bone."

He sheds his jacket, loosens his tie, and rolls up his sleeves. His face reddens. "The missing enzyme," he explains. He orders more items without asking me and flirts with the waitress. He scours his memory for big words and constructs entire stories around them.

"When I take photos, I like being in nature, and I try to unite with it," he says. "It's good for my, how do you say, mental equilibrium."

I reward his efforts with a nod and a smile. "Do you do photo shows?"

"Oh no. I'm a Sunday photographer. Even my wife refuses to look at my photos. So I don't get them printed anymore. I just like taking them."

"Now that's what I call a hobby."

"I believe there are two kinds of Sunday photographers. One takes photos of birds and plants. He won't be successful. Birds and plants don't change. Years later, someone else can take a better photo. The other takes photos of Fuji-san. He will be very successful when the top of Fuji-san blows off and photos are the only thing left of the mountain."

The crags around his eyes deepen. He orders *ocha* to round off the meal. He slurps his tea, which isn't that hot and doesn't need to be slurped. "It tastes better if you slurp it," he says. So we both slurp tea. He nods, satisfied with my progress.

Outside, his face glows like the red lantern by the door.

"Do you have time on Monday, 15 July?" he asks.

"I'll be in Korea."

"When are you coming back?"

"I might not."

"*N.*"

And we part ways with a handshake and a nod. No phone number. No address. Only memories.

32

BUN IN THE OVEN

Izumi hangs her purse on the backrest of a chair and sits down with a sigh, dabbing at her nose and forehead with a folded and ironed handkerchief.

"Ryōko is getting married," she says.

"Who is Ryōko?"

She reaches for my glass of iced coffee.

"I'll buy you one." I get up and buy her a glass at the counter. It's hot and humid out there, and if I don't get her something cold right now, I can kiss my iced coffee good-bye. When I put the glass in front of her, she takes several audible gulps.

"Aah," she says and sets the glass down. "Ryōko is one of my ex-colleagues. She grew up in Brazil and attended international schools. Returnees like her often don't fit in. Their Japanese skills aren't sufficient. They disregard rules—"

"Oh no!"

"People resent their forwardness."

"Oh my God, they're forward?"

"Yes, but she isn't that way. She has overcome all that." And she tells me that Ryōko met her fiancé's parents during Golden Week, something she'd dreaded and delayed for three years. His parents are traditional. As expected, the entire event, which had been choreographed based on ancient customs, was a disaster.

Then there's another ex-colleague, Hiro, a guy who fell in love with Thailand, learned Thai, moved to Bangkok, and married a Thai girl. "He came back a month ago on business, and seven of us former colleagues had dinner together."

And on and on. She's breathlessly recounting vignettes that have real people in them with names. And I'm speechless.

"Tonight, I want to show you a special sushi bar," she says. "It's an insider place."

It's near Shiinamachi Station. A handful of people queue outside in the rain. When it's our turn, we duck through the door—the door is so low even she has to duck. The sushi chef chants a greeting. We squeeze onto two of the eight barstools that are sandwiched between the counter and the wall and order his specials posted on wooden plaques on the wall behind him.

He writes nothing down. He fillets fish, butterflies shrimp, slices an octopus arm, molds rice, and assembles sushi pieces—all while accepting new orders. He reaches over the counter and places the first few pieces on our boards. There are no chopsticks. You eat with your fingers. He works with precision and speed and places more pieces on our boards and on the boards of others.

I ask him for more ginger. He reaches over the counter and plants a dollop on my board. He doesn't ignore me and doesn't pay particular attention to me but treats me like a regular dude. A rare honor.

"I invite you to my room," Izumi says.

I'm stunned. Sweet raw shrimp dissolves on my tongue.

"Next Tuesday?"

"Awesome."

"You might meet my mother."

It's a gigantic leap forward. Or more likely, a farewell gift.

The only drink is *ocha*. I slurp because it tastes better that way. The guy next to me also slurps. We have something in common. We nod imperceptibly. A bond of sorts. Two slurping guys at some sushi dive. I feel integrated.

"Please don't slurp," Izumi says.

"Why?"

"*Oyaji* do that,"

Oyaji are uncool middle-aged men, despised and ridiculed by every girl in Tokyo. You never, ever want to be called *oyaji* by a girl. It's absolutely the worst thing that can happen to you in Tokyo.

Sated, we vacate our spots. Insiders know this isn't a place to hang out after the meal. "You eat and leave," she says. The chef tells me the price. It isn't nearly enough. But I pay, and he accepts my money without demur.

"He miscalculated," I say outside in the rain. "It's way too cheap."

"It's his normal price. Once you know this place, it's hard to eat sushi anywhere else."

She hooks her arm under my arm that is holding up the umbrella. Tokyo's transformation from daytime sea of ugliness to nighttime center of flashing energy has already happened. I'm in heaven. I had a delightful meal at an insider place, and she has granted me a peek into her life.

"I love you," I say into her ear.

"Which reminds me," she says, "I need to get some facial cleanser."

We cross the street to an am/pm, and she buys a bottle of whatever. Back outside, she says, "It seems you were telling me something."

"Um, I can't remember. Must not have been important."

Thursday, June 27.

Our long weekend in the Bandai-san area begins with cropped nods at Asakusa Station, where we meet at 9 a.m. Rather than taking the faster JR line, we execute another one of my ideas and take the Tobu line north past Nikko through the mountains to Aizu Tajima and then change to the single-track Aizu Tetsudo line.

The self-propelled railcar hugs steep forested mountainsides and meadows that drop from view, and it stops at villages without stations. On uphill climbs, the diesel motor under our feet knocks and vibrates, and everything rattles. But when the engineer, decked out in uniform and white gloves, throttles back the motor on downhill stretches, the noise abates, and you can hear the wheels hitting the expansion joints. *Clickety-click, clickety-clack,* they go.

I love trains like this. They infect me with travel fever, and I dream of spending days or weeks crossing some vast continent to the relaxing rhythm of the wheels. Kids in school uniforms run around giggling and pointing at me. Others stare at me from a safe distance. A girl gets up her courage and approaches me.

"Where are you from?" she asks in Japanese.

"America."

"Where are you going?"

"Bandai-san."

"What are you doing here?"

"I'm studying Japanese. Are you studying English?"

"Not yet." She smiles, backs away. She has exhausted her courage, and I my Japanese.

The train terminates at Aizu Wakamatsu, famous for the twenty teenage samurai who committed seppuku on a hill nearby in 1868 during the Boshin War. One of them survived and told their story. They saw smoke and assumed Tsuruga-jō, their castle, had been set on fire and their lord killed. So they did what their loyalty code required of them. They were mistaken, however. The castle wasn't burned down until six years later, and their lord lived into old age.

We visit Tsuruga-jō the next day. Its stone walls and moats have survived the fire, but the wooden superstructure with its five-story keep is a replica. We visit lacquerware and pottery workshops, a samurai house, and a sake brewery. Groggy from the sake tasting, we take a bus up to the Bandai-san plateau and get off at a cluster of nondescript buildings, one of which is the *ryokan* where we have reservations.

A woman in kimono welcomes us with a stream of verbiage while we take off our shoes and put on the infamous one-size-fits-all-Japanese vinyl slippers. She leads us upstairs. It's a bit drab, for the money. But when she opens the door to our room, we enter a different world.

A Japanese-style room. Posts and beams of polished wood. Sliding doors of wood and rice paper between the entrance area and the tatami area. An ink-brush mural. A calligraphy scroll in an alcove. She recites a litany of rules. *"Hai, hai, hai,"* Izumi says. Tatami with edging made of gold and indigo brocade. Low lacquer table and two legless chairs in the center. Scent of dried rush. Reed fibers embedded in the walls. A window area with plank floor, two rattan chairs, and a rattan table. View of the garden—a rivulet cascades between shrubs, mosses, and rocks.

The woman bows, backs off the tatami, steps into her slippers, and backs out the door. Izumi brews *ocha* with hot water from the thermos. We sip it and eat the tiny sweets that are artfully arrayed on a lacquer plate. And we're infused with a cosmic sense of *aah.*

A *ryokan* is a procedure, not just a building. The next step, after rules, *ocha,* and *aah,* is the bath downstairs, one for men, the other for women. I've boned up on the *yarikata* of the bath and know how to do—until I sit down on one of the low plastic stools in the wash area and discover I don't recognize the katakana on the three dispensing bottles. Perhaps they're using fancier terms, like *head and shoulders* or whatever instead of the plain *shampoo,* which I'd recognize.

The three guys simmering up to their necks in the pool are scoping me out. They've heard stories about the size of gaijin equipment, and now they want to see for themselves. One of them carries a folded washrag on his scalp. I shampoo with whatever is in the mauve bottle, and when my eyes are closed, I swear I hear snickering. As per *yarikata,* I scrub myself with whatever is in the pink bottle and rinse off thoroughly.

Then I inch into the steaming pool. Near-boiling volcanic water gurgles from a rock outlet into it. You can barely see the garden through the fogged-up floor-to-ceiling windows, and condensation drips from the ceiling. Another guy arrives, perfunctorily splashes some water on his torso, and gets in the pool. He doesn't touch the three bottles, doesn't scrub himself, doesn't wash his hair. What about *yarikata?* Mystery after mystery.

The climax is dinner, which is served in our room. Dressed in identical, crisply pressed yukata from the *ryokan*—that's the way you dress for dinner at a *ryokan*—we sit on legless chairs and watch the two waitresses as they overlay our table with a profusion of handcrafted bowls, plates, and pots. They explain each delicacy, and when they're finished with their presentation, they bow, back off the tatami, step into their slippers, bow again, and shuffle out backward. We pour each other sake, strategize sequences, and eat one bite here, one bite there, luxuriating in the panoply of flavors, textures, colors, and aromas.

"Your hair looks different," she says an hour into it. She isn't very observant. If I shaved my head, she might not notice for half a day.

"I think I washed it with antibacterial body soap."

"Why?"

"Gaijin error." One in an endless series.

In 1888, Bandai-san erupted and blew off its top. It annihilated entire villages, filled in valleys, dammed up creeks, and created a plateau of marshes—now Bandai Asahi National Park. Its crown jewels are a series of mineral ponds with stupendous colors. We go see them on Saturday and hike some other scenic trails. At night, we check into a pension to escape the confiscatory rates of our *ryokan*. Sunday morning, it's raining. We slow-walk breakfast at the pension and read in our room (sounds of teeth being brushed filter through the wall, another testimony to Japanese construction technologies). It's still raining when we sprint to a ramen shop for lunch. But when we come out, the rain has stopped.

We rent mountain bikes and ride up a muddy road into Nakatsugawa Gorge until we get to a sign on the other side of an old tunnel that warns of landslides. We stop. My point is that we can go on because the sign is rusting and has been there forever and is therefore not applicable to today. Her point is that a sign is a sign. This being irrefutable, and also nonnegotiable, we turn around. But the tension is superseded by laughter as we descend at full speed, purposefully splashing like little kids through puddles and sending mud flying every which way.

"I can't go to dinner like this," she says when we're back in our room. She looks down on her mud-caked jeans.

"Well, put on something else."

"That's all I have."

But she has a plan. Which is to read in bed while I do laundry downstairs, based on the logic that she doesn't have anything to wear to do laundry in. I take off my muddy jeans, put on my shorts, and carry our clothes down to the laundry room. But my good intentions collide with the kanji instructions on the machines and the three sheets of supplemental handwritten instructions taped to the wall. Japan, the country of endless instructions.

"I need your help," I say back in our room and toss her my khakis. She puts them on. They're colossal on her.

"I'm not leaving this room," she says.

"You look foxy in them."

"I don't want to look foxy, and I'm not leaving this room."

"You can wear them to dinner if you don't want to wear your muddy jeans."

We shuttle to the laundry together. While our clothes are in the dryer, we take a bath downstairs. We even make it to dinner on time, a six-course

French meal. It's the beginning of the countdown, though we don't mention it. Our last Sunday night together.

Monday, July 1.
On the JR express back to Tokyo, she dozes off. It's evening, and we've had an active day. We're ideal travel companions and thrive on physical activity, nature, food, and reading on rainy mornings. And yet, in six days, she'll be Watanabe-san's. A juxtaposition of facts that are not juxtaposable. He accompanies us wherever we go, though I'm able to get rid of him for a few hours here and there. Then he's back, a shadowy figure, watching us with disinterest and patience, knowing his turn is coming.

And I steel myself for the moment she has to get off the train. But when she gets off, it's still too sudden, and I haven't steeled myself nearly enough.

At midnight, I call Don Colson from the pay phone outside the Weekly Mansion. I don't use the phone in my room for international calls. Weekly Mansion rates are exorbitant, and they've rigged the system so it blocks my calling card.

It's good to hear his voice. My condo is fine, he says. A maintenance guy broke down the door because he heard water dripping inside. He'd apparently misheard, but for a few weeks the busted door was all that separated the hallway from my belongings.

"When I came by and saw it, I threw a hissy fit," Don says. "But it still took them a week to fix it."

"Thanks for your help."

"No problem. Want to know the latest?"

"Sure."

"Ginger's got a bun in the oven."

"N."

33

SANCTUM SANCTORUM

Izumi picks me up at Soka Station. We walk down the main street, then some side streets, then a street that runs along an open fifteen-foot-wide concrete sewer canal. It's part of Soka's network of open sewer canals. Pumps and sluice gates flush river water through them and disgorge the mix untreated back into the river—a common system in Japan, and no one seems to be outraged by it. Izumi pointedly ignores it; therefore, it ceases to exist. She's telling me the story of her house. Her parents built it in the seventies and later added three rooms upstairs. It's a one-generation house to be replaced by a new structure in thirty years. We cross a bridge over the sewer canal. She's right: you're far better off ignoring it. But whatever you do, don't look at what's floating in and on the liquid. As we zigzag through some alleys, a woman pedals by on a *mamachari*, groceries in the wire basket in front, a boy in the baby seat in back. Someone rhythmically whacks a futon. We back against a wall to let a mini-truck pass. Neither linear Western roofs nor curvy-pointy Japanese roofs have chimneys. She lets go of my hand.

"Why?" I ask.

"The neighbors have enough to gossip about."

At a house made of bluish prefab materials, she unlocks the door and calls out *"Tadaima,"* an expression you call out whenever you enter your own home. All manner of shoes are scattered in the low area of the entry. More are crammed into a shoe rack. Slippers are lined up against the edge of the elevated area. A leafy plant, a clock, some brochures, two books, newspapers, pens, a notepad, and a collection of knickknacks are more or less arranged on a credenza against the wall. A coat rack full of coats and jackets occupies the opposite wall.

Rapid-fire Japanese bursts from the back of the house, and seconds later, a woman in a brown short-sleeved blouse, an olive skirt, and flowery pink slippers scuffs around the corner. Yoshioka-san. She crackles with spirit and energy, her hands fly about, and she nods and laughs and shakes her wavy collar-length hair. Her eyes that dart between Izumi and me instantly perceive everything. You can't hide anything from a woman like her. We exchange fixed expressions. She offers me corduroy guest slippers.

All this is a bit awkward for me as I'm still bent over from the hip, trying to untie the double knots of my shoelaces. Japanese, who constantly have to take off their shoes, never untie shoelaces. They keep them loosely tied and slip in and out of their shoes at will. For them, shoelaces are just decoration, as evidenced by the laced-up shoes around me.

We follow Yoshioka-san into a small living room and sit down at opposite ends of the black leather loveseat, as far apart as possible, a charade we produce for her. She talks alternately to me and to Izumi at warp speed and boils over with effervescence while she brews and serves *ocha*. Instead of relaxing on the matching chair or ottoman, she fidgets on the piano stool next to the Queen Anne china cabinet. The piano stool belongs to the Yamaha upright jammed in between the back of our loveseat and the wall.

When she addresses me, she does so at a more casual linguistic level than the polite level I've studied, which is certainly appropriate, but a lot of the words change, and I don't even recognize her verbs as verbs. Once it becomes clear that communicating with me in Japanese is hopeless, they banter with each other. Her voice runs up and down the register to convey surprise, pleasure, or concern.

"She's glad you came," Izumi translates after several minutes.

I ask if I can see one of her dolls. She jumps up, runs out, and seconds later places a stooped fifteen-inch man with ruddy cheeks on the coffee table. He buries his hands in the pockets of his herringbone overcoat and smiles at a dachshund that is dressed in a tartan vest. His face and posture recount his life. The details are exquisite. I half expect him to bend over and pet the dog.

"This is totally good," I say because I haven't learned the word for *awesome* yet.

She gushes with excitement and points with her pinky at specific areas, how she crafted his face from cloth and what she did to shape each wrinkle and dimple.

"She's particular about details," Izumi translates.

Sushi is delivered. I had some *onigiri* in Tokyo because I didn't expect lunch, but there's always room for sushi. Yoshioka-san eats a piece, flits in and out, unable to sit still. When she does sit still, they discuss me and fish, from what I understand.

"She's pleased you enjoy a variety of seafood, not only salmon and tuna," Izumi says.

While they're talking, an appliance in the corner catches my attention. A portable kerosene space heater with electronic dials. When it's on, it exhausts its fumes into the room. Which solves the mystery of why houses don't have chimneys. They don't need them because the Japanese don't mind breathing toxic fumes. Then the china cabinet catches my attention. It houses a TV, some crystal, three bottles of cognac, a set of gold-rimmed china teacups, some souvenirs, and surprisingly, a ten-volume set of leather-bound books.

"What are these books?" I ask in Japanese at the next opportunity.

My question baffles them. They confer with each other.

"We don't know," Izumi says.

"Can I take a look?"

"*Hai, hai, dōzo,*" they say in unison, laughing at my silliness.

It's a massive anthology of historical essays in English from the late 1800s to the early 1900s, some of them translated from French and other languages. I tell Izumi. While she recounts my findings in Japanese, Yoshioka-san makes a long chesty sound of wonderment that starts low and rises two octaves.

"Who in your family is interested in this?" I ask in Japanese.

They have a drawn-out exchange. Yoshioka-san's voice rises and falls several octaves in a single breath, similar to the chanter in a Bunraku play.

"We have no idea," Izumi says in English. "We've had it forever. We don't know where it came from. Maybe it was part of an inheritance. For us, it's just decoration."

When I have to go to the bathroom, Izumi shows me the way. A computerized john! She delves into its features—temperature settings for the seat, temperature and power settings for water to be sprayed at your bottom, front or back, man or woman—though they're inapplicable to my situation. I recognize two kanji, *big* and *little*. At least something makes sense.

"We just got it," she says. "It's quite practical."

"I understand, but I want to do this by myself."

She retreats. I do my thing, succeed in activating the *little* flush, and remember to exchange the orange plastic toilet slippers that have to stay inside the bathroom for my corduroy slippers that I left outside the bathroom. I find the niche in the corridor where the washbasin is and remember to duck under the rail of the accordion door. I wash my hands. Triumphant because I've accomplished so much without disrupting the household, I step back into the corridor. *BANG!* An explosive clatter shoots through the house. I see stars, grope for what hit me on the head. The fucking rail of the accordion door.

They blast out of the living room. I apologize profusely for the structural damage I've done to their house. They ask if I'm okay and apologize for the accordion door and console me, and when the tohubohu settles down, Izumi asks with a smile that promises mysterious treasures, "Shall we go to my room?"

We climb a steep staircase that leads to a single door and take off our slippers. With some ceremony, she opens the door. A girl's room. I'm not sure I can define the girl touches, but they're everywhere. It's a corner room, larger than the living room, with two big windows whose sliding metal shutters rattle softly in the wind. It has a twin bed, a desk, a chair, a component stereo system with a TV, bookshelves, an electronic piano, a chest, mementoes, more things, boxes, a clothes rack—yet there's still some open floor space. And there she stands, smiling, in the middle of her sanctum sanctorum.

I inhale her molecules. Clearly, she fought a ferocious battle to tidy up, and traces of skirmishes she lost are evident here and there. I can tell she isn't neat by nature. We sprawl on the floor and flip through photo albums. She names friends and tells stories. And there's her father, a handsome man with two little girls. But he'll never be allowed to know about my existence and about the deviant ways of his daughter. I try to kiss and undress her.

"Not in my room," she says categorically.

She plays piano. I sit on the floor and listen. She's perched on the edge of the piano stool, back arched, concentrating. I'm inside her soul, cosmically comfortable, and wonder why she kept all this from me for so long.

A jingle and then a female voice emanate from a speaker horn on a utility pole not far from the house.

"It tells children it's time to go home," she says. "And it's time for us, too."

Otherwise her sister, who is two years older and also lives at home, might see me. Or her father might. Which would be, I don't know what—shocking, embarrassing, chaos producing. His younger daughter with a gaijin!

Downstairs, I exchange a few fixed expressions with Yoshioka-san, and while I'm bent over to tie my shoelaces, she avalanches me with Japanese.

"She wants you to come back," Izumi translates.

We smile and exclaim more fixed expressions and bow a bit and say *bai-bai* and wave as Izumi and I back out.

Izumi takes one of the two *mamachari* that are leaning against the side of the house and pushes it as we walk back to the station. She's smiling, and she seems proud and happy that the whole event went so well.

"That was awesome, being in your home and meeting your mother."

"She likes you."

"I can't believe how much energy she has." The only problem is that I won't see her again. Does Izumi have the same train of thought? I doubt it.

"She spends every free minute in her studio," she says. "I'm a total fan of her work."

And Watanabe's shadow hovers behind us. Son of a gun!

Outside the station, our lips barely brush. She mounts her *mamachari,* rides over the curb, across the street, up the curb, and weaves on the sidewalk between pedestrians, other bicyclists, utility poles, signposts, and store placards, her tiny ass seesawing on the saddle with each stroke.

Saturday, July 6.

I've done the legwork for my onward trip—including getting visas for Vietnam and China. But I couldn't get a visa for Mongolia. They don't issue visas to independent travelers, the lady at the consulate told me. That's the first official setback.

Because the guidebooks say that credit cards are useless in most of Asia and that you should have lots of dollars in all denominations on you, I walk into my local Sumitomo Bank branch to get a major cash advance on my credit card—the clerk inhales between his teeth with a conscientious hissing sound as he aligns the stacks of dollars in front of me, each stack of bills sealed in plastic pouches that have the Sumitomo logo printed on them. Back at the apartment, I deposit some of them in a money belt to be worn inside my underwear, hide others in my daypack, and stuff the remainder into the sock that contains the roll of dollars I brought from home. It's called diversification of assets.

And one morning, Takadanobaba Girl jars me out of my thoughts as she steps from the shadow of the JR underpass. She walks toward me. Our eyes meet above the stream of black hair. She smiles. I want to tell her that I'm leaving, that I won't see her again. I want to wish her good luck with whatever she's doing in Takadanobaba. But no sounds come out of my mouth. She doesn't even slow down anymore. She has given up waiting for my words. Her breasts bounce past me, and she's gone.

I've been meeting Izumi practically every day. She's canceling appointments, rearranging her schedule, and somersaulting through hoops in order to be with me, now that we're running out of time. Every day has a melancholic tinge.

Yesterday afternoon, she came by, leaned her dripping umbrella against the wall by the door, planted a kiss on my mouth, and handed me a bottle of wine. I recognized it: one of the bottles of Chenin Blanc she bought at the wine-tasting in Vouvray the day we met. She draped her skirt over the TV while I opened the bottle, and soon we were wrapped around each other. You can't help thinking she's trying to make up for the opportunities she has squandered. At any rate, I'm blooming under her new dedication.

Last night, we went to a dining bar at the top of an office tower. Our table was by a window. Beneath us was the neon spectacle of Shinjuku. A dish of horse mackerel sashimi was decorated with a single *shiso* leaf. With my chopsticks, I tore the leaf into two neat halves and deposited one half on her plate.

"Wow, you've mastered the way of chopsticks," she said.

"Oh no, I have a long way to go," I said with a big smile.

Yet I still had to ask a waiter which of the three doors was the men's room because I couldn't read enough kanji to decipher the writing on them.

After breakfast, I pack a big box. At the bottom, I layer French and Japanese novels and books on ukiyo-e, Japanese sacred architecture, Japan Inc. and its corruption, and Japanese sexual practices as researched, I don't know how, by a Brit. Then, as I add the linen jacket and other stuff I bought, a piece of paper with a name and a phone number tumbles to the floor. Uehara Yasuyo. She approached me at Ikebukuro Station, a friendly soul in a confusing world. I should have stayed on the train with her. I should have had a cup of coffee with her. At least, I should have called her. I chuck the piece of paper into the trashcan.

I expect Izumi to start crying as she watches me prepare for departure. But she doesn't cry. She doesn't even watch me. She watches a cooking show on TV, a close-up of five dumplings dancing in boiling broth.

I lug the box to the post office and send it home. At lunch, we chat as always. Perhaps we interlace our fingers more tightly than normal, but overall no one can surmise that this is our last afternoon together.

"How much longer are you going to travel?" she asks back at the apartment as I'm working the French press.

"Four months."

"That long?"

"From Vietnam to Marseille overland is a long ways. And I'm planning to go hiking in the Dolomites with my brother. In October, I'm doing another homestay in la Fare les Oliviers, same family as last year. After that, I'm finished."

"I envy you."

I envy you is a translation of a fixed expression. Why she says it eludes me. Weeks ago, I suggested she travel with me through Russia to France. It meant nothing to her. We planned on doing Vietnam together, but she cancelled. Instead of envying me, she could be traveling with me.

"What are you going to do when you get home?" she asks.

"Haven't thought about it."

I know exactly what's going on. She's comparing me one last time to Watanabe-san, who has a solid career, predictable income, recognition in society, etc. I can never beat him on his turf, and it makes zero sense to try. I hand her a mug of coffee. But we don't finish our coffee. We're desperate. Or I'm desperate, and she's going along.

Then we don't have the energy to go far, and we don't want to be on a train where we can't touch. So we lumber to a dining bar five minutes away. It's intimate and dim. The barman remembers us from our prior visits. We've become regulars. We drink a bottle of Côte du Rhône. I'm excited about Korea and Vietnam and whatever comes afterward and blabber about it. Yet I know I'll miss her, and I know Watanabe-san's shadow will hover nearby every time I think of her. And there's no contradiction and no dilemma in any of this because there's nothing to choose and nothing to decide.

"Do you want me to write while I'm on the road?" I'm hedging. She'll be with Watanabe-san and might not welcome hearing from me.

"I'd love that. And how can I reach you?"

"At my brother's in Germany. I'll be there for only a day or two around September 10. So if you want me to receive your letter, you have to make sure it gets there before I do."

And as I'm speaking, an ingenious plan materializes before my eyes: Grammar as a Weapon. The Japanese prize vagueness above all and consider personal pronouns unnecessary and forward, even confrontational. On the suspicion something might be obvious, they omit it. This linguistic self-effacement and obfuscation is, to the never-ending perplexity of the American learner, part of grammar. And I'll use that very grammar against Watanabe-san. He can't say *I love you* in Japanese. He has to eliminate the personal pronouns *I* and *you*. And *love* doesn't exist in Japanese. It's expressed with *big like*. But *big* is still too forward, so he has to omit it. Thus, if his heart demands he say *I love you*, he has to say *Like*. She'll understand, and it won't be necessary to say more. Yet for her, it won't be the same. She longs for *I love you*, and she'll get it from me, in my letters, postcards, and phone calls—and maybe she'll rebel against the rules and strictures of her society and against the odious *yarikata,* and maybe she'll pursue her passion. Voilà, my plan.

34

WISHFUL THINKING

Rain makes irregular metallic dripping sounds. Crows caw in the school yard. Male and female voices of a talk show bounce up and down next door. We're lying in bed, entwined. Tears roll over her cheek, and I kiss them away. She wrests herself out of my embrace, sits up, and carefully adjusts her right contact lens. Which stops her tears.

I fix coffee as usual, but nothing is usual. It's our last breakfast together. Every act is melancholic. While she's in the shower, I do the dishes and empty the fridge. When she comes out of the shower, she's wearing my moist white shirt that brings out her features.

"Can I keep it?" she says. "It'll remind me of our leisurely mornings."

"I want you to keep it."

Now I can imagine her in her room, after her bath, dressed only in my shirt, though I know she'll never do that. She'll just keep it as a memento hidden in a box somewhere. No way that she'll ever expose herself to members of her family in a shirt that sports my name in indelible grease pen on the bottom of its front tail—written by hand at the cleaners back home. And most certainly, Watanabe-san will never be allowed to see it.

I pack while she gets dressed. I cram some socks into the porcelain mug with foliate motif that I bought in Ekoda on my first day, wrap it with a

T-shirt, and stow it in my duffle bag. It'll be my travel mug. I wrap wine-glasses, French press, tea set, and the other coffee mug with the wet towel Izumi used and put them into a plastic sack. She has agreed to take them.

"Why is the rice in the trash can?" she says.

"It's left over."

"You can't throw rice away."

"I can't?"

"Rice is sacred."

"Oh, sorry." I pull the bag of rice out of the trash can. It weighs at least eight pounds. "What am I supposed to do with it? Take it to Korea with me?"

"I'll take it."

"You think it's worth lugging across Tokyo?"

"We don't throw rice away. We treat it with respect."

We deposit the monstrous plastic sack—monstrous because it now also contains eight pounds of sacred rice—at the reception. She'll retrieve it later.

"Today is Tanabata, the Star Festival," she says on the train to Narita Airport. "Do you know?"

And she tells me the story. According to Chinese legend, there was a weaver princess, Vega, who wove the most beautiful robes out of clouds. She fell in love with Altair, a simple cowherd, and their love was so strong that her father, the Emperor, allowed her to marry him. But when her love caused her to neglect her weaving, the Emperor banished them to opposite shores of a big river, the Milky Way. Only one day a year were they allowed to cross the river and be together. That day was Tanabata. But if it rained on Tanabata, the river would swell up, and they'd have to wait another year.

I wonder what the message is. All her stories have a message. *The Makioka Sisters* did—a powerful message, namely her self-arranged marriage to Watanabe-san—and I didn't get it. Is it that Vega and Altair can never again be with each other because Tanabata is in the middle of rainy season, and each year the river will be swollen, and they'll have to wait another year? Is that her message? That sense of false hope?

From that point on, we fall into long stretches of silence. I'm thinking how unbearable her situation must be—to trade in a guy you love for a guy society hands you. And I know she loves me because her body loves me, and her body can't lie; that much I'm sure of. The rest I'm speculating on.

Urban ugliness under a gray sky rushes by the rain-streaked window. We sit facing each other. She's serious but not sad, and occasionally she smiles. Our legs touch. I don't speculate on what she's thinking. That would be too painful.

But in the background behind these convoluted morose thoughts, something else is happening: I'm vibrating with excitement. I'm going to Korea and then to Vietnam. And from the Mekong Delta, I'll be traveling north overland to Hanoi and on to China and, if I can get a visa, across Mongolia to Siberia. Then I'll turn west. I'll cross Russia, the largest country on earth, and won't stop traveling until I get to Marseille at the southern end of France. I'll dive into the cultures along the way and meet people and see their lands, and I can't think of anything I'd rather do, outside of being with Izumi—but that's not an option.

We go up to the departure area and hug and kiss at the barrier. People with baggage stream by. Her tears moisten my upper lip, and this time there's no contact lens to fix. The temptation is enormous to utter palliative promises no one can keep. Yet I'm searching for something to say to soothe the wounds, something that isn't a promise, something that conveys some sort of hope, but nothing comes to mind because there's no hope that has *us* in it. But then my mouth goes off on its own.

"We'll meet again," it says. It doesn't make sense, and it isn't a promise. It's a hunch at best, or wishful thinking or a dream.

Her lips form a thin smile. And it isn't a response.

We separate. I pick up my bag and pass the barrier, turn around, wave, and she waves, and we turn around and go on with our lives.

I don't come out of the stupor until bus 601 from Kempo International Airport to the Insadong area in central Seoul dies on a ramp inside the airport. Welcome to Korea. We sit in the swelter while the driver tries to flag down the next 601. It doesn't stop. But the second one does. As I climb in, the driver of the dead bus says to me, "Excuse me." But he doesn't say anything to the Korean passengers.

We stand in the aisle. My next task is to get off at the correct stop. Stops aren't announced, and the writing on the bus-stop signs is so small you have to be within a few feet to read it, but it's in Korean, so you can't read it anyway. Even if you could, you can't get to the exit because people and luggage block the aisle. Nor can you count stops, as you can on a subway; if no one gets on or off, the bus blows through without stopping, and you never know there was a stop, which happens at the first two or three stops, and my count is already off.

To solve the problem, I need to do something radical. I ask the girl whose side I'm awkwardly pressed against if she speaks English. "No," she says, which is encouraging. I show her my bus map, put my finger on my stop, and ask her to tell me when I need to get off. She studies the map, nods. Hers isn't the only body I'm pressed against, but our exchange has detached the shield of anonymity, and we're both relieved when she nudges me a stop in advance to go fight my way toward the exit.

From the bus stop on Chongno Avenue, it's a few minutes on foot to the Central Hotel, the least costly hotel the travel agency in Tokyo had on its list of "international hotels." I made a reservation for only one night, figuring that once in Seoul I'd look for a *yogwan,* a cheaper type of inn. It's a rundown place whose only signs of life are a clerk at the reception and four Russian guys under a sign that says *Turkish Bath.* I drop off my duffle bag and go reconnoitering.

Buses and cars clog up the streets and honk, and people agitate on sidewalks—a welcome whiff of unruliness after three months of iron discipline in Tokyo. The subway into the center is a cinch; everything is bilingual. On the street, it's a different matter. Like in Tokyo, addresses are based on a numbered block system, and few streets have names. But unlike in Tokyo, where it's hard enough to find things, the block system here is further handicapped by out-of-sequence building numbers. Building 298, for example, might be next to building 4. Some sort of chronological order. You can't find anything based on addresses, my guidebook warns correctly.

However, every time I unfold my map, someone stops and tries to help. At City Hall Plaza, a mega intersection crossable via a maze of tunnels, I don't come out at the right exit. I unfold my map. A girl with a rectilinear body stops and asks in English if she can help. I tell her the name of a high-rise building—due to the absence of a functional address system, everyone uses landmarks.

"Go in tunnel, turn left—" She reconsiders. "I show you," she says.

We reenter the tunnel system. She introduces herself. Mee-Young is her name, which I try to pronounce several times, and each time she guffaws.

"My boss trades with New York," she says. "Sometimes I have to talk with the Americans. But I don't understand them. I need to practice

English." She graduated with a degree in merchandising, and this is her first job. Her sentences dribble out like this:

"I was happy, how you say, money on finish of month?"

"Paycheck."

"Paycheck?"

"Yes, paycheck."

"I was happy get first paycheck."

We exit the tunnel system.

"My boss is mad because someone messed up. I'm afraid of him. He's strict and old-fashioned. As punishment, we all have to stay late next week and redo everything."

She lives with her parents. Her older sister has gotten married recently. "I'm twenty-three and don't have pressure yet. That starts at twenty-six," she says. "Korean girls are conservative. They like one man. You understand what I mean?"

Why is she telling me this? Is it discouragement or encouragement? Is she drawing a line in the sand, or is she promoting her faithfulness?

"I understand," I say.

My first impressions of Seoul. I circle back to find a *yogwan*. As I stroll up Insadonggil past cafés and antique shops, I recognize a *yogwan* sign on a two-story building at the far end of an alley. Two men in slacks and short-sleeved white shirts stand in front of it. One of them wears a tie and has a briefcase in his hand. They stop chatting.

"Are you American?" says the one with the briefcase.

"Yes."

"That's good."

He barrages me with questions—what state I'm from, where I'm going, and so on—and doesn't let up until I ask him similar questions. Floodgates open. He's from Puyo. He's a professor at a university in Taejon and studied linguistics in Florida for four years. His name is Sung-uk Kim.

"Mr. Kim," he helps me out as we shake hands.

I'm distracted by the brick steeple behind the *yogwan*, an unexpected sight.

"It's a church," Mr. Kim says. "Thirty percent of Koreans are Christians. I'm proud of that, though I'm Buddhist. The mix makes Korea a free society, unlike China. The Chinese may be okay, but I don't want anything to do with the Japanese. Americans are best."

"Actually, I'm looking for a room for a few nights, starting tomorrow."

Mr. Kim says something to the other man. "He's the owner," he says to me.

The owner smiles broadly, and we shake hands. He leads us up the exterior steps, past two-foot-tall earthen kimchi jars, to a hallway. "My family," he says about the first two doors, which are open. In one room, two children in T-shirts and track pants are napping on top of a blanket spread out on the vinyl floor. Then he shows us two rooms upstairs, one Korean style with a sleep-on-the-vinyl-floor arrangement, the other Western style with a double bed.

"Only the Western room is available," Mr. Kim says. "It's a fine inn. I'm staying here, too. I recommend it."

The bed has a bottom sheet, no top sheet, and a silky quilt-like blanket. A GE air conditioner blocks the small window. The owner switches on the TV and clicks through several flickering Korean channels to prove it works. The walls of the tiny bathroom are decorated with black mold and triangular flies.

"The room has everything," says Mr. Kim, who has taken over the selling process. "It's quiet because there's no traffic. And the price is correct."

"How much?" I ask the owner.

"25,000 won," Mr. Kim says.

I pull out my credit card. They both laugh. When the hilarity of my credit card has worn off, I count out the cash. We all smile, and the owner and I shake hands again. On the way out, he demonstrates how to use his homemade aquarium-like water filtration contraption by the entry, which appears to be more dilapidated, with things taped and wired together, than effective. And those are the only formalities.

Mr. Kim suggests we go to a tearoom down the alley. It's an atmospheric place with low tables and ottomans. The waitress, ecstatic to have an American in front of her, practices her few words of English on me—until he cuts her off in Korean. We sip pine-needle tea.

"I want to attend a linguistics conference in California," he says. "I came to Seoul on Friday to apply for a visa, but the US Consulate rejected my application. I'll try again tomorrow. If they don't give me a visa tomorrow, I can't go to California for the conference. I don't understand why they give me these hassles." He praises American universities, which are the best in the world, and raves about the fun he had, and a breath later, he laments

American morals, or rather the absence thereof. "I want my sons to go to college in America," he concludes, "but I want them to grow up in Korea so they learn morals."

When the waitress lays the check on the table, I go for it, but his right hand nails down my arm while his left nabs the check.

"He who gets the check has the honor of paying," he says, holding it up triumphantly.

"At least let me pay my part."

"Now that's incredibly rude and obnoxious."

"What is?"

"Offering to pay your part."

A few hours in Seoul, and I'm already responsible for a cultural calamity. But we overcome this somehow. We stroll around. It's almost 9 p.m., and I'm starving. I invite him to dinner, but he'll have to choose the restaurant, I say, because I can't tell a restaurant from a plain door in a wall. He accepts, and at the only restaurant that I recognize as such due to its shop-window full of plastic *soba* dishes, he says, "Here's your Japanese restaurant. They're becoming very popular."

It looks like a chain restaurant, down to the three girls in identical shirts behind the counter. As in Japan, the illuminated menu board has photos of each dish, but the writing is in Hangul, and the numbers are in Chinese. We're the only patrons. I'd rather eat at a Korean restaurant, but we're already inside, and I can't figure out how to unobnoxiously ask him to choose a different place. Perhaps he's trying to do me a favor because I mentioned I'd spent three months in Japan. He helps me order, but when it's his turn, he doesn't order for himself. "I'm not hungry after all," he says.

I eat while he talks, and I wonder why he isn't eating with me, whether cultural differences, despite his years in Florida, have caused a problem between us, or whether he just isn't hungry, or whether my stay in Japan has rubbed him the wrong way, or whether he misunderstood my invitation and didn't want to get suckered into paying for dinner.

One of the girls takes away my glass of ice water. Surely she'll refill it and bring it back. But she doesn't.

I concentrate on eating with stainless-steel chopsticks, a devilish invention. They're so slippery that eating noodles with them is impossible. Thank God for the spoon—something you don't get in a *soba-ya* in Japan because you're supposed to lift the bowl with both hands to your mouth and slurp the broth. But with the help of the spoon, I'm actually able to get some of the noodles into my mouth.

Until the waitress comes back and takes my spoon away.

"What's going on?" I ask him.

"They're closing. It's nine o'clock."

This is one complication too many, and I capitulate, though I haven't eaten half my noodles.

"Call me when you're in Taejon," he says once we're outside. "I'll take you to an authentic Korean barbecue restaurant. Every foreigner has to eat Korean barbecue at least once." He writes down a phone number. "I might be in the States. But try anyway."

The day that began in bed with Izumi ends alone in my room at the Central Hotel where a six-foot-tall red Hangul syllable is blinking outside my window. Twelve hours without her are like a week. Is she telling Watanabe-san this very moment that I've departed?

A winch with harness on a hook by the window catches my attention. The steel cable from the winch is fastened to the wall. Instructions are in Korean, Russian, German, English, French, and Japanese. A fire-escape device. You strap on the harness, climb out the window with the winch in your hands, and let yourself down. The device seems to be for one person. What do you do with your wife or lover? Sacrifice her? I lift the winch off the hook. It must weigh thirty pounds. I think about letting myself down the seven floors to the street and hand-cranking myself back up. While I diddle with it, I glimpse at Izumi, sitting on the bed, dressed only in my moist white shirt, observing me the way she does when I diddle with mechanical devices. I'm going nuts already.

35

ABSURD DEGREE OF FREEDOM

A pudgy woman in red pumps, navy skirt, and white blouse chases after the bus as it pulls out of the express bus terminal in Sokcho. The driver stops and lets her board. Her luggage is a hefty purse. She scans the available seats, sees me, does a nearly imperceptible double take, and maneuvers her fanny into the seat next to me. Her gold necklaces and bracelets clink faintly. Her makeup is subtle compared to the theatrical makeup of girls in Seoul, with their black-lined lips and all. An accountant at Hyundai, perhaps.

She doesn't speak English, not even *yes* or *no*. I switch to Korean and my phrase book. We establish after a tedious struggle that she's on her way to Pohang and I on my way to Kyongju via Pohang. After that we give up; it's simply too exhausting.

The road winds like an endless roller coaster along the mountainous coast of the East Sea, as the Sea of Japan is called in Korea. Trees alternate with sweeping vistas of whitecaps, cliffs, and desolate beaches dotted with concrete barriers, concertina wire, antennas protruding from bushes, and half-buried pillboxes. And beyond the haze of the choppy sea is Japan, where Izumi and Watanabe-san are doing their Sunday morning thing.

Koreans have a special place in their collective heart for the Japanese. I learned that in Seoul. Every English-speaking guide chick you listen to so raptly in temples and palaces talks about the Japanese at length and portrays with unforgiving bitterness the ravages they perpetrated when they ruled Korea from 1905 to 1945—though I imagine that the Japanese-speaking guide chicks tone it down a bit for the throngs of Japanese tourists.

I also learned about Japanese prices. Those are the posted prices in museum shops. They're sky-high, and I must have raised my eyebrows. An observant saleslady rushed over and whispered in English, "Don't worry. Japanese prices. You pay a lot less." A form of multigenerational stealth reparations.

During my five days in Seoul, I met Koreans who wanted to practice English and foreigners who flocked to the sights. I even had a date with Mee-Young, the rectilinear girl I met the first day. She insisted on having a baked potato at Wendy's, an incomprehensible choice amid the wonderful food culture in Seoul. Then we promenaded. Our last stop was a café on Chongno, where they kicked us out at midnight when all bars and cafés closed simultaneously.

Mayhem reigned on the street. Subways and buses had stopped running, and people formed a wall at the edge of the sidewalk and yelled their destinations at the taxis rolling by. Mee-Young wriggled into the lineup and also started yelling. Occasionally, a taxi would stop, and someone in the lineup would pile on top of the people already in the taxi. If too many people needed to go the direction the taxi was going, brief scuffles broke out. A policeman in the middle of the street flagellated his arms and blew a whistle, but he was just decoration. Suddenly, Mee-Young got tangled up in one of the scuffles, and when the taxi pulled away, she was in it along with a bunch of other people.

The next morning I called the number Mr. Kim, my Ekoda roommate, had given me.

"Mr. Kim, please," I said to the woman who answered the phone.

"Yes, excuse me. Many Mr. Kim."

"The engineer Mr. Kim."

"Yes. This is engineering company. Many engineers."

"I'm sorry. The engineer Mr. Kim who was in Tokyo last April."

"Yes, thank you." She connected me.

"Hello," I said. "Are you Mr. Kim, my roommate in Tokyo?"

"Roommate?"

"Were you in Tokyo last April?"

"Yes."

"Did you live in Ekoda?"

"I'm sorry." Click.

Wouter the Dutch guy was right: staying in touch is an illusion.

The sun comes out, but the East Sea isn't a blinding blue surface that stretches into the horizon, like the Pacific on a sunny day. It's grayish green, cold and hostile. We're two hours into the ride along this harsh stunning coast, and I'm gazing at the waves when my neighbor shifts in her seat, rubs her thigh against mine. A startling sensation, a woman you don't know rubbing her thigh against yours and not pulling it away. Her shoulder touches my arm. I'm wired. She wants to talk. She wants my phrase book. She flips through it, scours it for useable phrases, but doesn't accomplish anything by the time the bus pulls into a rest stop. We get off, and she disappears. The cool briny breeze from the East Sea is a godsend after the smoggy swelter of Seoul.

Back on the bus, she hands me two cans of beer and a bag of rice crackers. I'm surprised, uncertain. What am I supposed to do with this? With a gesture, she urges me to drink. I hesitate. How do you deal with this politely? Refuse three times before accepting? Offer her one of the cans so we can drink together? Or would that be incredibly rude and obnoxious? So I say *thank you* in Korean and start drinking. She rewards me with a smile.

It stimulates further efforts. She finds a useful Korean phrase in my phrase book and puts her finger on the English. *How old are you?* I flash my ten fingers four times. She nods, adds two fingers. She's forty-two. I find the Korean word for *children.* She holds up her index finger. She has one. She points at me. A boy. She counts on her fingers. Seventeen. She has no husband. Whether she's widowed, divorced, or single is beyond our communication tools. I'm into the second can of beer she keeps nudging me to drink, when she takes my hand and presses it on her breast.

"Um—" I say.

She says something, repeats it, repeats it again. A question. She shortens it. What is she asking me? She shortens it further, strips it down to a single word. *Sex?* She lets go of my hand on her breast and searches feverishly in the phrase book but finds nothing. I search the phrase book as well but can't find anything on the subject either. Unbelievable that they'd print a phrase book that doesn't have anything about sex in it, not even the word *sex*, though it has a whole section on dating. *Do you mind if I smoke? Have you got a light?* I mean, come on.

She looks around the bus, but there's no privacy, not even on the back bench. She must be starved for sex. Korean society is strict on women. I'm a foreigner. With me, she can have an affair. No one will know. She wants to get banged, and she has chosen me to do it. Sometimes life is elegantly simple if you let it be.

She cups her hand over my crotch.

Waves roll up a sandy cove bordered by cliffs. Farther out, the choppy grayish-green sea fades into haze.

She makes an appreciative sound.

Maybe she isn't an accountant at Hyundai. Her hand on my crotch is unnerving and pleasurable at the same time. It renders my brain dysfunctional.

She repeats the word.

Money? I ransack the phrase book. *Money* is so basic, so fundamental to every aspect of our lives, but it isn't in the goddamn phrase book. *Credit card, currency exchange, traveler checks, dollars, pounds*, and *cashier* are, however. I can't think of anything more useless than this phrase book. Our entire society is based on sex and money—and they aren't in the phrase book.

Rhythmic changes of pressure.

I want her to continue. I want her to stop. I give up flipping through the phrase book.

She kisses me—perhaps to humor my Western desire to be kissed. She must have watched some Hollywood movies. But Koreans of her generation don't kiss. That's what I've read, and her kiss is proof. She sticks her wooden tongue into my mouth and leaves it there unattended. And her lips are lifeless, too. I don't need to do this again. But her hand is unnerving.

She says that word again.

Money! I pull a 10,000-won bill from my pocket. About twelve bucks.

She spreads out the fingers of her other hand, the one not on my crotch. She wants five of them. 50,000 won.

I shake my head, say *thank you* and *no* in Korean.

She curls in her thumb: 40,000 won. Circular pressure changes on my crotch. Her salesmanship is flawless. She says something with *yogwan* in it. 40,000 won plus the *yogwan?*

"No," I say in Korean.

She lifts her hand off my crotch, leans back, and shuts her eyes. As she recedes into the background, and as my simmering hormones cool off, the coast and the East Sea take hold of me, and I dream of traveling to the end of the earth.

On my last day in Seoul, I plopped on a shaded bench at Tapkol Park. Guys loitered on benches or squatted on the steps of the pagoda or played go. Others circled lazily. Two maternal figures were selling something. I pulled *Korea* out of my daypack. A guy sat down at the other end of the bench and scooted into my personal space. *Korea* fascinated him. He leafed through it and asked a laundry list of questions. When I asked some in return, his gregariousness bloomed, though every word was a battle. He bought two small bottles from one of the maternal figures.

"Drink," he said, "it's good." A ginseng drink. Active ingredients: caffeine, alcohol, and sugar.

His hand landed on my knee. A guy sat down on my other side. More guys accumulated around the bench. They examined *Korea*, discussed the photos. The guys who'd been playing go came over, too. They rested their hands on my shoulders and nattered among each other and urged the original guy to translate. I would have loved to be able to speak Korean. We laughed and tried to understand each other.

But I was worried. I didn't know what this was all about, or what it would lead to, or why there were so many guys pawing me. I got antsy. I said I had an appointment, tapped on my watch. They urged me to have another ginseng drink. But gradually I extricated myself, unsettled by so much friendliness.

Later that afternoon at my *yogwan*—I'd just gotten out of the shower and was cooling off in front of the AC—the phone rang. The owner of the *yogwan*. Would I come down for a cup of coffee, he asked in English, which I understood after his third effort.

They were sitting on the floor. Well-trained, I took my shoes off at the door. A fan churned the muggy air—only guest rooms had AC. The owner patted the floor next to him. The seat of honor. He introduced the woman, his wife, and the other man, his brother. He enumerated his and his brother's kids. He ignored the grandmother who clattered with a kettle in the kitchen corner. She wore an earth-tone longish skirt and a loose tank top. She didn't wear a bra.

She might have been in her fifties. She came over with a mug of Nescafé. As she bent down from the hip, the cloth of her top drooped, exposing her white pendulous breasts down to her brown nipples. Maybe her status as grandmother allowed her to do this, or she didn't have a husband, or I was just a foreigner and it didn't matter what I saw, or she thought nothing of it. She offered me the mug with both hands. Her arms pushed up her breasts and presented them to me.

I stared. Was she doing this on purpose? Was she aware of the impact her breasts had on me? Did it please her? Everyone could see what she was doing, but to them, she wasn't there. Aroused, I took the mug from her dark wrinkled fingers that didn't match the smooth white skin of her breasts. I said *thank you* in Korean, and she said something and smiled and straightened up. What life must a woman have led to have those breasts, a middle-aged face, and old hands?

The owner asked about my family. I invented one to have something to talk about. Nothing depended on the truth, and I had no reason to confront them with the debacle at home in my former life or with the absurd degree of freedom in my current life.

"You like in Korea?" he asked.

"Very much."

He became serious. "Many problems in Korea." He glanced over his shoulder.

"What kind of problems?"

He tried to say something, couldn't think of the right words, said a few things to his brother, who couldn't think of the right words either.

"Many," he finally said to me.

Were we within range of North Korean artillery? I'd visited Panmunjom in the DMZ thirty miles to the north and had seen the theatrics of North Korean and South Korean soldiers glaring at each other across a few feet of sticky air. If it weren't a reminder that the war still isn't settled, it would be just another tourist attraction. It *is* a tourist attraction, however. You go there by tour bus and watch a finely choreographed show that gives you the willies. But you have to have a non-Korean passport. Why Koreans aren't allowed to see the show eludes rational humans.

His wife asked him something. He lightened up, translated, "You like Korean food?"

"I love it."

They all smiled. They'd understood. I listed some dishes. They nodded and commented.

"How long in Korea?" he said.

"Two weeks."

"Other country in Asia?"

"Bali and Japan."

"How long in Japan?"

"Three months."

He grunted and translated. They murmured, didn't like it.

"Three months in Japan and two weeks in Korea?" he said.

"I only have a fifteen-day visa." I pulled my passport from the money belt under my jeans and showed them the Korea visa. They passed it around. It satisfied them.

"After Seoul, where?" he said.

"Sokcho."

"Hmm, Soraksan," they said in unison, even the grandmother.

"Mountain is beautiful," he said.

"Beautiful," his brother confirmed.

"Fish in Sokcho is very good," the owner said.

When my mug was empty, I perceived a wisp of restlessness. The break was over, and they had to get back to work.

My neighbor wakes up as we pass Pohang's rusting industrial hulks and shiny miracles of modern manufacturing. She shifts in her seat. Her hand lands on my thigh and creeps up. Reaches my crotch. Cups it. My thoughts grind to a halt. Rhythmic circular pressure changes. Appreciative sound. She curls in thumb and index finger of her other hand: 30,000 won. She makes a precise gesture. Final offer. Plus the *yogwan*. She says something, maybe, *Don't worry, it'll be worth every won.*

Everybody gets off at the bus terminal. It's hot. The air is thick with humidity. Where's the cool breeze from the East Sea when you need it? She strides to the edge of the lot. Across the street is a *yogwan*. Undecided, I tarry by the bus. What are the laws? If I get apprehended with her, will I rot in jail for thirty years? Will she scream *RAPE* in Korean to extort more money? Will a thug in her room rob me at gunpoint? She pivots back toward me, says something, maybe, *Aren't you coming?*

Ha, me and my doubts!

Made in the USA
Lexington, KY
20 October 2012